RADICAL REGENERATIVE GARDENING AND FARMING

RADICAL REGENERATIVE GARDENING AND FARMING
Biodynamic Principles and Perspectives

Frank Holzman

ROWMAN & LITTLEFIELD
Lanham • Boulder • New York • London

Published by Rowman & Littlefield
A wholly owned subsidary of The Rowman & Littlefield Publishing Group, Inc.
4501 Forbes Boulevard, Suite 200, Lanham, Maryland 20706
www.rowman.com

Unit A, Whitacre Mews, 26-34 Stannary Street, London SE11 4AB

British Library Cataloguing in Publication Information Available

Library of Congress Cataloging-in-Publication Data
Names: Holzman, Frank (Frank James), 1952– author.
Title: Radical regenerative gardening and farming : biodynamic principles and
    perspectives / Frank Holzman.
Description: Lanham, Maryland : Rowman & Littlefield, [2018] | Includes
    bibliographical references and index.
Identifiers: LCCN 2017020320 (print) | LCCN 2017022104 (ebook) |
    ISBN 9781538105993 (Electronic) | ISBN 9781538105986 (cloth : alk. paper)
Subjects: LCSH: Organic gardening. | Biodynamic agriculture.
Classification: LCC SB453.5 (ebook) | LCC SB453.5 .H65 2018 (print) |
    DDC 635/.0484—dc23
LC record available at https://lccn.loc.gov/2017020320

♾™ The paper used in this publication meets the minimum requirements of American National Standard for Information Sciences—Permanence of Paper for Printed Library Materials, ANSI/NISO Z39.48-1992.

Printed in the United States of America

Contents

Introduction

WHEN YOU ENTER A GARDEN you are elevated to a calming, relaxed state. In this sanctuary your mood transforms as you become part of this special place of beauty. A garden possesses elegance and the magic of nature—a wonderful mixture of art and life sciences embraced by spiritual realms. The gardener enhances life as it flourishes unbridled, leading you down the path of the natural world.

The gardener creates a place that is an oasis with its flowery smiles and perfumes that arouse even the smallest insects; the tastes and textures of a garden nurture the soul. It buzzes with life's vibration. I have worked with blind gardeners who helped me become more aware of the smells and feels of each plant. I spent time with a girl who could not see or hear but who shared the special smells of her favorite plants. A garden is like no other place, delicate as a gentle breeze brushing across a petal, with the force of nature that entices every being with a desire to be part of this mystical paradise.

Organic principles are the best way to manifest this beauty. Organic methods work with the natural flow of nature and not against it. They require an understanding of your surroundings so that you can use the dynamics of a given area to your advantage. Nature has all the components to work with, or else forests and jungles could not exist. Getting to know your adversaries gives you power over them. Likewise in a garden, understanding all the cycles of life that exist there allows you to coexist with them.

This is to say that organic gardeners and farmers are more aware and better educated than those thinking in a one-dimensional view. Sustainability means first that you understand the abundance of resources available to you so that you can assess what is around you and how to use it.

Being sustainable is a process whereby you protect your resources by being sure you always give back more than you take away. In organics the soil is our greatest resource. We feed the soil, not the plants. Soil is what produces abundant gardens and farms. The gardener produces good soil rich with balanced nutrients. If you are moving forward in a positive direction, then you will see your soil become healthier each year. You will know this because the garden produces more abundant yields of higher quality and with less work. Problems become minor because of the balance taking place and the gardener becomes the facilitator of this balance by being one with the garden. The caretaker of a rich radiant garden or farm is a good steward of the soil. A rich garden holds an abundance of wealth; there are many things to profit from in this place. As the garden becomes vibrant so does the gardener. As you enrich the soil beneath you, it in turn enriches you. Heal the soil and it heals you.

Society can produce dysfunctional humans. People are imbalanced because their surroundings are as well. I have worked in horticultural therapy and seen it do wonders with all sorts of people. I have set up barrier-free gardens for those with disabilities and have seen people with severe disability become beams of light in their garden plots. When I went through some difficult times, gardening kept me more centered and focused and gave my life meaning. Life attracts life. Living things are attracted to living things.

Gardens are a vibrant force of life that feeds us spiritually as well as physically. As the gardener starts out on this journey, first year gardens are like infants. But within this new world the possibilities are endless. Creating a garden is a step-by-step process, beautiful and innocent. Nature offers a great world of hidden surprises and you never stop learning. For when gardeners stop learning, they become compost. To become rooted, or perhaps routed, into the garden is a long-term relationship and commitment. To become an integral part of your surroundings takes time.

Finding your place through a natural process is centering. Developing this relationship is important. It connects us to this place called Earth and with who we are. It also connects us with where our food comes from and how it grows. It is like no other relationship you have with humans or pets. In the beginning it is an investment, but given time it pays off and rewards you severalfold.

It takes a commitment to develop the soil beneath your feet. It is a gradual development. Over time you find your place in the scheme of things. You become the soil on your hands and have compost in your veins. Being truly organic is a lifestyle. It is a philosophy of holding soil sacred. It invites you to find your place through the natural process. The garden and the gardener grow together year after year. The knowledge you gain cannot be found in a classroom. You get out of it what you put into it. And it is forgiving because life heals all wounds.

It takes a slow and steady pace as you move through the seasons and you get into the rhythm of life's cycles. You develop skills. Your senses become keen; your taste buds become more acute. But most of all, you become aware of your role here on this planet and how to flourish in its abundance.

Being a good steward of the land requires being sensitive to the complexities of your given ecosystem. It involves how insects and even diseases fit into the garden or farm. Predators must be in balance with their prey. Weeds are guardians of the soil and provide habitat for creatures unknown. The soil is in a constant flux of change, and each season is unpredictable and different from the last one. This is the real work.

In other words, it is a labor of love. Gardening must be done as a passionate endeavor. There are certainly easier jobs that pay more money, but if you do it with integrity you will achieve satisfaction and a quality of life. An example is when I tell people how to plant a tree. You take a twenty dollar tree and put it in a sixty dollar hole. If you are going to do it, do it right the first time. Quality in your work produces quality in what you grow.

I used to get asked, "How do you compete with the big supermarket?" You don't. You maintain a level of quality that they cannot. That is what is meant by the real work. It is easy to get frustrated with the slow progress of healing a piece of land and the slow development of the farmer or gardener. If you are dealing with soil that has been abused by misguided individuals, it is easy to perpetuate that way of thinking and dump your share of chemical abuse on the soil and pass it on to the next person. Or you can break the pattern of ignorance and give it a positive turn by caring for it yourself and those around you. It is a choice of maintaining a high level of quality for yourself as if you deserve it too. If this is your vision, then this is what you will manifest. A garden or a farm is a place that is enhanced with an abundance of life, not just food, and deserves the respect that all life deserves. It starts and ends with the soil.

When I was twenty years old, I was very fortunate to discover something that I had a passion for. A beautiful garden is a reflection of the passion one has for their work. That passion has led me down many paths pursuing my education and to many parts of the world to do my work. Each garden or farm opens up new doors of knowledge, and each season brings new opportunities to improve upon.

I got my start as a maintenance gardener on large estates on the San Francisco peninsula in California. It is critical to have a good perspective on maintenance in order to proceed with design. I dealt with landscape architects who knew nothing about maintenance. They made major mistakes not understanding how to incorporate care for the landscape they were designing. I did this work while taking horticulture classes at the local community college. I was introduced to horticulture as the fine art of agriculture. Later I attended the University of California, Berkeley. Agricultural studies gave me a technical understanding. Ecology was introduced as the household of nature. While there, I also discovered the Integral Urban House in Berkeley, which was part of the Farallon Institute. I learned to think of food as part of the landscape through edible landscape design. Later, I realized that food could and should be the main focus. Appropriate technology was being used as a tool to work with nature in an efficient and resourceful manner. This fits in well with the concepts of permaculture principles.

All my previous learning prepared me for biodynamic/French intensive methods, which had a strong following at the University of California, Santa Cruz. It was not being taught at the school itself but within a small pocket on campus called the enchanted garden; Alan Chadwick was the creator. There biodynamic farming was combined with French intensive gardening methods. Biodynamics exposed me to a more spiritual perspective of agriculture and horticulture. This is where I developed market gardening ideology. This is also where I examined the energy exchange of the plant world, and how the soil breathes of life and the pulse of the universe.

Alan Chadwick was, among many other things, a messenger for the work of Rudolf Steiner. Alan was a horticultural genius with amazing insight. His system is whole and flows full circle. It addresses the sensitivities of all beings and how to interact with them to create the whole farm. This can be done on many minute levels. It is an approach for integrating whole systems, and I use it to incorporate all the modalities I have learned. I studied basic landscape concepts and small-scale farming design, permaculture principles, and integrated pest management or IPM, which was introduced to me by William and Helga Olkowski.

As a student, I was introduced to a wide variety of perspectives. As an apprentice, I learned it more experientially. As a journeyman, I could develop my own style with unique challenges. Teaching invites me into group dynamics where I continue to learn. Yet being in a garden is where I am embraced by the spirit that brought me here. In the pages ahead I wish to share the passion, insight, and experiences that have made my life very rich.

The first chapter introduces ecology. It examines how to emulate nature as a way to establish a farm. This is the basic principle of agroecology. The next chapter explores design concepts and principles as a way to bring together science and creative elements. Chapter 3 discusses compost and composting techniques that allow the gardener to complete the cycles of fertility. Chapter 4 delves into the importance of soil. It is a biological science that is often overlooked. Chapter 5 follows with an examination of the amazingly beautiful and graceful plant world. After that we look at plant and seed propagation in chapter 6. Next, chapter 7 examines entomology as an important component of any functional farm or garden. The book then moves into the underworld of pathology and all its mysteries in chapter 8. Chapter 9 introduces the concepts of biodynamics and how it fits into everything. This is followed by chapter 10, which looks at maintenance and finding balance, before the final chapter goes full circle to give a complete perspective on how it all works as a whole, combined with appropriate technology concepts.

1

Transitioning Ecology into Agroecology

The ultimate goal of farming is not the growing of crops, but the cultivation of human beings.

—Masanubo Fukuoka

IN THE LATE 1960S AND EARLY 1970S, ecology became a popular buzzword and the subject of much study around campuses in the United States. An increasing awareness was growing around concerns about our natural environment. It was the birth of the ecology movement. Previous writings brought awareness to environmental concerns. *Silent Spring* by Rachel Carson inspired much of the ideology being embraced. Recycling, renewable energy, and bans on synthetic chemicals used to grow our food were all topics being addressed.

In 1970 the first Earth Day was established as an awareness campaign. With all the concerns about cleaning up the environment, most folks had little idea about where their food was coming from. It was a generation that had been disconnected from its food source.

During that same time, the Green Revolution was in full swing. Large chemical companies were setting up programs, mostly in developing countries, to persuade the local farmers to buy into a packaged product that would drastically change the way they farmed. The idea was to convince these farmers to use newly, developed hybridized seed that would produce better yields. In order for this program to work effectively, farmers would need to purchase the tractors and new equipment and start a program using synthetic fertilizers and pesticides. It was a complete package.

This strategy was a program that would create dependence on the chemical companies and the banks loaning the money. Farmers were convinced to sell the soul of their farm for the idyllic dreams of modern society. This program would completely alter the face of farming in these countries. As a result, the farmers lost hundreds of years of gene pools that had been passed down to them. The seeds they inherited from their elders would become extinct.

It was sold as a package deal. In order to farm with the newly developed seed, they needed synthetic chemicals in the form of fertilizers and pesticides and a tractor that was previously not needed. The farmers became burdened by loans to pay for their tractors and equipment. Many of these farmers had no idea how to use these new methods of farming and never before needed a bank loan. But most importantly, the soils became toxic from the chemicals used. This provided an inexpensive source of food to export to the United States and Europe. Killing off nature's balance created a dependency on the chemicals to do the work.

This was the same program used to change farming in the United States in the middle of the last century. Small-scale farming, the heart of agriculture, became agribusiness that was corporate sponsored. During this time, pockets of young people became interested in getting back to the land and growing food for themselves and their families. The land grant colleges taught only chemical farming concepts, so there was a new movement to grow food naturally. This required people to reinvent the wheel and discover new methods of growing without synthetic chemicals. This new approach meant learning from nature, not dominating it. It became a more sensitive approach of developing an understanding of how nature really works; it is the idea of working with nature not against it.

The ecology movement at Berkeley was largely promoted at the Berkeley Ecology Project. It highlighted publications on exciting things to learn about the environment, such as recycling, tree planting, and organic gardening. The community gardens were hosts to radical concepts, where signs were spray-painted with ideological sayings like "Squash the State" and "Give Peas a Chance." Ecology as a science was being introduced on campus. The curriculum of ecology was relatively new. In an ecology class at UC Berkeley, I was introduced to the complexities of ecosystems. Off campus, environmental issues were often viewed as to their human and often politically negative impact on the environment.

As my education evolved I began to understand how my awareness of the environment would affect my view of life sciences. After all, I was in Berkeley and it was the 1970s. It was easy to adopt what was called a biological approach, which later became geared more toward sustainable practices. With experiences in community gardens around town and the Integral Urban House, there were a lot of different perspectives on what was being taught at the university. As my awareness of the environment could be applied to land use through agriculture and horticulture, it started to become clear how we all play an important role in this world we live in. Reading books like *Radical Agriculture* by Richard Merrill did a lot to raise my consciousness. I later studied horticulture in Merrill's class at Cabrillo College.

Ecology was popularized by Eugene Odum, an American biologist considered the father of ecology. He did a lot of his fundamental work while at the University of Georgia. Along with his brother Howard he published *Fundamentals of Ecology*. The term *ecology* was first coined by a German biologist, Ernst Haechel (1834–1919). The common science is human ecology. This is the study of human interactions as it relates to societal conditions.

Ecology comes from the Greek word "eco," meaning house—so study of the household. Ecology is the science of relationships between organisms and their environment. We are part of that broader environment; the broader environment is referred to as macroecology. It is a mixture of microcommunities that blend together and operate as one organism. Plants have the amazing ability to trap the sun's energy through photosynthesis and manufacture food, which allows the rest of us to live.

The ecosystem is composed of producers, consumers, and decomposers. Each environment has a unique set of dynamics that is intertwined and cohesive. It consists of many levels of plants, animals, insects, and microbial communities living symbiotically. The ecosystem represents many stages of growth, and it is ever changing and transforming. Biogeography is the study of the distribution of species and ecosystems in geographic space as it relates to geological time. Organisms and biological communities vary and morph along gradients of latitude, elevation, isolation, and areas of habitat.

When humans move into this circle, they are upsetting the existing balance. It is important to try to minimize our impact on that balance. In other words, don't jump into the biological pool with a belly flop or a cannonball. Step into it gracefully. You don't have to be so loud. Everyone will already know you are there.

The key is how to protect and enhance this group of microenvironments so as not to upset the fragile balance. It hosts a large range of resources ready for you to discover. Before you plant, conducting an assessment of all existing life and their habitats will be beneficial. You'll want to consider insect and earthworm populations, temperature gradients, small animal habitats, and water reservoirs. If you have mushrooms after a good rain, the soil is rich in microbial and fungal life.

Analyzing the land requires knowing the history of what has gone on there. Understanding negative impacts due to land degradation from overgrazing, pesticide pollution, soil solarization, and depletion or contamination of groundwater will help you develop a plan for healing it. Understanding the history of a piece of land helps a lot. Abiotic factors such as fires, severe droughts, and other weather extremes also need to be taken into account. These issues will become more prevalent in future analysis due to climate change.

Soil, water, and perhaps leaf tissue testing will also give you valuable information about what toxins are in the soil. The county cooperative extension service can provide a basic soil test of macronutrients and pH levels. Water on the land is crucial for growing food. Both air and water flow in formless ways. Because of this, pollution knows no boundaries. Canada is on the receiving end of much acid rain and air pollution from the United States. Water is easily taken for granted. It seems endless.

New Mexico offered me a different perspective. They use ditch irrigation. When the water is gone, there is nothing until the ditch rider shows up again. Horny toads seem to know how to find pockets of water that are hidden from plain view. Regardless of where you are, water cycles need to be completed with an unobstructed flow; stagnant water won't attract the life you need. A pond can be a good resource. It is like a biological funnel. There can be habitats for reptiles, frogs, lizards, all are very beneficial. Water can be stored for future use. A creek can be used to run a ram pump to push water from a nearby spring up a hill to a holding tank where it would have gravity flow for many uses. Water can be stored in a variety of ways from ponds to tanks to underground cisterns.

In Belize, all rooftops funnel water into storage tanks. Bamboo is sometimes used for rain gutters. This is a good example of water harvesting. Water everywhere needs to be cared for as a living resource. When working with polluted or toxic water, plants can be used to detoxify the water. It needs to be set up as a leach field of sand or loam. The plants don't just absorb the chemicals, but actually break them down into harmless compounds. According to the Woods Hole Oceanographic Institute, the following plants will absorb heavy metals from water: *Nymphaea alba* (water lily), *Phragmites australis, Sparganium erectum* (bur reed), Iris *pseudacorus* (yellow flag iris), *Schoenoplectus lacustris* (bulrush), *Carex acutiformis* (common sedge). Oxygen suppliers consist of *Stratiotes aloides* (water soldier), *Hydrocharis morsus-ranae* (frogbit), and *Acorus calamus* (sweet flag reed). Phytoextraction plants consist of sunflower, mustard, canna lily, willow, and Salix, among others. Some of these plants can be invasive. Water is filtered through them in a leach field and put back into the system as clean water. This process is called phytoremediation and imitates what takes place in a swamp. There are habitats that attract life from the outside as well, especially during migrations. One example is birds. If you have orange crown warblers, yellow-breasted chats, or thrashers, you are in luck. They have huge insect diets. Hedgerows are often their habitats; don't destroy them.

The idea is to enhance biological activity and mimic nature by copying what already works there. Leguminous trees can provide a good source of nitrogen. Plantings at their base can take advantage of this. Existing plants can be used as indicators of the soil. Russian thistle thrives in soils low in calcium, iron, and organic matter. Lambs quarters look for loose soils, rich in calcium and phosphorus. Dock (*Rumex crispus*), blackberries, and plantain signify acidic soils. Dock is also a sign of iron in the soil. Buttercups and willow thrive in wet soils with a high water table. Yarrow can indicate potassium and sulfur. Dandelion, horsetail, and mullein are attracted to high silica. Moss indicates poor drainage.

A balanced ecosystem maintains a constant cycling of water and nutrients. This confluence is important in order to maintain consistent patterns. From time to time balance is disrupted by outside influences such as weather or internal ones such as seasonal patterns and population explosions, or perhaps a tree falling. Chaos is the upsetting of balance. It brings about dramatic change and change is inevitable. In biodynamics, chaos is viewed as a sign of new growth and evolution. If you maintain an awareness of your environment, you can be prepared for change. You can even direct it. This is called sensitive chaos.

By keeping aware of weather changes and monitoring insect populations and paying attention to changes in growth, you can gain insight. Through this, you can become a functional part of the dramatic wheel of life. For this to happen it is important to identify appropriate energy paths and not to obstruct them. Where does the air and water flow and what is the path of the sun? Nocturnal activity of insects and animal is also good to observe. This can be a fun activity with kids.

It is much easier to destroy ecosystems than it is to restore them. For instance, left to its own accord, nature requires two hundred and fifty years to make one inch of topsoil. Ecosystems are fragile. Losses of habitats can be devastating and the loss of available resources can be just as devastating and time-consuming to amend. The approach to ecology should not be met with fear but with love. In a natural system, weeds are great soil builders. Synthetic fertilizers are not. It takes life to enhance life. Organic matter does this.

An ecosystem is a fragile biological community of interconnected organisms working within their physical environment. A healthy forest or jungle is a good example of diverse plants and animals. The primary components are the plants that manufacture food from inorganic substances using photosynthesis. They are defined as autotrophic. The rest of us cannot synthesize our own food and depend on complex organic substances. We are heterotrophic and depend on plants to live.

The ecosystem develops in the same way. It regenerates itself as it goes along. It is built on niches of habitats for the inhabitants that move into it in succession. This succession is the progressive replacement of one biological community by another. New life forms are often carried in by wind and water. As the order evolves, natural selection is occurring. Habitats are developed by disturbances and changes. These successions build and develop in a gradual and orderly process until they reach a climax, which is when the habitat becomes stabilized.

The system is at equilibrium with environmental conditions, yet always changing. The ecosystem contains flora and fauna of a variety of species structured into a complex hierarchy of interactions that work symbiotically. The overall size contributes to its stability along with maintaining buffers. The ecosystem in a climaxed state can maintain itself until there is disturbance brought about by nature or human involvement. The balance of maintenance is always in a state of transition.

Diversity and succession fluctuate but not evenly. Rapid rates of growth take place during bloom times or at peak growth periods. Diversity depends on potential niches and using them as they become available. Diversity usually grows during early and middle stages of succession and declines in the climax stage. Increased diversity does not translate into stability. It means that the system is in a state of growth.

There are short-term gains compared to long-term physical growth. This is one way to measure the stability of a forest. Plant communities grow in ways that work in symbiotic patterns. For instance, a leucaena tree is a fast-growing leguminous tree of the tropics. It can be introduced to an area that has opened up in the canopy due to a fallen tree. Growing leafy vegetables or herbs at its base would be beneficial. A maximum biomass takes place when much of the energy of the forest is stored in the mature trees. The fallen tree becomes home to many forest floor dwellers. Later, it becomes a food source for many generations of decomposers. Energy coming into an ecosystem is in the form of sunlight used by chlorophyll producers and rain. This is represented by the plants in the forest, like trees, grasses in a field, and algae in a pond. Other producers like the carotenoid-bearing purple plants that assimilate carbon dioxide from sunlight are also important. They demonstrate a way of dealing with stress.

Producers also include microscopic bacteria, which obtain energy by oxidizing simple inorganic compounds and of course the decomposers that help complete the nutrient cycles. As the forest matures, nutrient cycling is so important to maintain. That is part of the role of a fallen tree. A dead tree can contain a large amount of life. Insects dwell in cavities that later become homes for birds. Weather, especially extreme weather, is a cause for rapid changes in the forest. There are advantages and disadvantages to everything. Too much rain supports some forms of growth. Yet for other species, it will cause them to perish due to the growth of disease cycles. Disease can also be seen as the culling of weaker plants. Cold temperatures and a good frost will inhibit insect populations. Sustained frost will slow microbial development and bring a slow start to spring. It is a balancing act that always moves like a pendulum. Climate change is creating a serious challenge to keeping those changes in balance. A large forest of tall trees helps create its own weather by trapping in moisture and releasing it in the form of rain. All of these factors play a role and feed into one another.

The energy created in an ecosystem is stored in its biomass. Trees in the forest are a good example. One of my favorite places is a jungle floor covered in rich green foliage. This is biomass in a less stable form. It is more transparent with the rapid exchange of life. In a forest, the nutrients can be tied up in the biomass for a number of years, such as with the trees.

To access the health of an ecosystem you must assess several factors. Look at the water shed. Where are the drainage and catchment areas? This should be easy to find. Look at the diversity of species and age. Old growth is the gene pool and the makeup of the forest's history as well as its future.

Ponds and streams are vital to an ecosystem of size. Check the water's pH and dissolved oxygen. A creek with a drop in it is a good way to get oxygen into the water. Check the riparian buffers along creeks. Look at the invertebrates in the stream.

Bird populations give a lot of information. The types of birds in a habitat can tell you about the presence of insects in the woods. Wildlife diversity is very important. An upper canopy along with a lower canopy helps provide diversity. A healthy leaf litter is a continued state of decomposition and provides nutrient cycling for everything above. The budget for nutrients is not usually taken into consideration. This is an assessment of the economy of nature. It is well to access the nutrient content of the biotic components in a measure of time.

The producer into consumer into decomposer chain is often greatly disrupted by humans. The extreme, yet common, example of disruption is when someone clear-cuts a forest and then replants it with only one type of species or even a clone. They have taken a forest and turned it into a tree farm. Forestry companies do not distinguish between the two. This is another indicator of imbalance—representing the three Ps: people, pollution, and poverty. People are mostly, if not entirely, consumers. As they move into an area, they tax its nutrient base. Pollution is a by-product of all ecosystems. Once the pollution gets to a level that the plants can no longer tolerate, it becomes a problem.

At this point the system cannot support the demands of the consumers. Without having a natural order of balance, people take from each other as they did the land. This creates poverty, which is a consciousness more than an economic indicator. I often hear that the main problem with the environment is that there are too many people on the planet. There are, as long as they live the way most of us do. But in reality, this planet could support many more people if we could learn to exist in a more sustainable manner.

As a case in point, the Midwest plants hundreds of thousands of acres of corn and soybeans to be used as feed, which is then sent down the Mississippi River on barges en route to New Orleans to end up in various parts of the world. Those grains are used as feed for livestock. Used differently, that land could feed the entire planet. The exchange in energy is one way to calculate what an ecosystem produces. A natural order also has an incredible resilience.

After a clear-cut, pines often grow back and dominate the landscape. Now that they are a monocrop, they become the target of pine beetles. The pines eventually deteriorate and die and deciduous trees fill in to take their place. As plants and animals have to adapt to their damaged environment, so do we. In a garden, it is always important to establish a barrier for deer. People often ask why the Native Americans didn't have to use deer fences. That is because hundreds of years ago there were natural predators that have since been killed off. And if there was an occasional deer in the garden, it became part of the next meal.

The natural order does not mean the pest is eradicated. If you set up birdhouses for birds of prey, they will not eliminate all the rabbits, for to do so would eliminate their food source. They only lower the numbers. The natural order of things can be convoluted to match our perception of how things should be. A forest fire cleanses the forest floor, fed by the winds of change when it becomes too cluttered with branches and fallen wood. A heavy rain replenishes and feeds the plants below. What is often viewed as mild erosion can also be seen as redistributing the nutrients on the forest floor.

It is hard to understand exactly what all is happening in the course of an ecosystems evolution. Actually, the producers of this system produce carbohydrates, not energy. The waste produced is what feeds the secondary producers or decomposers, who are the main recyclers and fulfill the cycle. In that way, there is no real waste. When we step into the picture, the view changes into what can be taken out for our benefit. Done properly, we need to make sure that we are contributing equal to what is taken to maintain a balance because we are otherwise not contributors.

This can be described as agroforestry. Agro, meaning an agrarian element, has now been introduced and that changes the whole perspective. Generally agroforestry involves planting a crop in the forest. There are many examples. Ginseng or golden seal is usually planted on the north slope of a wooded hillside. Cinnamon trees are another example. They are understory and it takes eight years before the bark is ready to harvest. Coffee is a very common crop that became popular as the demand for more exotic coffee increased. It is now grown all around the equator under a canopy.

Sometimes existing wild plants are found and harvested, such as herbs. This is referred to as wild crafting and these products are considered to be higher grade than what is grown. This is a common practice in wet areas like Oregon. Truffles are a much desired delicacy that brings in a high dollar. As far as I know, they cannot be introduced easily. There are people selling trees that are inoculated with the spores, but I do not know about their success rate. Pigs are often used to root them out. I met some folks who raised pigs and decided that having them root for truffles will pay for them to live there. Sometimes muscadine grapes grow wild in the woods. Harvesting them and eating or selling them could be considered agroforestry. They are good for the wildlife and attract many birds, which can be useful.

Agroecology is a method or group of methods for growing crops with these same principles. Agroecology was first introduced to me at the Farm and Garden Project at the University of California, Santa Cruz. This was part of the legacy of Alan Chadwick and where biodynamic/French intensive gardening was introduced at the enchanted garden that Chadwick started. Agroecological methods require working with these systems by designing for wildlife, food, and restoration.

One important aspect to consider is what resources are there and what this land is capable of providing within a reasonable capacity. This is an assessment of the land's carrying capacity. Carrying capacity is based on water, soil, and space with adequate sunlight. Once you have used up 50 percent of the available resources, then you are at peak consumption. Resources need to be generated at least at the same rate of consumption. The best way to do this is through the composting of unused materials. You can get ideas of humus levels by examining the topsoil. You can also dig straight down a spade's depth to view the soil profile.

In Georgia and the Southeast United States, there is not much topsoil. It was cotton farmed hundreds of years ago and most of the topsoil is in the Gulf of Mexico or the Atlantic Ocean, depending on which way the creeks flowed. Look at the lush growth around the area and notice what type. How much water is there and how is the water situated? The overall health of the area and what is currently being supported there tells you what you have to work with.

Four elements (soil, water, sun, and air) need to be in place to serve the needs of bringing life onto the land in a way that is whole and completes the cycle. In examining the carrying capacity, look at all the resources for green growth, dry growth, wood, and existing food and water. If you take the land beyond its carrying capacity, it is hard to restore loss of nutrients and depleted land. Often the land has already fallen into a state of depletion and this will be an uphill battle. Do not make your work harder than it needs to be. It is best to move into a place that has been fallow so that it has started to recover.

One of the main principles of agroecology is the cycling of nutrients. The goal is to put back more than you take out. Consider the idea of sustainable yields rather than maximum yields. In using concepts that utilize appropriate technology and efficiency, one can still maximize use of land without maximizing the nutrients. By using biodynamic/French intensive methods, yields can be four to six times greater than with conventional methods. And you can see dramatic soil improvements each year. Besides, if you really enjoy this work, why would you want to exhaust your nutrient base?

This is the very foundation of health. How are you ensuring the land's future as a way of ensuring your own? Think in terms of the land producing energy, recreation, and valuable habitats while securing your own sustainable food security. There are many ways to use your resources to their fullest without having a negative impact. For instance, water can keep you and your food cool, store heat, make energy, grow food (like watercress and fish), irrigate crops, clean, and quench your thirst. Soil can be used to store food, keep it warm and cool, provide ovens and houses, heal wounds on trees, and be used botanically in the garden to grow abundant food. And there is so much more.

The idea is to be as self-sufficient as one can within reason. This can be a difficult objective in its entirety, yet something to consider when putting the whole operation in perspective. To be able to provide for food, housing, fiber, medicine, and energy needs may not always be an efficient use of your energy. Driving around in your car is certainly not efficient and an incredible waste of nonrenewable resources. Socioeconomic factors play a role in determining your lifestyle needs and appropriate use of your time. If one's objective is self-sufficiency, it is important to realize that a developed community of resources is much more valuable than developed skills.

Days need to be measured in accomplishments as well as enjoyment. Embracing community fosters both of these. Keeping systems as close as possible should be a primary objective. In doing this it is best to start small and branch out in an efficient manner. One key principle about nature is that it operates at optimum levels of efficiency or else it does not survive in the overall scheme.

Imitating nature is the fundamental application of agroecology. Biomimicry involves innovative design concepts that imitate the architecture of nature. Many design concepts are taken from nature. Eggs are a good example; they are structured to absorb pressure. Or as streams lose elevation they add oxygen to lower sections that need it to maintain the life below. Trees provide a trellis for vines. This attracts birds that also help eat insects in the trees. Leaf litter on the forest floor is made up of layers in various stages of decomposition. This encourages the development of mycorrhizal fungi. The filaments of these fungi can be seen as you open layers of the forest floor. The use of polyculture plantings of the upper canopy provide filtered sunlight for smaller plants that offer benefits for the trees above. These concepts can be re-created in the garden. We'll look at this in more detail in the design chapter.

Designing a system that also fits into social economics can be very challenging indeed. It can and should be a gradual process. Nature moves along a different current than that of modern society. How do you and a piece of land flow in a confluent direction? It really is a long learning process and a beautiful one. Start by not wasting anything. Consider your needs and scale down to what is absolutely necessary. Putting unused plant material back into the soil is a direct form of this.

There are many composting systems you can incorporate, as described in the chapter on composting. One key element is to mimic nature with diversity and integrating many modalities. In a healthy forest, you never see oaks in one area, ash in another, dogwoods in another. Nature depends on their integration and so does the healthy web work of a farm. By maintaining diversity and a rotation of usage, you also keep the soil healthy. Part of this is because of the nutrients you take out, but also because of what you put back in.

Each species of plant has a different chemical makeup and each one attracts different life forms. Some of these are left behind and add to the diversity of the soil no matter how minute. A healthy community is represented by various species and age groups. Older trees contain the gene pool and younger ones are the future. This is the difference between a natural forest and a tree farm and you don't need a farm to grow trees. Imitate nature by interplanting to break up the continuity and attract diversity. Some examples might include planting a row of fruit trees across a field or through the middle of a garden. This is popular when using espalier methods. Another idea is to plant yarrow under fruit trees to attract lacewings and damsel bugs or alyssum to attract hover flies and *Stethorus* beetles.

Another interesting example is the method developed by Masanobu Fukuoka in his book *The One-Straw Revolution*. His yields were much lower than conventional ones. Yet if you look at his input of energy for what he got out, there is no way to compare with the efficiency of his work. Some of us work very hard and hopefully love it. He gave minimal effort but got amazing results with little input of energy. His observations of his land were very keen, but it took him a long time to get there. He invested many years of work and inherited many more years from the generations before him. In *The One-Straw Revolution*, planting methods imitated nature by scattering seeds among the native plants and incorporated the use of his livestock (mainly ducks) for insect control.

This is a great example of a long-term commitment that can bring you to a place of minimal impact. To be so connected as to be able to facilitate a close relationship with nature is something to strive for in working with a piece of land. This is more difficult in production farming but it allows you to grow your food without as much effort. This is doable anywhere. Some places are much more challenging than others. In nine years of work at a community garden in Atlanta, I was able to see a small piece of land become very alive and abundant. It started out as a damaged piece of land that would hardly support weeds, with bricks for subsoil left over from the foundation of a house. The garden was an experiment in soil building. With a lot of hard work, a committed crew, a serious composting program, and cover cropping, we saw the soil become lush with life. It provided a wealth of food that fed the families involved. After several years, it got to the point where it needed little cultivation. This is how no till systems need to be addressed.

Most of us have marginal soil to start with. The soil needs to be brought to a place where it no longer needs intense care. If you start with little you have to give it a lot to get a lot. There are definitely worse soils in various parts of the world. Farming requires a serious amount of investment. Seeing land become healed and restored into what it can be is incredibly rewarding. Some land may have more open areas than can be used efficiently. Introducing trees, especially along perimeters, is very valuable. Forested areas hold moisture, retain warmth, create habitats, and of course, provide wood, wind breaks, and privacy. This is also a way of providing for future generations.

Soil Reclamation

Stopping erosion is the first problem to address to regenerate the land. Layers of brush or a Waddell fence of woven branches can be used, along with a small berm of soil. This should be seeded with clover and grasses as well as plantings of vines like *Vinca major* or *minor*. Soil compaction can be resolved with deep-rooted plants like dock, lamb's-quarter, or alfalfa. In nature there is no room for tractors. An efficient garden can be designed the same way. The next step is to establish a ground cover. Native grasses and field plants lend themselves to this. Next put in small trees, shrubs, and vines. There are many berry producers that work well for this, such as mulberry, muscadines, ground-cherry, elderberry, and so on. Leguminous trees are also good soil builders. Once that is established, taller trees can be planted that will become the upper canopy.

Trees also provide shade for animals. Animals add another dimension to the ecosystem. Utilizing them effectively can be very resourceful and add to the full circle of your farm. Goats can keep a field cut and fertilized. They are wonderful recyclers and can be used on kudzu effectively. If you use goats for consecutive years, they will starve the roots and kill the plants. They can also do major damage like clean the bark off of trees. They are best tethered in a field. Chickens can be run through a field to reduce insect populations before planting. Ducks are used extensively in the Pacific Northwest where slugs and snails are a real threat.

Livestock and Their Uses

Animals should be rotated to avoid overgrazing and for diversity. Carnivores do not fit into an ecosystem well. They easily upset the balance. This is hard for pet lovers. Animals have to be monitored carefully to avoid having an overwhelming impact. Sheep will eat the grass down to stubs. They need abundant rainfall. The rule of thumb is, if no one in your area has such an animal, it might be for good reason.

Animals in general need a lot of room. It is easy to fantasize about them without providing for them correctly. The idea of plowing a field with water buffalo sounds very romantic, but you need to live in Southeast Asia. This sounds a little absurd, but some folks attempt to practice just as outrageous ideas.

It is a balancing act to measure the care required for them compared with what they offer. Planting a row of trees through a field changes the continuum of that field. Nitrogen-fixing trees can be beneficial to plants planted beneath them that also appreciate the shade. A row of espalier fruit trees is practical and esthetic, if you can provide the time to do the regular pruning required. A tree resonates with life and is a grand statement as it grows in a field. It becomes a magnet for many life forms. Birds can be seen sitting in them, monitoring the ground below for insects. It can also host a bird's nest.

A row of trees adds a contour to the air flow across a field. Make an assessment of the four elements—soil, sun, water, and air movement—and consider how to harvest from them. Of course the soil is the primary resource and the one you can affect most readily. Full sun is needed to grow most crops. The sun can also be harvested in many other ways, to cook, dry, heat, and make electricity.

Water is important both below and above ground. Irrigating crops is critical since the rain cannot be relied upon. Above the ground water is a valuable resource as a biological component. It attracts many useful insects and reptiles, provides water for birds, and so on. A clean source of air brings with it all the changes to make life very refreshing. By imitating what takes place in a healthy forest, a garden can become just as efficient. Nutrient cycling is done by not allowing waste. Unused crops are either recycled in a compost pile or plowed into beds, which encourages worm populations. Cover crops are a good way to add nutrients and life into beds. Their roots attract rich microbial activity. Cover crops are a way to create mycorrhizal fungi in the soil.

This is one way to imitate a forest soil as it lays the foundation for dynamic life. Although it is hard to not disturb with annual crops, it is something to aspire to in perennial beds. Alfalfa is an option here. It does an excellent job of protecting the soil. Nitrogen-fixing plants are incredibly valuable in any season to come. Green manure is an excellent way to build soil. When walking through the forest or jungle, one is awed by the intensity of life. This can be an inspiration for us in the garden. A bed of tomatoes reaching across to join a bed of pole beans to create a canopy, or vanilla beans climbing over to meet the branches of a bread fruit tree creates a jungle effect in your own garden.

Do not plan it that way and let it surprise you with its eager growth. You may get some complaints about how hard it is to navigate. Yet the beauty that it creates is rich foliage lush with life. This is what summer is all about. It's as if the plants are making a statement. They are in the middle of their time doing what they do best. And you may want to throw some compost at their feet and say thank you. There is also a subject of adaptation. The plants in the garden become adapted to the soil and environment they are in. Each place and every established garden has its own set of dynamics. This is what works in a forested ecosystem.

Being Truly Sustainable

When you plant seeds that came from plants that grew maybe fifty feet away, they are adapted to that given area. This is a big asset for their adjustment and development in the given area. Being truly sustainable also means staying local. Being ecological offers a pragmatic approach to growing. Blending into an existing forest with trees and shrubs is a good transition. Use fruits and brambles for this. Imitate what a forest does with stacked polyculture plantings. This resembles the forest by utilizing the upper canopy for shade and smaller plants that can occupy the area underneath. Growing sunflowers with beans or okra and winter squash also imitates forest plantings.

Planting tall or staked plants down the middle with smaller plants on the side is another concept for efficient use of space. This could consist of cucumbers on a trellis with bush beans on either side. Using vanilla to grow up onto a trellis of fruit trees that are grown in the vase method will allow sun to get inside the middle of the tree. This could be done with strawberry guava or lychee.

Niche Gardening

Going back to the ecosystem mode, you can utilize niches the same way forests do. This could be seen as niche gardening. Finding out what works best in a garden is best done with trial and error. Allow tall grass to grow at the edge of beds to provide habitats for spiders. This works around taller plants like squash, tomatoes, peppers, and beans to some extent. It does not help for small leaf crops like mustards (Asian greens), lettuce, turnips, cabbage, and other greens, which are a habitat for snails and slugs. Those areas are best kept clean of weeds. Grapes also do not fend well with grasses because of the leafhoppers they attract. If aphids are a problem in fruit trees, it might help to grow plants that attract ladybugs like fennel, Queen Anne's lace, or tansy. If the aphids are being placed there by ants, then tansy would also be helpful. Plants like borage at the edges attract beneficial wasps, or try a towering dill or angelica growing up in the middle of the bed. Buckwheat grown around squash provides another beneficial habitat for wasps.

It is common to get a little bird damage on the more mature peas when trying to get seed from them. Netting may help with this. Late cabbage or broccoli can benefit from these birds who might like some caterpillars to go with their peas. Creating these habitats involves monitoring. Maintaining them does also. The grasses need to be cut periodically to move everyone around and keep everything in motion as the season evolves.

Maintaining permanent areas under trees and growing areas with compatible plants is important to consider. Indonesia is home to beautiful terraces used as rice paddies. They are maintained with such care. The farmers take what was passed down to them with a lot of respect. The terraced rice paddies are set in permanence with turf growing on the sides of the terrace. They use a drainage system that allows the water to flow through a small hole down to the bed below. It is beautifully done. There is also room in strategic places for an occasional banana or coconut tree in the corners.

This is an example of intensive agriculture and a wonderful use of steep hillsides that would otherwise be hard to utilize. Because the paddies are flooded periodically, they provide habitat for lots of amphibians. The flooding does a good job of keeping weeds out of a grass plant that would not hold up well against weeds. The frogs sing you to sleep at night. All the work is done by hand. Each village relies on the local rice harvest.

Being Local

Planting with native seeds and plants that have adapted to your area helps prevents problems caused by invasive, nonnative plants. This is a good idea when planting anything. When looking for fruit trees or shrubs, the first choice is to find local sources. The nursery people know more about what works in a given area as well. This means planting trees that already grow in your area. In 1990, I organized a tree planting program across the state of Georgia. I was inspired by Andy Lipkis of Tree People, who planted one million trees in Los Angeles. I didn't plant anywhere near that many. It was the twentieth anniversary of Earth Day and the objective was not to plant thousands of trees, but to get thousands of people planting trees. This was a wonderful program for me. It was part healing the earth and part sharing my passion to do so with others. Planting young trees is a positive step into the future. You are not planting them for yourself but for your children and even more for their children. It is especially rewarding to work with schools since children are great teachers with their upfront honesty.

Hopefully, some of them were inspired by the event to take on a similar project one day in the future. This is what I previously mentioned as doing the real work. As this work becomes who we are, it also reflects out into the community. It is contagious. This is one reason to practice biodynamics; it is a more spiritual approach. I was approached by a passerby one day as I worked in my garden. He asked me if I went to church. I replied by saying that I was in church. Nature is my church. Being sustainable is something to strive for. Saving your own seeds is part of the picture of self-sufficiency that closes the system. Watching a piece of land transform into a healthy vibrant environment is something to strive for. Exchange energy from the land rather than many miles away. Discover the wealth of the land by using the resources for the raw ingredients that you would normally buy at the store.

In the forest or jungle everything is done intentionally. It all develops with function and form. It has a purpose or it cannot exist there. So it makes sense that one's involvement with a piece of land needs to be done as an intentional act. A thoughtful plan helps to avoid future problems. Pulling weeds without a clear plan can create erosion. There is never a weed problem in the forest. Killing insects when there is no sign of damage causes an imbalance. Creating corridors that allow movement into and out of a field supports wildlife, climate, and air and water flow. Developing interdependent systems like composting and other nutrient cycling helps enrich the entire surroundings.

Having broader community-based concepts like seed saving and community-supported networks like cooperatives and community supported agriculture (CSA) groups also support a healthy life cycle that forms a foundation for the support needed to complete the energy being generated on a farm.

Eventually, completing the cycles of a closed system gives you the optimum resources that agroecology is all about. As you transform a piece of land, you become transformed by it. These cycles are generated and regenerated as the journey of life evolves.

2

Design

Though the problems of the world are increasingly complex, the solutions are embarrassingly simple.

—Bill Mollinson

THE VISION OF CREATION is exciting and challenging. This is where the journey begins with a new opportunity to develop a piece of land. It is like painting with the palate, only the canvas is three-dimensional and alive. The imagination can flow with passionate ideas that explode onto paper. The mind gets filled with colorful flowers, favorite fruits, the heavenly scents of lavender, and all that.

But wait. Am I doing it right? There are so many things to consider. Where is the best place to put it all? There are many right ways to lay out the most beautiful plans, and many more wrong ways to go about it that lead to costly learning experiences. One thing is for sure. There is no possible way not to make mistakes.

That is how we often learn and each endeavor comes with its own lessons. What are your objectives? How do your wants fit into what the land wants? Each piece of land is suitable for growing something amazing, but how do you fit it into what you want to grow. Each given area has a flow. How do you flow with it? It is like any relationship. There are compromises that make the transitions easier and it all takes time. It is good to have a one-year, two- or three-year plan. It helps also to work with what is already there. Gardens require ample sun, water, and soil. The most efficient way to trap the sun's energy is with plants.

Energy Cycles

Energy is cycled back into the soil in the following pattern: sun energy → plants → food → green manure → compost → soil, and back to plants. Is there enough water to support the growing you are doing? Rain cannot be relied on; you will need another source. Soil often needs to be nurtured back into a healthy state. It may also need remediation and this takes time. Make sure not to inhibit nutrient cycles. Nutrients like carbon and nitrogen, water, oxygen, and gases released from the soil flow in cycles. Plastic over soil prevents it from breathing. If you have stagnant water, then you have a drainage issue. When everything can flow in cycles, life flows freely. This is important for the overall health of the soil. Don't reinvent the wheel.

Conquering nature is one of humanity's great mistakes. Having a harmonious relationship with the natural environment around you is the key from the beginning. Most importantly, how do you make it healthier so it provides for you the way you want it to, long term, which is a more sustainable approach? Look at the whole picture. To get an overall perspective, you may need an aerial view from a tree or hill.

Making keen observations is a subtle task. It takes time to enter into an intimate relationship with a piece of land. Sitting quietly at the edge of a field can offer insight into how the various species function in their environment. It is a good investment of time to make useful observations that will pay off later. Notice how the slope of the terrain impacts the growth of the plants living there. Look for corridors in the openings in the woods along the edge of the field. It would be good to spend the night out in the field to see who shows up. It is also useful to observe how the field wakes up before sunrise.

Developing a Relationship with the Land

First, it is important to do an assessment of the existing plants. If native plants exist, try to work with them by incorporating your ideas into the already existing landscape. Perception in the garden is a developed sense.

The art of listening, smelling, and sensing the energy of the plants requires being open to your surroundings.

Research what conditions these plants grow in so that you can better understand what is best suited for the given area. The slopes are important for water and air flow. Bottom areas are always colder and wetter. Cold air contains more moisture and falls to the bottom; these areas will frost first and last and stay cooler. This is the law of convection. It helps to measure temperatures in these microclimates.

Divide areas up by the species that exist there. Bottom fields should be different than the high spots. A taller, denser ecosystem stays cooler during the day and retains heat at night. Look at the spot after a good rain to examine drainage problems. The sun's orientation is very important. Ideally, it is best for beds to run north and south for sun exposure on both sides. But east to west beds can use the sun differently, with small plants at the front sweeping to large ones in the back. You design it to look like a family portrait with the tall ones as backdrops sloping down to the small ones in the front.

Observe what trees are along the perimeter of the field you plan to work in. If you have oaks or nut trees, for instance, you will have squirrels. Black walnuts put a toxic acid into the soil to keep anything from growing around them and competing for nutrients. The ecosystem around a field exists well into the woods surrounding it. This is where the animals and insects come from that will visit your garden at night. Understanding who is there will be the first step in how to exist with them, like the invasive plants, which can often be nonnatives. This is an indication of an imbalance. Getting rid of them would be a long-term goal.

Always start with a pencil, paper, and a big eraser so you can make a lot of changes. It is easier to make changes on paper and a lot less costly. A landscape design is an expression of oneself, like in any art form it reflects one's personality. What do you want to convey? Design is as much about personality as it is about needs. A garden should invite you in.

In China, they follow the concept of feng shui. It involves movement of energy that flows in and out, without obstructions. Entrances consist of beautiful invitations with wide borders that funnel you in and sweep you through its corridors and on to another perspective of a garden that is rich and radiant with life exploding out from all areas. There is a central focus, or often several, such as a tree or a tall group of plants. Use plants that will lead up to this point, for example, a row of lavender on each side of a wide path or a bed of flowers with a small tree located at the end of the bed. There is definition but not like a manicured landscape. Allow plants to be a bit unruly to demonstrate a balance between a cultivated garden and one that also embraces nature. Nature is always the predominant leader. Try not to obstruct its flow.

Healthy plants want to grow freely and so give them room for this by understanding their needs for space. It is also good to fill up areas where plants have open voids. Basic landscape design involves form and formation. Form is the shape. Each plant has its own shape. Formation is the arrangement of these shapes. Some plants are more vertical; they work well as foundation plants to define end corners and so on. They can work well with horizontal ones that are oval or columnar. Use ground covers and spreading plants for the base to fill in the puzzle. Define corners with tall plants, which soften edges and borders along the front of beds. Use this with a consistent row of short plants. This gives it a defining edge.

There are many plants that complement each other. As you lay out the garden, you can get a feel for this. Follow your instincts and invite comments from others. Paths need to be easy to navigate. Try to avoid straight lines. Paths should sweep along like a dance. Use a more rounded pattern, but not to the point that you get lost or create a maze. Creating a circular design by using beds to form an arch can help define an area. An inner circle may resemble the outer perimeter of the garden. This can be used to form a clear definition as you transition from one area to another.

Design beds that are contoured with the slope of the land using space efficiently to allow you to get the most out of your design. Create shade for the benefit of your plants. This will protect them from heat and wind. A hedgerow can also serve as a windbreak. Windbreaks can be suited for different situations, and it is good if they serve more than one purpose. Elderberry (*Sambucus*) or *Rosa rugosa* is useful as a light windbreak but will not hold up against strong winds. Quince (*Cydonia oblonga*) or thornless blackberry work better for more challenging areas. These also provide a good fruit for you and wildlife. A windbreak needs to be pruned to encourage solid growth and just not top growth. A double windbreak can be used in a serious situation. Many types of brambles like blackberry are sturdier for strong winds. It will have to be maintained to prevent it from spreading.

Keep in mind that if you wish to trap the energy of, say, the wind, it is only to release it gradually. That is why plants work better than a wall where heat is released gradually. Ground covers and low-growing plants open up the atmosphere more easily. This provides air circulation above the landscape. There are places to trap air at beginnings and midway, yet allowing for air flow is very important.

One basic principle is to allow for the flow of air and moisture. The movement and fluidity enhances a healthy environment. Open up for sunlight to penetrate around and through plants. This is especially true for perennials. Trees are much healthier if opened up to allow air and sunlight in. Make sure to allow breathing room around plants and create the living mulch to protect the soil and the moist gas it gives off. Living mulch is what takes place when the plants are mature and leaves just overlap a little to create a canopy. This protects the soil, keeps out weeds, and helps develop the microenvironment just above the soil.

Keeping good air movement around plants is important. This can be advantageous on a wet year. Plants that are prone to diseases need more air flow. Use cut grasses as light mulch around young transplants to protect the soil but still allow it to breathe. They will decompose by the time the plants mature and develop a canopy over the bed. Seeing earthworms near the surface of the soil after a gentle rain is a good sign of porosity and fertility. Chances are the field you are working in is rounded also. Work with this shape. Contours along hillsides help ease the drop of elevation. Cover crops like white clover can be established in paths if there is not too much competition.

One farm I know leaves a path just wide enough for a lawn mower. The clover is spread onto the bed with the lawn mower's spray. This can work in a place with low-growing seeds. Work with existing shapes of the trees around you. Work with irregular shapes by adding continuity for balance. When there are too many straight lines, break up the continuity. Move away from horizontal straight lines at the tops of plants. Plant the same plants into small groupings in a traditional landscape design pattern.

Keep in mind that plants are round and do not need to be planted like square pegs. Plants fill in best in staggered patterns. Colors that complement each other allows for the painting of this landscape. Yellows move into oranges that move into reds well. Purples become blue and so on. Hedgerows and herbs can be used as herbaceous borders that are attractive and practical. For instance, a wide corridor can be edged with a small row of herbs like sage or prostate rosemary. Alyssum, yarrow, or lemon balm could also be used to provide habitat for beneficial insects.

Hedgerows also act as a filter to catch what is moving across a field in the air, by water, or on four legs. They encourage biological diversity. Hedgerows can be made up of a variety of plants or staggered plantings in a continuous line. A creative design for a hedgerow is one that serves multiple purposes. It can serve as a windbreak. It can also be edible for humans and wildlife. Here is a short list of possibilities: elderberry (*Sambucus*), gooseberry (*Ribes grossularia*) or currants, quince (*Cydonia oblonga*), rose hips (*Rosa rugosa*), blackberry (*Rubus*), pineapple guava (fejoa), rosemary, green tea plant (*Camellia sinsensis*), aronia berry (*Malus floribunda*) or chokeberry, lingonberry (*Vaccinium vitis*), serviceberry (*Amelanchier*). Work with the topography. You can also use tall growth as a catchment to trap air flow as it moves downhill. In the case of a hedgerow, they are planted in tight space. Otherwise, being practical is a dimension of design that is going to lead to its success. Maintenance needs to be considered as you can minimize your work by choosing plants that fill in a space well but don't compete for that space and are best suited for the area as they mature.

A watering system developed early will keep watering plans organized, followed with the use of mulch and living mulch. Keeping plants together that have the same water and sun needs is also important. Consider how the plant will look when mature. When I was working in the city parks in California in the 1970s, it was easy to observe ivy planted under shrubs. It may have been job security. How will neighboring plants blend together? How will they benefit each other, both physically and with nutritional needs? The existing balance or lack thereof needs to be assessed.

Permaculture Principles

Manifesting changes is a step-by-step process of careful planning and execution. Permaculture is a whole system that takes the entire environment into account. It ties together all the components to allow them to work together. It involves the use of ecosystem concepts and places plants into zones. An ecosystem is a structure of management of the natural laws. Everything is there to learn from. It can be seen as a small-scale existence nestled in a larger-scale system or web of life. The idea is to imitate patterns of nature. Take into account the functionality of each thing.

When planning, try to use plants that are multifunctional. For instance, planting clover or vetch under fruit trees provides a good cover for the soil. It builds the soil and provides nitrogen, and the flowers attract bees. Chives can also be very beneficial. It helps as a preventative for fruit scab, attracts beneficial insects and discourages harmful ones, and is a culinary herb.

A good place to start is with your base. Start with the place where you wake up and put your feet on the ground. This is the center of your universe. It should be a close walk to the area that needs the most attention, like annuals, vegetables, and those you use and work with most, a salad garden or herbs for the kitchen. As you branch out, move toward perennials or plants that are less demanding as the zones expand.

Try to maintain diversity all throughout the growing areas. The idea of planting only one plant creates a monoculture. All of one plant attracts all of one pest. A forest is very diverse, consisting of a community referred to as an ecosystem. It has a large host of families, ages, and sizes that compete and exist together. Try to emulate this in your design. The perimeter of the field where the garden is going to be is where small fruit and other shrubs can grow, and then fruit trees are lined around the field as you graduate into the existing woods. Areas that are protected from the wind can be used for tall plants that might be susceptible to wind damage. Shaded areas can be a zone for plants that benefit or tolerate shade, especially for afternoon shade. Areas of elevation need to be considered. Plants that benefit from higher spots usually need more drainage and in bottom areas you will often find plants that prefer wet soils. It will be beneficial to follow this pattern so the plants can take advantage of this when the summers are dry. Because of temperatures and moisture, needs for drainage should be considered.

Having a pond is a valuable biological resource. It is often the missing element on smaller lands. When creating one, remember to have a source of water and a place for runoff. This way it will not be stagnant. The best ponds taper into a depth of a foot or more. Using plants around the edge attract a wide variety of insects. Rocks can be used as landings for bees, dragonflies, and the like.

Elsewhere in the garden, groupings of plants that have mutual needs and are symbiotic in nature are useful. How do the plants interrelate? Plants themselves have interesting patterns, like the head of a sunflower or the shape of all flowers. They are elegant in their simplicity. These patterns are useful in providing water runoff or helping with pollination by wind. Use these patterns to design your own plantings. This is sometimes referred to as a mandala garden. A mandala is a circular or semicircular layout around a center. Using herb circles as the center is both esthetic and practical. Surround that with intensive plantings of vegetables, herbs, and flowers in an integrated approach. Along the parameters plant shrubs and trees.

Leave room for a few weeds. Much of what we call "weeds" grow in areas with similar soil and water needs. These plants catch and store energy that can be used by the gardener if cut when they are young and used as green manure or mulch. Some have deep roots that cultivate the soil. Others attract butterflies and desirable insects. Remediation is important because most areas are in need of some help from previous damage.

Observe weaknesses in the system. Erosion is an obvious one. Damage to the existing wild plants is a sign of poor health of the soil beneath. The weak soil of the given area produces plants that are being targeted by insects and diseases that are attracted to weak plants. By designing the area efficiently, you can minimize weeds, help store water in the soil, and maximize use of the area you are planting in. Plants can be used to help catch water. You will find the area with tall lush grass to house the earthworms.

If there is a creek or running water on the land, it is important to protect that area with riparian buffers of plants that prevent erosion from overflow during heavy rains. Native grasses work well for this. Along areas with a gentle flow one could introduce watercress. Along areas that flow even less would be a good area to introduce Cyanobacteria or blue-green algae. This could be collected in small amounts as a nitrogen source for beds. Unless a stream begins on the land, there is always the issue of contamination from the land above. It can be difficult to own one's watershed. Bioremediation can be done with plants like *Azolla* (duckweed fern). It is another plant source for making biofertilizer. This plant also removes chromium, nickel, copper, zinc, and lead. Water is an important part of balancing the biology of a piece of land.

Another concept to consider is polyculture plantings. This concept uses understory plants to utilize and protect the area beneath the ones above and using space efficiently. Growing tall plants with shorter plants under them is efficient and compatible. An example of this would be to plant dwarf or semidwarf fruit trees with slightly more space than usually needed. Halfway between you can plant a smaller shrub, like a blueberry bush. The base of the tree could provide space for flowers like larkspur or *Echinacea*, which would be beneficial for the tree above. At the base of the blueberry, calendula or clover are well suited. This way you are filling in the areas along horizontal levels and vertical ones and working with compatible plant communities that exist well together. Growing mints under some of the fruit trees can be used to discourage ants that will climb the trees and do damage. Tansy is also useful in discouraging ants. Wormwood (*Artemesia*) will discourage caterpillars.

It helps to group plant communities together that have similar needs for water, sun, and soil pH. In agroforestry, it is useful to try to introduce plants that will grow on the forest floor or that use the existing trees as a trellis and also use plants that will enhance those that are already there. Observe and emulate nature. Muscadine grapes climbing on the trees is one of nature's examples. Coffee is a good example of an agroforestry crop. It is also important to minimize impact. Estimate just how big an area you need. What are your food needs? It does not take that much room to provide for your needs if done efficiently. Doing a lot with a little is a good philosophy to follow. It is easy to get ambitious and later get overwhelmed. I am often asked, "How big of a garden should I do?" How big of a garden can you do well? Don't lose sight of what is important, doing quality work and having fun doing it. That's what brings quality results.

Design should involve a multitude of factors. The creative challenge is the desire to express yourself fully by resigning to the passion that is in you and to enhance the beauty that is already there. It requires perspective from many different angles and a thorough examination of your ultimate vision for what it will be. There are many stages of development, which can take years to accomplish. There is an organic growth of development and style that is gradual and ever changing.

This is combined with appropriate technology, which is the creative art of using what you have and utilizing available resources to their fullest. In the 1970s, I was able to visit and get involved with the Integral Urban House located on 5th Street in Berkeley, California. This is where I was first introduced to edible design concepts. I also met Bill and Helga Olkowski and was later introduced to the practices of integrated pest management.

There was an apple tree in the backyard with a bench under it. Around the bench was a planting of creeping thyme. It was a beautiful setting to sit and enjoy the many features of this house, like solar design, rainwater harvesting, and much more. It was a creative use of land that was also esthetically pleasing. I wondered why all yards weren't designed this way. I later realized that most people do not want to get out of their one-dimensional thinking. This place has since inspired several other urban homesteads. Some incorporate chickens, rabbits, beehives, and even fish.

Edible Landscaping

Edible landscaping is a creative way to work a combination of food and esthetics into an area of existing structures or landscapes. Edible landscapes incorporate food, ornamentals, and herbs in a colorful display. It is a little more decorative, emphasizing looks that also include production. Many plants lend themselves to this use: purple kale and kohlrabi, romanesco broccoli, savoy and red cabbage, rhubarb or rainbow chard. Lettuces are good edging along beds with a wide range of colors to choose from. Herbs are easy to work into a display. Garlic chives provide a very nice flower in the fall. There are many variegated herbs, purple basils, or sages that complement flower beds very well. Rosemary is a good foundation plant. I met a woman who grew her own dye herbs mixed into the flower beds.

Many plants are also used medicinally and give a beautiful display in landscapes. Then there are many edible flowers such as nasturtiums, daylilies, hibiscus, anise hyssop, bee balm, borage, and angelica to name a few. I have known people to grow their own saffron, which is a beautiful crocus. All fruit trees produce beautiful flowers in the spring. Blueberries can be used as a hedge very effectively. They can be seen through, which is sometimes desirable. This is a psychological barrier. There are other berries that cut out visibility if so desired. Jerusalem artichokes provide a nice backdrop of yellow daisies and are a good food staple. Asparagus and rose hips (*Rosa rugosa*) are also good background plants. Many berries and kiwis or grapes can be used to climb over arbors or fences. Cucumbers and even luffa sponge vines with their bright yellow flowers work well on fences. Strawberries work well as a ground cover in the front of a flower bed. Onions and garlic can be tucked in around flowers and serve to help keep insects away from those that are harder to grow. Purple bush beans blend in well. The use of a mixture of scarlet runner beans and grapes can be used to keep sun off a greenhouse in the summer.

It really depends on the imagination of the gardener. If you have a use for an edible plant it can be incorporated into the design. In the tropics, there is a large selection of plants to choose from. Katuk (*Sauropus andogynus*) can be used as a hedge. Its leaves make a nice salad. Chaya (*Cnidoscolus acronitifolius*) adapts to corners as a foundation plant. Jicama (*Pachyrhizus erosus*) and Malabar spinach (*Ballella alba*) work well as ground covers. Vanilla bean (*Planifolia ochidaceae*) is a wonderful orchid vine grown on a structure or another plant. Keep the trellis no taller than you can reach. It flowers and sets bean once it starts growing horizontally. Callaloo (*Amaranthus cruentus*) is a great green for hot climates. Its relatives are amaranth, a nutritious grain, and the troublesome pigweed (*Amaranthus palmeri*). Taro (*Colocasia esculenta*) is a wonderful lush landscape plant. Its root is commonly found in dishes around tropical parts of the world. Other plants include culantro (*Eryngium foetidum*), a close relative of cilantro, and New Zealand spinach (*Tetragonia*), which works well with purple beans. Winged beans (*Psophocarpus tetragonolobus*) can be used on a trellis as a backdrop.

Succession Planting

Back in North America, succession plantings are part of the plan when using annuals. Leafy greens can be replaced with summer flowers or herbs. You can have timed plantings for year-round effect. For instance, a full season design idea could start with a bed of tulips, followed by purple beans and daylilies in the summer, and then red Russian kale for the fall with an edging of pansies. In the South, one can utilize three seasons and some use of the winter. It gets too hot in the summer for the cool weather plants that are used in the spring. As summer plants die back, it is time to replant the cool plants again to carry you into winter. Sprouts, such as sunflower, can be used when in transition between plantings for a week or two until the next transplants are ready. Be aware of toxins in the soil. If your house has a history of being sprayed, or there may be paint chips around the house buried in the soil, it would be wise not to eat anything along this area. Check it out first.

Restoration and Recovery

Land recovery and restoration is an involved process that takes time. If you are working with depleted soil, where even weeds have a hard time growing, it might be good to plant a cover crop there first and work it in before any serious planting. Legumes are the most practical way to put nitrogen into the soil. White clover lends itself to marginal areas. Compost has many features that can remedy very poor soils. If you have limited resources, and things are really bad, you can take horse manure and spread it on a piece of land, till it in, and it will sprout whatever the horse has eaten. This can be used on ground where even weeds have a hard time. Ideally, it is good to feed the horse grains you want to grow. This is for places in need of vegetation. Erosion requires plants that will hold the soil in place.

On steep slopes, a first aid remedy is to take used sticks made into a woven fence, add a thick layer of mulch to stop run off, and then plant with a ground cover. This can be done every four or five feet down a slope. Ultimately, a combination of shallow and deep-rooted plants works well. Start at the top and work down. Terraces might need to be put in place. Hedgerows are another possibility for less dramatic areas. Often the soil is very imbalanced and is in need of not only nutrients but also proper pH and more life in the soil. Sand, hard clay, or rocky soils do not support plants without some form of humus. A living farm or garden needs life in the soil to support it. Diversity and the use of native plants help to do this. It might be necessary to start small. Depleted soil is often the result of over-grazing, overcutting, or other misuse of the land. Over time, land restores itself, but this could take years. Any attempt to put life back into the land is rewarded with positive results. There is a great need to do this work all over the planet and not nearly enough workers doing it.

In tropical clear-cuts, which can be seen all over developing countries, we developed a system with many stages. The first stage involves planting fast trees like leucaena as a nitrogen-fixing tree along with hardwoods, some nut bearing. Then planting easy trees and shrubs. Mulberry, passionfruit, and acerola can be grown fairly easily. Beans can be interplanted to enrich the soil. As the large trees grow, bananas and palm heart are introduced. Eventually, coffee, breadnut, and bread fruit can be established for semi-long-term use. As tall trees become established, fruiting vines can be trained to grow on them and bananas are planted as understory plants with semishade. Reclaiming land is an art and a science that has wonderful rewards.

Companion Planting

The science of companion planting is a valuable tool. The most important part about developing a garden is doing what works best for the plants you wish to grow. Using plants that are compatible in a given area is an intriguing science. This is how plants connect and disconnect in the plant world. There are several components to companion planting. It is best to try to integrate more than one of them to get optimum or dual use for your plantings. Physical companions are those that provide an immediate and practical use. An example of this is using a plant to trellis another. Sunflowers make a nice place for cucumbers to climb onto. Corn lends itself for pole beans or field peas to climb. Pole beans can also climb onto okra. The next part of physical or spatial planning is to fill in empty spaces to avoid providing room for weeds and to use space efficiently. This is a very important part of the French intensive method. Most leafy greens like lettuce or spinach have spreading and horizontal roots, similar to how they grow above the ground. Root crops grow in an opposite direction, mostly vertical. Plant lettuce with the usual spacing, which is about six inches, in staggered rows. Then plant carrots or radishes very close to them. They will grow without competing for space. It is kind of like Jack Sprat and his wife. They only need one seat on the bus. They fit well together.

Beets and small Chinese greens work well together. Turnips and spinach, cabbage and daikon radish are also good choices. Radishes mature quickly before the greens cover the space around them. Another example is to plant turnips between cabbages. The cabbages require one-foot spacing. The turnips are ready for harvest as the cabbage leaves begin to close up the space. Here you basically get two crops out of the same space. Other spatial combinations are tomatoes, which are generally trellised above the ground, and herbs. All that space on the bed under staked plants is a great place for small herbs that enjoy the shade, like chives or parsley. Peppers and eggplant work for this also.

The next component of companion planting is biological. Biological uses are those that work along chemical lines to either ward off insects that are undesirable or to attract insects that are desirable. This is the most popular aspect that most people think of when companion planting is mentioned. Plants that provide a strong deterrent are easy to find with your nose, but using them correctly is more of a science. Marigolds and nasturtiums repel aphids, leafhoppers, and thrips. Rue (*Ruta graveolus*) repels Japanese beetles. Geraniums sometimes work for squash bugs. Garlic will deter a wide range of insects. Ants do not like tansy.

There are also plants that attract wanted insects into an area of the garden. These are usually host plants for predatory insects that feed on the ones that feed on your plants. Borage is a useful plant around tomatoes. It is a host for the braconid wasp. This wasp will parasitize tomato hornworms. If you have ever seen tomato hornworms on your tomatoes, you know the damage they can do. If you have ever seen one with what appears to be rice crispy on its back that is the pupae of the braconid wasp. The wasp stings the worm and plants its eggs into the worm; the eggs parasitize the worm until they are ready to hatch and emerge as more wasps. Do not disturb this. At this point the worm dies and your plants thrive. Many of the umbellifers, like Queen Anne's lace, dill, yarrow, and angelica attract many predators. They need these plants to live in. Yarrow and alyssum are good candidates also. They attract lacewings and pirate insects. As another example of the dual purpose of companion planting, sunflowers provide a place for the cucumber to climb on and offer shade. But they do something else: sunflowers are a host to ladybugs, which clean the cucumber plants of aphids.

Another component of companion planting is botanical. Botanical methods involve how plants exude chemicals into the soil to alter their surroundings. For instance, mustard emits oils that are toxic to some insects and diseases, and in this way they are helpful to beans growing nearby. Marigolds are toxic to nematodes, so are African black oats. To some degree, rye can also be effective in this manner. Castor beans give off a substance that is toxic to gophers and moles and keeps them at bay. Elderberries are reported to work also. Mint and pennyroyal release oils into the soil as a deterrent to carrot worms.

Nutritional companions are important for providing nutrients into the soil for other plants to absorb. Buckwheat is believed to help activate the release of calcium in the soil. Legumes fix nitrogen from the atmosphere and store it in their roots. As roots break off or when turned into the soil, they provide essential nitrogen. This is especially true for cover crops like clover and vetch. Plants with long roots like lamb's-quarter and dock can cultivate the soil and help nutrients move to the surface to become more available to shallow-rooted plants. Alfalfa can have twenty-five-foot roots and is a great plant to have along the side of a bed for this purpose. Frost is also a great cultivator. Yet plants do it continually during the growing season. Some plants help enhance the flavor of the plants around them. Carrots like tomatoes as well as peas. I have always grown basil around tomatoes. I cannot say for sure that it works, but I always harvest the most amazing taste with both. The relationships and disrelationships between plants vary from place to place and season to season because other factors, like climate, are also very influential.

Therefore, designing a garden is an ongoing experiment that offers many insights to the magic of your garden. When planning a layout, it helps to separate plants into groups. Beds are divided up as follows (but keep in mind, I never like to devote a bed to only one type of plant). For the overall garden, 25 percent in perennials is a good goal. This saves a lot of labor in cultivation. These beds need a lot of attention for weeding, topdressing, and culling plants that need replacing.

Because of market demands combined with personal needs, it is hard to give equal percentage to different types of plant crops. Planting around 15 to 17 percent in legumes (peas, beans, etc.) works well. And an equal amount to leafy crops works well for balancing. Root crops get slightly more with at least 17 percent. For instance, a collection of garlic, onions, and sweet potatoes are smart food for the winter. Fruit vegetables should have about 20 percent of the space because of big crops like tomatoes, cucumbers, and melons. Flowers for market receive about 20 percent. This represents two-thirds of the overall growing area laid out into beds. The other third is in established fruit trees, grape vines, and wildflower areas. Wildflowers are another element for creating biological balance. A field of hay can be approximately four times larger. This provides material for composting and could provide feed for animals.

In the South, there are three seasons to grow in without protection. Spring and fall are similar with leaf and root crops being primary plantings. Summer is mostly fruiting and seed vegetables, along with flowers and herbs. Winter does work well for roots and leafy vegetables if you use a cloche or coldframe. Coldframes can be designed to fit over beds, or you can use hoops covered with plastic and cloth for nights dropping into the mid-twenties. They are needed for the extreme winter temperatures. Of course, these need to be uncovered when the sun comes out. Plants do not like extreme temperature fluctuations. Spinach, kale, collards, and parsley hold up well down to the low twenties. Mature roots like carrots and Jerusalem artichokes that are entirely underground are stored well in the ground until they are needed.

There are many types of garden designs, each having a different objective. They should all have elements that work for esthetics, production, practicality, and maintenance designed into them. Entrances are an important part of welcoming people into a garden. A pergola of post and timbers to support kiwi vines or grapes planted on the corners provides a nice entrance. It becomes a canopy that could have a shaded bench inside. Keep in mind that if you use kiwis you need one male plant to pollinate the females. Another idea is a gazebo planted with different colored roses. Cherry or other trees with beautiful flowers create a nice entrance. Develop a mini-meadow of wild flowers as part of an entrance.

Learning Gardens

There are many types of concept gardens that provide a large range of possibilities. Learning gardens can be very creative and fun, especially children's gardens. The most creative is the edible playground garden. It is designed for learning and having fun. Having fun is an important component to learning. This garden can make use of many recycled materials. It can be done inexpensively and is limited only by the imagination. Sidewalk reinforcement wire can be recycled from construction jobs. A cucumber tunnel could be made with the wire. Bamboo can be used to set up two teepees, one for cherry tomatoes and one for pole beans. Growing bamboo is not recommended as it is too invasive. It is better to find someone trying to control their patch and help them by doing a harvest. A large area can be used to create a sunflower maze. A swing set can be used to support vines like grapes or kiwis. Set up parallel wavy walls with wire to support small melons. It's a wall o' melons or beans. Make a hutch shaped like an igloo from various branches and bamboo for scarlet runner beans or any other vines. Finally, build an entrance that consists of two parallel boxes. They are joined at the top with a piece of lattice for sugar snaps with bedding plants like lettuce, radish, nasturtium, and so on.

Let the children plant it so they have a sense of ownership. In most cases, if they plant it they will eat it, and take great pride in it. Children are easily receptive to creating and connecting with nature.

Barrier-Free Gardens and Horticulture Therapy

Another very rewarding garden concept is a barrier-free garden for people with disabilities. These gardens are quite simple to make. You can construct tables with boxes that have sides that are maybe six inches high. Drill holes in the table for drainage and fill the box with soil. The height is measured to accommodate wheelchair access. Set up blocks and stands for five gallon buckets, large pots, and bushel baskets with soil for larger plants like tomato, pepper, eggplant, bush squash, and so forth. Make sure there are holes in all containers for drainage. Many types of containers can be used; you could even use an old toilet for bush cucumbers or squash. There are many plant varieties suited for container gardens, making it easy to work with. Allow the participants to bring their own containers to plant in. This invites creative recycling into the mix. We have used old boots, furniture, and all sorts of food containers. One garden I visited provided a suitcase of cucumbers. Maybe they were planning a trip and didn't want to leave the cukes behind. These gardens fall under the description of horticulture therapy. They involve learning experientially.

To become embraced in natural surroundings allows one to breathe, relax, and be fully part of what you are doing. It can be a healing place as well as a learning environment. Being disconnected from other living things is unhealthy for all of us. Nature has a way of making us reconnect with life that is very healing. Horticultural therapy is a contemplative moment that can last for an entire bed that bridges space and time.

An herb garden is another concept garden that is easy to set up. Many herbs are easy to grow. They are often low maintenance and have low water needs. There are many that are shade tolerant. Gardens can be set up in the formation of wheels, spirals, semicircles, or whatever the imagination allows. Plants can be divided into categories, like medicinal and culinary, or by regions of origin. Medicinal herbs sometimes prefer wild environments to grow in. Herbs can be grouped as they relate to astrological symbols. Herbs are unique in that their beauty is simple and confined, yet hardy. This is an opportunity to design a beautiful landscape.

Cut flower gardens are usually thought of as being for a private residence. But this is not necessarily so, for the earth smiles with its flowers. They are food for the soul and need to be on display in public places to add a smile to each environment. This is where color schemes are part of the design. The mature size of the plant needs to be considered. There are many flowers that need staking once they start to bloom if you plan to use them as cut flowers. Cutting them or at least deadheading them encourages more blooms. Staking can consist of a piece of wire placed horizontally on stakes about three to four feet off the ground. This works well for cosmos, tall poppies, or *Ammi majus*. With gaillardia or venidiums, the wire needs to be much lower. Most people start with zinnias, marigolds, cleome, and celosia. Dahlias usually need individual staking. If wind is an issue, staking and/or windbreaks may need to be in place for them. There are many flowers that are easy to plant and grow. Larkspur, nigella, celosia, zinnias, and cleomes are easy to broadcast into a cultivated bed.

It is also important to take maintenance and hardiness into account. This is all about being creative and what the end results will look like. Most importantly, in all gardens try to keep a balance of creativity alongside function and practicality. For instance, alyssum along the edge of the bed will attract *Stethorus* beetles and tachinid flies. Flowers, of course, add color to a garden and draw the visitor in to investigate what else might be worth the visit. The placement of tall flowers in corners of gardens brings a bright addition and complements everything around it. It is always a combination of the art and science of what works in both realms, and doing it with passion provokes a quality of work.

3

Compost

What It Is, How to Make It, How to Use It

Compost is life into death into life.

—Alan Chadwick

COMPOST IS THE BASIS FOR organic farming and gardening. From the smallest kitchen gardens to large production farms, it is vitally important. It supports renewed growth and nutrient cycling. It is fundamentally the most important way to improve the soil. It does this on three levels. First, it improves the tilth in soil. It loosens clay soils; it provides oxygen and helps digest the most dense clay soils. It helps build texture and structure for sandy soils and increases water-holding capacity. It is the best and longest lasting soil conditioner you can find.

Second, it provides balanced nutrients that are sustainable and slow released in a way no chemical fertilizer can match. More importantly, it enhances the life of soil by introducing beneficial microorganisms. Depending on the raw ingredients used, compost contains all the macro- and micronutrients needed for plant growth.

Third, compost contains an enormous population of microscopic plants, animals, bacteria, and fungi. One square inch of compost can contain over one hundred million beneficial microorganisms. They exist in a state of dynamic equilibrium that is ever changing. Some compete for food while others live symbiotically.

Compost produces compounds that stimulate growth in plants. It is a concentrated structure of biological, chemical, and mineral nutrients that work together to create an ideal soil for growing plants. Its molecular structure binds together in a way that makes it more resistant to harmful pathogens. It contains major and minor nutrients in stabilized forms.

Physically, the microbes glue the soil together into aggregate particles. They also coat soil particles that bind together chemically into negatively charged colloids. These colloids contain negatively charged ions or anions that attract positively charged ions or cations. Electromagnetically charged minerals like phosphorous and potassium become available to the root hairs and are taken up into the plants. These chemical bonds help facilitate healthy fauna. The microscopic colloids also help the soil develop a crumbly structure. These colloids have a jelly-like structure.

Compost has excellent water-holding capacity while providing channels for air circulation. This creates ideal conditions that allow the soil to hold water well, as it also drains well. This structure allows the soil to breathe and facilitates circulation of water and air. This encourages roots to grow deeper and helps develop the aggregate structure of the soil. Compost helps prevent soils from drying out by improving reserves for water. The microorganisms absorb water themselves and create a thin film at root tips to prevent them from drying out. It prevents soil erosion with life-giving properties binding the soil together. By binding the soil together biologically, nutrients are not washed away. Compost can absorb twice its weight in water. Aeration is extremely important for plant roots. Beneficial bacteria and fungi release oxygen. This aids in the release of nutrients. Compost contains many small plant forms that release an abundance of carbon dioxide into the soil as well.

The introduction of biological life forms moving about in the soil creates capillaries that further add to the soil's structure. These microorganisms encourage earthworms and other decomposers to break down organic matter into a form that plants can readily absorb. Compost is the ultimate recycler. Nature does not waste. Humans are consumers, accumulators, and very wasteful. Composting is a way to complete cycles efficiently while putting back into the soil what we depend on.

Once this process is started, it is easy to continue with establishing healthy soil development. The continued use of compost will make the poorest of soils rich and vibrant with life that plants can flourish in. Humic acid contains many properties that enhance the soil on several levels. Humus is the end product of decomposition. It is stabilized organic matter that provides balanced nutrients that plants can easily assimilate. It creates a buffer by binding to toxins making them less soluble in the soil. It helps balance the pH. It inoculates the soil with microorganisms that build mycorrhizae formations along the roots with bacteria and fungi that work symbiotically. The bacteria feed on exudates that the roots release. This is the symbiotic relationship between soil and plant roots that is needed for healthy growing to take place. The bacteria also break down minerals the plants can absorb and utilize directly. Some of these bacteria work to parasitize harmful bacteria that would otherwise suppress growth or cause diseases.

One example is beneficial nematodes that attach to harmful nematodes with a whole host of harmful organisms. Humus feeds plants lacking in chlorophyll, further enriching soil life. Humus holds nutrients in check and provides the slow release for root uptake. Its effect on overall health allows plants to take up and utilize nutrients more effectively. Humus contains antibacterial and antifungal properties that both buffer and attack pathogens. It introduces many beneficial life forms that enrich the soil food web with what soils need to become lush with life-giving properties. It is the main facilitator of recycling nutrients back into the soil.

Compost can contain 60 percent humus. Humus also contains fulvic acid that transports minerals and acts as a catalyst for nutrient transformation and growth stimulation. Catabolic metabolism is the breakdown of complex molecules into simple ones to release energy. Humus is the binding of these molecules back into stable compounds that are readily assimilated.

The process of decomposition has been taking place since plants have been on the planet. In the fall, leaves from trees drop to provide next year's nutrients. Ecosystems are in a constant process of nutrient cycling as a way to sustain themselves. In the compost pile this process is greatly expedited. This process is faster and more concentrated. This helps prevent a loss of nutrients.

In workshops, I often compare building the compost pile to making a cake. A lot of it depends of getting the right ingredients and putting it together in the right proportions. There are many methods for building compost. The one referred to here is the Indore method. It was developed by Sir Albert Howard, one of the fathers of organic philosophy and an inspiration to the beginning of the organic movement. He worked as an agronomist in India from 1905 to 1934 and developed the method in Indore, India. One basic principle is to balance the carbon/nitrogen ratios of the pile. All substances need carbon and nitrogen to break down.

The ideal ratio for efficient decomposition is around 25 to 1, carbon to nitrogen. Nothing is pure carbon and nothing is pure nitrogen. Nitrogen feeds off of the carbon and provides the heat. Carbon provides the fuel. If the pile does not heat up properly, it is because of a lack of nitrogen. If you ever put your hand into a bag of grass clippings it is hot. That is a high source of nitrogen, about 15 to 1 carbon to nitrogen, but too dense to make compost. Sawdust on the other hand is 500 to 1 carbon to nitrogen. That is way too much carbon and too dry to break down properly. Chicken manure is high in ammonia, which is why it burns your nose to smell it. Ammonia breaks down into nitrogen, but it can use some help to do it. Air and water assist the carbon molecules to do this (see table 3.1).

Manures are a good source of nutrients because animals do not digest food totally. Much of it is passed through them. With the addition of digestive enzymes, digestion happens more readily once it leaves their body. Another way to look at compost is by wet to dry ingredients. Manures are often the source for nitrogen and are best used in their wet or fresh form. Old or rotted manure will not contain enough nitrogen to heat up properly.

TABLE 3.1
Carbon to Nitrogen Ratios of Raw Organic Materials

Organic Material	Carbon to Nitrogen
Coffee Grounds	20:1
Corn Stalks	60:1
Cow Manure	20:1
Fruit Wastes	35:1
Grass Clippings	20:1
Horse Manure	60:1
Newspaper	50–200:1
Oak Leaves (Dry)	60:1
Pine Needles	58:1
Rotted Manure	20:1
Wood Sawdust	600:1
Straw	80–100:1
Table Scraps	15:1
Plant Materials	12–20:1
Poultry Manure	5–15:1

Source: University of Florida IFAS, http://ifas.ufl.edu/.

What you want to look for is a high ammonia content. Hay is a good source of carbon and provides much needed air into the pile (see table 3.2).

What we create in a compost pile is a very dynamic concentration of biological activity. This activity is aerobic and requires a great amount of air. It also needs a lot of water, because the life is growing and decomposing at an enormous rate.

Anaerobic decomposition is another process. It is not creating the same bacteria and fungi. Aerobic works best for manifesting life-giving properties. The materials you use are very important. Carbon sources consist of dry materials. Leaves are a good carbon source. Fresh leaves contain approximately a 40 to 1 carbon to nitrogen ratio. With dry leaves it's 80 to 1 carbon to nitrogen ratio. The biggest problem with leaves is they mat and prevent airflow in the pile. It would be best to shred them first. This can be done with a lawn mower.

TABLE 3.2
Mineral Analysis of Raw Materials

	Nitrogen N (%)	Phosphorus P (%)	Potassium K (%)
	2.4	.50	.2
	.66	.2	1.1
	8	9	3
	4	21	.20
	2	.50	1.2
	.29	.25–1	1.5
	15.30	0	0
	6–12	1–6	1–2
	.6–1	6–1 9	1.6–3
	.44	.35–1	.35–1.6
	.60	.45	.5–.8
	1–2	1–2	.6–1.2
	2.4	1.4	.6
	1.68	.75	4.93
	7	2	1

Source: Rodale Encyclopedia of Composting.

The nutrients in leaves vary depending on the tree. Maple, especially sugar maple, provides many nutrients, as does white ash and leguminous trees like hickory or locust. Fruit tree leaves are also high in available nutrients. Oaks and most deciduous trees are fine. Pine needles can be used if you desire acid compost, but it takes a little longer for the compost to mature. It is best to pile leaves by themselves and let them rot into leaf mold that is just decomposed leaves. This is often added to potting mixes or small planting areas.

Cardboard has the same matting problem as leaves and contains some glues that are toxic. Paper mats together incredibly well. Sawdust is way too carbon, as are wood chips, which are mostly wood cellulose, with even more carbon than sawdust. One common mistake people make is piling up wood chips, letting them break down, and then calling it compost. At best, this is soil conditioner and has little or no nutrients. Wood chips are also used as mulch on top of beds. They need a lot of nitrogen to break down. They suck nitrogen from the soil in order to break down so you lose a lot of nitrogen from your soil in the process. They should be used minimally in the garden and not in the compost pile at all.

Composting can be done very effectively with sawdust. It requires a lot of organic matter and a lot of turning, but it can turn out a good product. Dried plants can be a source of carbon as long as they are free of diseases that could be transferred into the soil later. Although many plant diseases may not survive the composting process, it is not worth taking a chance that they won't. So burn those plants or put them out away from the growing area. The use of sunflower stalks on the bottom provides ventilation. The center rots out and it becomes a vent tube. Jerusalem artichokes and other plants with semiwoody stems do not do this as well, but they can be good sources of carbon. Hay is the first choice, especially straw. It is more easy to find partially rotted hay that a farmer is happy to let you haul away. Be careful to only use rough-cut hay coming from an unattended field. It has not been sprayed or fertilized. This already has some bacteria and moisture in it.

Nitrogen sources provide more of a selection. Manures are often the most popular choice. Unless you have animals of your own, it may be difficult to find clean manures without traces of synthetic chemicals. These often get passed through the manure. Dairy cows pass the hormones they are given. Horses are given hormonal feed and deworming agents. Chickens are given a large list of synthetic chemicals that can upset the fauna of your soil. It can be challenging. I have fond memories of taking my very young daughter to the back of the circus to get elephant manure when the circus was in town. After researching more about how they were treated, that was stopped in exchange for finding better quality sources. It is important to use raw materials from clean sources so you are not bringing toxic materials into the garden.

Many years ago a group of us decided to steal spent hay from a large agribusiness operation. I ended up with a triple dose of bad karma. First, there was a bumblebee hive buried in the hay from which I received a serious bee sting in the face. About a week after using the hay to mulch sweet potato starts, I discovered it was full of weed seed, so I cleaned it out of the beds. The next day I discovered that I was covered with enough chigger bites to keep me itching for a week. It was a harsh lesson that I didn't forget.

You can also use nonanimal sources. Piles can be made with green manure like grass or clover with great results. When doing this, it is best to add a little soil to introduce some bacteria into the mix. Food will break down well in a pile although you should not use this in large quantities. Kitchen scraps do offer diversity and minerals. Eggshells bring in calcium. Coffee grounds, filters and all, and half-rotted vegetables work well as feed for hungry microorganisms. Be sure not to put meat or dairy into the pile. This does not do well nor break down.

Alfalfa meal can be used as a supplemental nitrogen source. Growing from non-GMO seed allows you to save your own alfalfa from old seed to avoid bringing in GMO (genetically modified organisms) alfalfa. The idea is to be as diverse as you can. Alfalfa (*Medicago sativa*) can easily produce 100 to 150 pounds of nitrogen per acre. Again, like in a cake batter, variety is the spice of life.

In biodynamics, it is preferred to use three different forms of manure from unrelated species of animals. Manures vary in nutrient capacity, as shown in table 3.2. For ammonia and nitrates, chicken or any other fowl is easily the highest, followed by pig, cow, goat and sheep, and then horse. For potassium, chicken is also the highest followed by pig, goat, horse, and then cow. For phosphorus, chicken is again the highest, with exception to bat, followed by goat, pig, horse, and cow. I often hear about sewage sludge as good compost. Sewage sludge makes good compost, but it contains toxic waste and heavy metals.

When I worked for the cooperative extension service in Georgia, they recommended putting commercial fertilizer like ammonium nitrate in the pile to get it to heat up. This has detrimental effects and kills off any possible way to build beneficial microorganisms. It is counterproductive.

If you happen to live near a coast with relatively clean water, seaweed can be an excellent source of nitrogen and trace minerals. It needs to be rinsed well first to clean the salt off. It is best to use your better judgment. With materials in general, if it is from a questionable source it is better to stay away from it.

The structure of the pile needs to be built according to what you need and what you can handle. There is a different approach to making a production compost. You start the pile and complete it that day. Nothing is added later on, to avoid inhibiting the process. These piles are often around six square feet by six feet high, if one has enough materials. It is good to build it as high as you have materials. The pile can reduce by one-third its original size when finished. It works well to have several people help build it, or at least one other person. It goes along much better. It is ideal to make piles with half a dozen people and the piles can be six by twelve by six. That would be a lot for one person in a day. The pile needs to be at least three feet in diameter. This way it will have enough thermal mass to manufacture the process and store the heat for proper decomposition. Start what you can finish in a day so the process will heat up uniformly.

Larger production compost is often made with a front-end loader. Start by putting a pole in the ground where the center will be. This is a ventilation hole. The pile heats up and needs a place to release this heat. It also allows air to get into the center of the pile. It is best to use a smooth pipe of around four inches in diameter and tall enough to extend well out of the pile. This will be taken out after a day or so. (Large tree branches can be used, which is all I often have in developing countries, but they are heavy and difficult to remove.)

Constructing a Compost Pile

Take a fork and loosen the soil where the pile will be. This opens the ground to receive the forces. The pile can lose as much as 20 percent of its nutrients through fluids into the earth. This does not have to be lost if you later use this area to plant on. Therefore, piles should move around to available spaces in the garden if at all possible. Many of my original locations were later planted with fruit trees. Another reason for opening the ground is because when the pile finally cools off, small insects and earthworms can easily move up into the pile to add to its completion. It helps to fork the ground lightly to encourage this.

Start by putting down a layer of brush or other thick material. If you have a lot of bachelor buttons, both wild and cultivated, that works well for this. Or sunflower stalks come in handy. This is followed by four to six inches of hay or another carbon source. Next, add about four inches of manure. If using green manures, put them down a little thicker so it is almost fifty–fifty. Then water the pile, wet down the dry, and wash the soil and manure into the hay. After this, add another six to eight inches of hay with three to four inches of manure and water down each layer. See the illustration in figure 3.1.

If you are in an area where the soil is acidic, or even if it isn't, sprinkle wood ashes or lime over the manure or nitrogen source about every third layer to balance the pH. A low pH or acid conditions can inhibit the development of the bacteria and fungi needed for proper decomposition process to occur. Use charred wood ashes because they also contain some potassium and are an excellent carbon source. Too much lime can formulate an abundance of ammonia and nitrogen can be lost. Put it on in handfuls. Add a thin layer of soil to every few layers. This contributes needed bacteria and helps contribute a colloidal content to the pile.

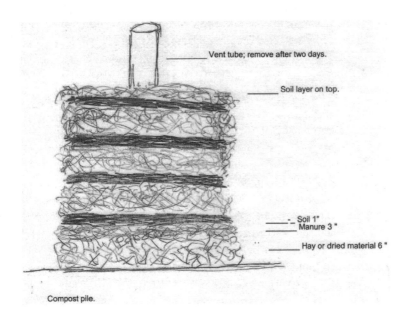

Vent tube; remove after two days.

Soil layer on top.

Soil 1"
Manure 3 "

Hay or dried material 6 "

Compost pile.

FIGURE 3.1

When several trees are planted in one season there is a lot of soil left over. Digging a hole three feet wide and thirty inches deep for a tree leaves a surplus of soil. That soil can be used for years as layering in a compost pile. It is kind of a holistic way of returning it to the land. The whole pattern is repeated for each layer. It is good to introduce green plants into the pile, especially those that retain a lot of water. Another good contribution is a layer of comfrey and stinging nettle (*Utica dioica*) incorporated into every few layers.

Other plants that are very useful include chamomile, dandelion, yarrow, and any legumes or grasses. This is a great way to recycle spent or dead garden plants that are free of diseases. Rock minerals like rock phosphate, granite dust, kelp, green sand, and bone meal can be spread over layers periodically. This adds to the mineral content of the pile and helps the minerals become digested before use.

As the pile grows taller, it is important to shape it to prevent it from becoming a pyramid. The pile should have a little bounce when layered onto. This way you know you are putting enough air into it. The balanced amount of air and water is needed to generate microbial growth. Once the pile has reached a height of completion, either due to exhausted materials or exhausted work force, it is time to cap it off. Put a light layer of leaves or hay followed by a light layer of soil. Once the pile is complete you have a towering mass of organic matter. It is a smorgasbord for all the various aerobic recyclers.

Phases of Decomposition

The first phase of the composting is the mesophyllic stage. This is where sugars and carbohydrates are metabolized. It involves the thermophyllic fungi that break down the epidermal layers of plant material. The pile also consists of fungi like Basiliomycetes and bacteria like *Bacillus* and *Heliospirillum*. Fungi are eukaryote organisms of complete cells. They aerate the soil and create pockets for others to inhabit; they also transport and store nutrients and break down lignin, the waxy substance that is hard for others to digest.

Fungi are more attractive to forest and perennial plants. They are seen as the more brown colors in the pile. This produces moderate temperatures and lasts for one or two days. The next stage is thermophilic bacteria. Heat-resistant bacteria like *Arthrobacter*, *Pseudomonas*, *Streptomyces*, and *Actinomyces*, and some fungi dominate this.

Bacteria are the primary decomposers here. Bacteria produce amino and nucleic acids essential for nitrogen in the soil. Actinomycetes are especially beneficial as a nutrient producer for plants. Bacteria are more attractive to annuals and areas of common cultivation. They invade the materials to further break it down to substances less recognizable. This phase can last one week to one month with temperatures reaching 150 degrees Fahrenheit or higher; 140 degrees is a minimum objective. This is hot enough to kill off weed seeds and most diseases. This pasteurization process is also very effective at roasting seeds in the pile. Although to be on the safe side, diseased plants should not be incorporated into the pile. Metabolic heat transfer generates the heat.

In other words, microorganisms are creating this heat by digestion and multiplying in the pile. Piles can reach higher temperatures, but anything above 160 degrees or so can burn off essential nutrients, so this should be discouraged. Once the pile has cooled off, you have entered back into the me sophyllic and third stage. Here similar fungi and bacteria enter into the pile to further break down materials. Protozoa and nematodes will later consume these bacteria and fungi. They will produce carbon and concentrated minerals. It is kind of like the big fish eating small fish. These are in turn eaten by invertebrates, arthropods, centipedes, roly-polies (*Armadillidium vulgare*), and earthworms that will eat everything small enough to fit in their mouths.

All these things are rendered to a completed form that is rich in humus. Turn the pile after two weeks or so to both aerate the pile and get materials on the outside mixed inside for uniform decomposition. Use the pipe for the first turning as it usually heats up again with the introduction of more air. The movement of gases in the pile is generally upward and into pockets. Water moves downward in the pile and into pockets. Circulation is important, which is one reason for turning the pile. After two or three weeks or when it begins to cool down again, I turn it once more. At this point, I hope it stays cool and do not use a pipe in the middle. I only water it during the turns if it looks very dry. After the first turning, I let it cool down, and then put biodynamic preparations into it before turning it for the second time. I generally have finished compost in about three months.

A large occupation of earthworms and roly-polies (*Armadillidium vulgare*) is an indication that the pile is finished breaking down. I have seen compost turned every other day and used in two to three weeks. This is done in Belize or Nicaragua where the topical heat helps manifest biotic growth and labor is cheap and in plentiful supply. Other methods of composting can achieve good results. Biodynamic composting is similar.

The pile is built in a trapezoidal shape tapering up and leveled off at the top. It is finished with a layer of soil or sod cover to insulate it. Sheet composting involves fewer layers, maybe only one or two feet high. This is covered with plastic or leaves and allowed to sit for several months; then it's plowed or worked into the soil where it is located. Compost bins allows you to be more organized and out of the way of growing areas.

Another good system is the New Zealand box method. This involves constructing panels made with screen or fence on frames. The panels are set up on three or four sides to contain the compost pile. The panels are built with hinges or tied together so they can be removed without disturbing the pile. It is a convertible box and can easily be built out of scrap material. It can be placed next to the pile to be turned into for each turning. Compost does not need sun. So if you have limited areas to grow in, why use it up with compost? There is also pit composting; this is more anaerobic and useful in tropical areas without as much rain.

Large-scale composting production can be done using similar methods as I use but with mechanical means. Long windrows are set up using dump trucks, shredders, front-end loaders, and overhead watering systems. The pile won't be as detailed, but a lot more compost can be generated this way. Not all compost is the same. The important thing to consider is the quality of your materials. I stay away from commercial waste that has traces of toxic chemicals. Cottonseed meal, for instance, is a good source of nitrogen, but where does it come from? It can contain substances you may not want in your garden, like chemicals that have been outlawed in United States for many years. The idea of making compost in a concentrated form that is insulated from outside elements encourages the use of as many nutrients and beneficial organisms as possible. It is also important to try to keep the pile protected from heavy rains so it will not become waterlogged. You can do this with covered frames so the pile can get the air it needs while it is still decomposing.

Once the pile is finished, keep it covered to further protect it from the elements. Do not let it dry out. The idea is to use it during that season, the sooner the better. The life in a compost pile is fragile and very susceptible to the elements, especially wind and rain. Keeping it on higher ground will keep it from soaking up water and becoming soup.

Composting can be done in many ways, as mentioned above, and used in many more. The finished product is rich in humus that is in a stabilized form. There is no better way to enrich the biology of the soil. Being elbow deep in compost gives me a feeling of being connected to the wealth all around me. I doubt anyone gets up to his or her elbows in 10-10-10 fertil-izer. It would not feel quite the same. It is good to put some compost in the soil before each planting to ensure that you are putting back more than you take out. This is a way of constantly healing and improving the land you are on. I cover freshly dug beds with two or three inches and immediately fork it into the bed deep enough to be covered with soil. Compost left on the soil exposed to sun and wind will quickly diminish to soil conditioner at best. Once in the bed, treat it as though it is planted with the finest seed, keeping it watered and mulched.

Using Compost

When planting large plants in holes, it is good to mix in 50 percent com-post to the existing soil before putting it back in the hole. Compost is also an important ingredient in potting soils. In this application, it is shifted to use only the fine humic particles. Topdressing provides nutrients during the growing season. A healthy amount put at the base of plants stimulates growth at various stages. This works to further make nutrients available throughout the season. As proteins break down they are formed into peptides and amino acids that are available to ammonia compounds to be restructured into nitrates and made available to plants. Biopesticides can be a useful way to prevent and disrupt diseases.

Compost is a main factor in this when used as compost tea. Compost tea is made very easily with water. You can make a tea bag with a potato sack, steeping the compost in a barrel of water suspended by a stick and tied off. You can just as easily throw some compost in a bucket and strain it later through a cloth. This way it can be put through a sprayer. If you add molas-ses, this mix will increase microbial growth and have a positive impact on the plants. Compost tea contains beneficial microorganisms that move into pockets of leaf surface and digest leaf exudates that would attract patho-genic organisms. They can also provide some nutrients as a foliar feed.

Combined with other plant teas, compost can be a catalyst for providing easily assimilated nutrients. It contains trace minerals necessary for plant growth. It also buffers and protects surface area of the leaf from pathogens. More so, beneficial bacteria and fungi attack pathogens and parasitize them by their overwhelming numbers that are present in the concentrated form. Make sure that the compost is fresh and from a good source by using qual-ity raw ingredients in the building of the pile.

In addition, the introduction of oxygen helps stimulate their effect. Stirring the solution before use can do this. Other microbial properties of the tea like yeasts, fungi (*Trichoderma*), and a variety of bacillus, phenols, and aminos inhibit the development of diseases. Compost can also be mixed with other botanicals to make them more effective against diseases and insects.

Compost has proven useful with diatomaceous earth for tree insects. It enhances the use of neem oil as a fungicide. Compost tea has been effective on early stages of bacterial canker, anthracnose, verticillium wilt, and early blight. It can be used with some success on *Phytophthora* late blight of potatoes and on root rot fungus. It has overall effect as a preventative used in a maintenance spray program throughout the growing season.

Working with compost is a wonderfully positive experience that allows you to be connected with the biological world on a microscopic level that is enriching to your soil. It also helps one to understand where we come from and where we are going back to one day. It is by far the most dynamic way to impact the garden. Plants grown in compost are far more nutritious and full of vitamins. It takes gardening and farming full circle. It is the best soil stewardship program one can establish. With continued use of a comprehensive composting program, the quality and quantity of yields go up. The balance it brings to the soil diminishes problems and creates a healthy environment.

I learned long ago that I do not grow plants, the soil does. People often tell me I produce beautiful fruits and vegetables, herbs, grains, flowers, and so on. You do this by producing healthy soils for them to flourish in. Compost can be used for soil remediation with very effective results. There are several species of microbes contained in compost that are effective in absorbing and breaking down toxic materials. They work on different principles. One process is extracellular. The microbes secrete enzymes to break down molecules into a simple form.

The next phase is intracellular, whereby the material is absorbed in a mineralization process. Bioremediation of water is a method of using plants to absorb and break down toxins. The process works by setting up leach fields. This can be done with boxes indoors or in a greenhouse. Many of the plants used are common to swamps and do this naturally in their native habitats. Here is a list of plant species you could use: *Nymphea alba* (water lily), *Phragmites australias* (a common reed, this can become a nonnative wet land grass), *Sparganium erectum* (simple stem bur-reed), *Iris phsuedacorus* (yellow flag iris), *Schoenoplectus lacustris* (club rush or bulrush), *Carex acutifornis* (sedge). Oxygen suppliers are *Stratiotes alvides* (water soldier), *Hydrocharis morsus-ranae* (European frogbit), and *Acorus calamus* (sweet flag reed).

Examples of phytoextraction plants include sunflower, mustard, canna lily, willow, and Salix. Water should be allowed to move slowly through these channels to be absorbed by the plants. The interesting thing is that these plants do not absorb the toxins and then become toxic themselves. They break down the materials into a molecular form that is no longer toxic. This is how swamps clean and regenerate the water flowing through them.

Compost can be from a wide range of manures and organic materials. In working with traditional farm animals as well as some exotic ones like elephant, camel, or even cricket manure, there is a lot of variation in their physical appearance and what they offer. In North Carolina, we made a pile with miniature horse, alpaca, llama, goat, sheep, chicken, duck, turkey, geese, and camel. We were visiting an animal collector. Fowl is a wonderful source of nitrogen, but when fresh it is in a high state of ammonia. It needs to break down thoroughly before use. It creates a very hot pile. Elephant and water buffalo manure are available in Thailand if you can get close to them. Elephant seems a bit like horse but is a better quality. Horse is readily available and sometimes the only choice. Goats are wonderful recyclers and will devour almost anything. They are a good choice to work with. Cow, although messy, adds a good diversity. It is good to stay away from dairies because of the hormones. Any organic dairy uses their manure to spread on the fields. Try to find cattle manure in the winter when they are feeding around a ring full of hay. Otherwise, it is impossible to gain access to them. Pig and sheep are excellent but difficult to find. Fisheries are a good resource if you get in touch with the right person. It may be possible to get zebra and rhino manure from the zoo.

We used to get very well rotted horse manure down a steep slope behind some stables. The stuff was so rotted it looked like spaghetti because of all the worms it contained. Because of its age it would not heat up, so it was used it to supplement the existing compost.

I have had many adventures building compost piles. I have encountered snakebites and beehives in rotted hay piles that mutilated my face. I have hauled manure in the trunk of my car. I once stepped into a pile of cow manure and went in up to my hip. Not realizing that there was a trench at the end of where I was standing, I was stuck and had to be pulled out. I was not a welcomed site when returning home. I have also had a lot of humbling experiences that I walked away from saying I should have known better. I have had many learning experiences to build from.

The leaf pile is another resource to pull from. Pile up leaves in the fall from sources where you know there are no traces of chemical sprays. Use only hardwoods and try to make it as diverse as possible. You can use pine needles if you need to make an acid mix for blueberries or something that likes a low pH. It generally takes a couple of years for them to break down. If you are in a hurry, they can be put through a shredder. This is an efficient use of a lawn mower with a bag attachment. This will speed up the decomposition to about half the time. The leaf mold at the bottom of the pile can be mined for use in potting soil mixes and to cover beet and carrot seed plantings. Keep in mind that because the leaves do not heat up they will contain seeds. This is one serious drawback. Leaves can also be added to the compost pile. Leaf mold contributes many bacteria and some trace minerals to the soil. They are a valuable resource that is there for the taking, using other people's waste that is a resource for you.

The burn pile is another form of recycling. This is a place for hardwood materials, like stems of lamb's-quarter, broccoli and cabbage stems, sticks, used up bamboo, and so on. Put diseased plants into the burn pile. This is also a good place for fruit tree prunings. Their ash is high in potassium. But do not burn poison ivy; the fumes are very dangerous to breathe. The ash from a burn pile is a milder substitute for lime that is used in building compost. It also contains some potassium and phosphorous. Spreading the ash is a good general way of cleaning up the garden or fields to discourage winter homes for rodents. Never compost toxic materials that you would not want in your soil.

Earthworms are an invaluable resource for any growing operation. As mentioned before, they are one of the most valuable assets to have around. They are working while you are sleeping. Once earthworms move into your compost pile, you have a finished product. You can set up worm beds out in the open, but it may not work in most environments, so it is best to build a box for them. I used fiberglass shower stalls laid sideways in Belize with plywood placed on the open end. Old bathtubs work well for this, too. It can be done on many scales. An old kitty litter tray allows you to set one up in the house. Rectangular plastic tubs are also very popular for this. A concern with fruit flies can be dealt with by putting window screen on the top. Vermiculture is a very efficient way to compost your kitchen waste.

Most people usually work with California red wigglers (*Eisinia fetida*). The local worms found in the soil outside are OK, but red wigglers are a more aggressive worm and give results much more quickly.

If setting up a bed outside, fork up the ground and place a partition around the given area to contain them. Something will have to be placed on top when finished to protect it from heavy rains and birds looking for a meal. Inside, include shredded cardboard cut into long strips along with a little shredded paper. This creates air pockets.

Next, place dry leaves, dried grass, well-rotted sawdust, or old mushroom compost. A good starter is to use older spent compost mixed with a little soil. Coffee grounds are a good addition. Well-rotted wood chips or leaf mold will make the worms very happy. Just make a nice combination of materials as a starter for them. You can add a few handfuls of rock dust, gypsum, lime, or decomposed plant or vegetable matter. Moisten the area down and add a pint of worms to a couple square feet of surface area. They immediately head down into the soil to avoid light. Add food materials sparingly at first. They will eat most things. You can give them one pound of food scraps per square foot but they get by on less. They do not seem to do well with citrus but they can become accustomed to it over time. Absolutely no meat or cheese is to be given. They cannot deal with it. Avoid giving them tomatoes, peppers, squash, or melons with seeds. The seeds will sprout and you will create a lot more plants than you want to deal with, especially in a potting mix. Eggshells are a good food for them to recycle. Citrus is at the bottom of their list.

If the soil gets a little dry, dampen it with a watering can. Worms need a good combination of air and water just like us. Before starting to harvest the soil of worm castings, feed them only on one half of the container for a couple weeks. This will encourage them to go to that side. Then you can harvest without disturbing the worms. It is a good contribution to potting soil mix. One can sow seeds into it without mixing and it does fine. It also works well to topdress around plants. A tea can be made like compost tea as a mild fertilizer. This is the best alternative for a small kitchen garden. Using the bathtub lends itself to collecting the tea.

Making compost is a laborious task yet it is a good way to connect with the elements of soil biology. It is one of the best ways to invest in a piece of land. The giant compost pile gives salutations to the end of a growing season and one of the first things to start in the beginning of a new one. It adds to the completion of the cycles of fertility.

4

Soil

The care of the earth is our most ancient and most worthy and after all our most pleasing responsibility. To cherish what remains of it and to foster its renewal is our only hope.

—Wendell Berry

SOIL IS THE GREATEST RESOURCE and most important component to a farm or garden. Healthy soil is crucial for the development of healthy plants and ecosystems and societies. This is the greatest source of biological diversity on the planet. It breathes and pulsates just like other living entities. It is an incredibly complex structure of minerals and living organisms that function as a living organism that exists on many levels.

When in a balanced state, soil can be viewed as an organism itself. Soil supports life both above and below the ground. There is a lot of emphasis on crop production and not enough on soil production and improvement. Improving the health of the soil is the first step toward developing the sustainability of our planet. Plants require a healthy soil in order to perform well. Plants are the scar tissue of the earth. Plants regenerate and protect the soil. Only humans scar the earth through the damage they do and prevent it from growing back as if they were abusing it for some form of satisfaction. The way we treat the land reflects on how we treat ourselves.

Radical soil conservation requires viewing the soil as a sacred living entity. This involves contributing positively to its health on a continual basis. Praising the land with continual offerings that nurture it would contribute to a much more healthy and vibrant planet. It is much easier to destroy it than it is to develop it to its healthy potential.

To understand the culture of soil is to understand ourselves and our purpose for being here. To work with soil is very therapeutic. As we heal the land, it in turn heals us. Understanding the true culture of soil is like knowing the difference between the dirt on your face and the soil in your hands. Becoming part of this living entity, which is thriving with life, forces you to become more alive. When soil is at its optimum state of biological activity, it breathes, pulsates, and multiplies at an incredible rate. This subterranean world is full of life. It could be compared to life in the tropical rain forest only on a microscopic level.

For instance, there can be a hundred billion bacteria per gram of dry matter along the rhizosphere where humus interrelates with the root hairs of a plant. A healthy soil is a balance of microecology and humus. Soils contain all the elements for us to live on the planet. This supports the plants that in turn nurture us. For soils are the intestines of the plant world. They contain the biological functions for plants to digest the foods they need. This is why it is best to feed the soil not the plants. Soil is very sensitive to the elements and should be kept planted or at least mulched with plant materials that will allow it to breathe at all times. Soil needs to be preserved as a valuable resource, because it is a finite resource.

Preserving the soil and maintaining its vitality is a great investment. Many people spend a large part of their lives investing in a retirement plan. Having a good soil economy is like money in the bank. The amending of soil, especially one of poor health, doesn't take long compared to what is sometimes a lifetime of working at an unsatisfying job. An investment in the soil is much more sustainable and secure. It is time well spent if you use the land. You cannot develop a solid foundation of any existence without good food and that requires good soil.

The direct link between sustainability and soil health is an obvious one. Throughout history, societies have crumbled when soils deteriorated through neglect. The greatest resource of the 1900s was people and the labor they provided. The greatest resource of our current millennium will be topsoil and the preservation of it. Our health reflects the health of our soil. There is a direct connection between our health and the degradation of soils where our food is grown.

This is happening now on a global level at a rate faster than ever before. Yet it can be rectified with putting good stewardship practices in the forefront of how we exist. All problems in the garden, whether it be disease, insect problems, or nutrient deficiencies, start and end with the soil. Being a good steward of the soil is a privileged job. If you work with the soil and consider the earth to be a sacred place, your work can be viewed as a spiritual one. A caretaker of land is an important role. It is the responsibility to our children and a gift from those before us.

Of the four elements, soil is the one we can impact most easily. Water and air are formless and not as stable, so therefore not as tangible as soil. Soil recycles wastes and filters pollutants and stores water and oxygen. Soil is a very important part of water cycling. Sixty percent of fresh water is held in the ground. Soil can regulate the flow of water as well as clean and purify it. This is how springs come about. Soil contains around 50 percent more oxygen than is found in the atmosphere. Air movement and renewal depends on soil permeability. This is determined in part by soil particle size, which affects pore size or macroporosity. The air in the soil needs to be at appropriate levels. This release of oxygen and other gases helps enhance plant growth as well as soil insects and microorganisms. Nitrogen gases are heavier than oxygen and so are more stabilized, but small amounts do escape depending on biological activity.

This is the dynamic life interactions that take place on the surface of the soil. It is where two worlds meet. It is a habitat for unique life forms. It is not as obvious as where the oceans meet the land, unless you can view it at the microbial level. The air is influenced by pressure above the ground along with pressure below, moisture, and soil temperature. Some of this is caused by biological activity and the climate above ground. The oxygen further stimulates microbial activity and the absorption of carbon dioxide. Water vapor is released through evaporation, but hydrogen is otherwise held.

This process is greatly enhanced by the diversity of plants with various plant sizes. By planting larger plants seen as crops with ground covers underneath or even some small weeds, you create the intense jungle atmosphere that protects the soil and keeps it porous as well as traps these gases and releases oxygen for availability to soil microorganisms living on the surface.

Smelling soil is something I have enjoyed as long as I can remember. When I was a child, I used to enjoy opening up the soil and putting my face into it to consume the gases released. A rich magical mix of oxygen and gases should exude something comforting to the nostrils. This is an important principle for French intensive methodology. A good example of cover is to use small clover plantings as a base with the main crop growing out of it. On a warm day, the interaction of a porous soil, breathing with intense interaction, is an example of the rich biological activity that balances the whole arrangement of a garden (see figures 4.1 and 4.2).

Carbon is an important constituent of all organic matter. Much of the energy provided for flora and fauna comes from the oxidation of carbon. The carbon cycle is important for producing materials that feed microbes and for stabilizing the functions of life in the soil. The carbon cycle involves a series of processes that allow carbon from plants to transform into either feed for animals or as plant residue that are digested with microbial activity back into the soil to further assist plant growth. Through this collective process, carbon dioxide is released and taken up by plants. Smaller amounts are released in the soil. This is used both as soil reactions with microbes and as gases producing carbonic acid. These are the carbonates and bicarbonates of calcium, potassium, magnesium, and other mineral salts.

FIGURE 4.1
French Intensive Planting. Chinese cabbage and broccoli.

However, most carbon dioxide in plants is acquired from the atmosphere through the process of photosynthesis. The carbon cycle is of major importance because it impacts all living organisms directly, including animals. Our dependence on it is critical. The carbon–nitrogen ratio in soil ranges from 8 to 1, to 15 to 1. This is quite different from the compost pile where the ideal is 25 to 1. These ratios are lower in arid regions and higher in humid regions with more rain and higher temperatures that do not fluctuate as much. Crop residues are a primary source of putting carbon back into the soil for farmers. Mulches that are left to decompose or be turned into the soil are another. Compost and cover crops provide important forms of carbon along with microorganisms that will further break it down. Soil carbon makes up around 60 percent of the physical matter of soil.

The relationship between soil and carbon is important to consider. Carbon is generally released in three different ways. Plant matter provides a lot of carbon. Plant structure is 50 percent carbon. Crop residue breaks down more quickly. The second most available source is through humus. Humus is more stable and slower to change the properties. Charcoal or burnt wood

FIGURE 4.2

is the third. This is a carbon sink because it is so slow to release the carbon. Wood ashes that contain the black charred wood is almost exclusively carbon. This serves as an activator for microbial activity and raises the pH to make it more alkaline. This is generally cycled through a compost pile but can be used as a quick fix directly in the beds if done sparingly. It is important to know how much you want to raise the pH so not to make it too alkaline. This is also a source of some potassium.

Carbon in the soil has a great absorption capacity. Organic soils can absorb thousands of pounds of carbon dioxide per acre from the atmosphere. This is an important player in curbing greenhouse gases and is often overlooked as a vital carbon sink only because soils do not often breathe this well. Soil contains large amounts of carbon. The soil's organic carbon content works as a buffer to help insulate it from extremes of temperature and moisture. This not only reinforces soil structure but improves water-holding capacity while creating reserves for water and biological nutrients. The organic matter works off of these carbons as a source of stored energy. Such compounds contain nutrients, cations, and trace elements that necessitate plant growth. The cations are positively charged ions that are attracted to negatively charged ions or anions. Plants absorb carbon from the atmosphere and store it in their roots where it is transferred into the soil.

The role of organic matter is important in preventing carbon from being released back into the atmosphere. The amount of carbon in the ground is around three times greater than that of the atmosphere above the soil. The vegetation of healthy plants can contain four and a half times as much carbon as is found in the atmosphere.

Soil Composition and Physical Properties

Although there are various materials found in soils, they are composed of four major components. For optimum plant growth, 50 percent should be represented by air and water. Minerals make up 45 percent, and the remaining 5 percent is organic matter (see figure 4.3). Types of soils that contain clay have the smallest particle size. Next is loam, which is really a combination of sand, clay, and organic matter. Sandy soils have the largest particle size (see figure 4.4).

A loamy soil would be the most ideal to work with. Sandy soils are the most challenging. They have nothing to hold them together and little or no

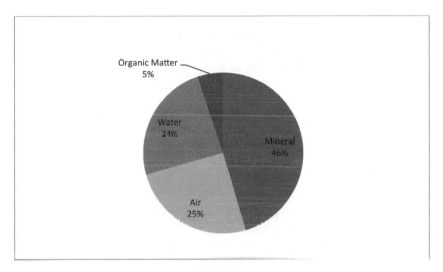

FIGURE 4.3
Average Composition of Silt Loam

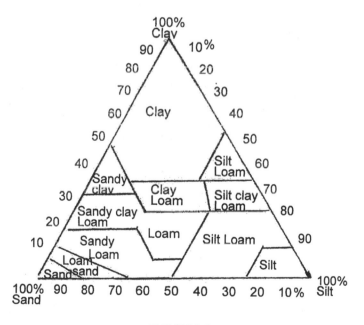

FIGURE 4.4
Diagram of Physical Components of Soils

water-holding capacity. Clay is the opposite with lots of aggregate. Clay soil holds onto a lot of moisture and when it dries out it becomes like a brick wall. Although harder to work, with the introduction of organic matter all those minerals can be broken down and released to a form plants can assimilate. The more permeable soils, like loam and sand, also lose nutrients more quickly. One advantage of clay soils is that they hold nutrients longer and so are a more stable nutrient base.

An ideal soil is one that is permeable, one that can be penetrated easily by liquids and gases. It is important to maintain porosity as part of its structure. It is important to understand how much cultivation a soil needs to develop a good soil structure. Knowing when to back off and do minimum cultivation so not to destroy the soil structure once it has gotten to an optimum state is of the utmost importance.

Different types of soils need to be approached differently. Heavy clay soils require a lot of work. Sandy soils require a lot of organic matter. Creating a good tilth requires cultivation, and maintaining tilth requires organic matter. Organic matter needs to be in a form that can be directly assimilated along with material that will break down gradually. Compost provides the former and cover crops the latter.

Whatever soil you are presented with, it is in need of attention and healing. To gain a perspective of the soil, it is good to look at the soil profile. By digging straight down with a square nose spade, you can examine the profile horizontally. The surface layer or topsoil is darker and contains most of the life forms. It can vary in size. You can find places with ten feet of topsoil in Oregon, seven feet in north Georgia and North Carolina, several feet more in Illinois, and down to zero in central Georgia. In the southeastern United States, one is lucky to find more than a few inches.

Below this is the subsoil and foundation for what is growing above. As the color changes, the organic content diminishes. This often consists of clay particles of a very small size and can go down to several feet. Below this is the substratum or bedrock. The parent material influences characteristics of the soil, the ability for air and water to penetrate the soil and be occupied by living organisms. This is important because the minerals are in an inorganic state that plants cannot easily assimilate. The organic matter digests these mineral deposits, breaking them down into a form that plants can absorb. The life that facilitates organic development is classified as macroanimals; such as small animals and insects like millipedes (*Parajulus*), sowbugs (*Trachelifus rathkei*), mites (*orbata*), earthworms, and slugs and snails.

Earthworms are so important. In rich soil, they can digest fifteen acres of dry earth per acre each year. Microanimals consist of parasitic nematodes, protozoa, and rotifers. These microscopic insects multiply fast in lush soil conditions. In warm weather, protozoa can populate to one million per gram of soil. Plant forms are made up of small plants, algae, fungi, actinomycetes, and bacteria. Some of these manufacture nutrients from sunlight; the others under the surface do not. Algae play an important role in rice growing. With close examination, you can observe their abundance in paddies in Indonesia where they promote high crop yields.

Fungi are very useful in digesting lignin, cellulose, and gums that others cannot. The mycorrhizae of fungus penetrate roots of tree crops and provide enzymes to aid in digestion. Mycelium creates a spider web of hyphae that feed protozoa and other microorganisms. This is especially true with abuscular fungi. Glomalin fungi helps build soil tilth by sticking soil together. This allows for crumbling by utilizing physical and biological systems to develop and intensify the capillary structure to grow in. This is part of the life force that is sought in biodynamics and develops a good soil economy. Actinomycetes are similar to bacteria and provide many nutrients. Bacteria can be found in the most numbers. They aid in oxidation and nitrification of enzymes vital to plant growth. Larger plants also aid in the development of organic matter through root decay and growth as they penetrate the soil. Organic matter stimulates activity in the soil and provides energy that gives off heat. It also draws in water and carbon dioxide. All this helps with plant growth. Humus is the by-product of decomposition. It coats clay particles and prevents them from holding together in a solid mass. It also provides enzymes and triggers hormones that stimulate growth through chemical interactions with minerals.

The clay-humus activity is responsible for much of the chemical activity in soils. Mineral composition is impacted by several factors in the soil. The acid alkaline balance plays a vital role. If the pH (probable hydrogen) changes, so does the availability of minerals. Hydrogen is a main factor in lowering the soil pH. Dryer climates tend to have higher pH. If the pH is too high, many nutrients become unavailable to plants. This may require the addition of sulfur and is more difficult to correct than a low pH. If the pH is too low, the addition of lime will correct it, but keep in mind that it can take six months for it to become effective. The more fine the ground limestone, the quicker it works. This is why it is best to test the soil in the fall and add supplements for the following spring.

Metabolism of nutrients takes place on a biochemical level. The electron transfer of nutrients is fundamental for metabolism. The organic matter contains negatively charged particles held together by carbon and hydrogen. These humates fix themselves for plant roots to absorb root exudates. The microbes provide enzymes that serve as catalysts.

The other important component is soil colloids. Colloidal matter is held in the small clay particles recognized as silicate clays and iron aluminum oxide clays. These are positively charged cations. The negatively charged ions or anions are attracted to these colloidal crystals. Some of the colloids have platelets that increase their absorptive capacity. The humates are chelated with amino acids that surround the minerals and make them soluble. They are carried by water molecules. This requires porosity in the soil. Oxidation helps facilitate this process. Photosynthesis aids in the process. The exchange of gases contributes to this as well. Oxidation is an important key.

Minerals can be viewed as macro- and micronutrients. Of all minerals, nitrogen is the most popular macronutrient. Because it is soluble in water, it is more volatile and is easily lost. Legumes have the ability to fix nitrogen from the atmosphere and store it in their roots. It needs to be regulated. Too much can be very damaging and too little can cause poor growth. It encourages above ground growth, dark green leaves, plump grain heads, and works directly with manufacturing protein. It works well if available to plants on a regular, steady allowance. Nitrogen is derived from crop residues, especially leguminous crops, manures, legumes such as clover and vetch, and of course, rich compost.

Fertilizers made from animal proteins are high in nitrogen. Feather, fish, and blood meal have high concentrations. I stay away from blood meal because I question where it is coming from, and it attracts animals like raccoons and opossums. Cottonseed meal is also high, but unless I know where the cotton is grown, I stay away. I have seen loads of DDT sprayed on cotton in Central America. It carries over into the seed. Alfalfa is a better source. Lightning carries an incredible amount of nitrogen. Eighty percent of the atmosphere that we breathe is nitrogen. Lightning magnetically pulls it in and dumps it in the soil or your house or trees.

Soil Minerals

Nitrogen starts out as ammonia. This is toxic to plants in its raw form. Nitrification is oxidized by azotobacter and nitrate bacteria breaking it down to nitrites and then into nitrates. This is then processed by actinomycetes, bacteria, and fungi, which plants take up. Nitrogenase is the process where nitrogen and oxygen fixes into nitrates using molybdenum as a chemical charge and rhizobium bacteria provide the enzyme for doing this. These nitrogen-fixing bacteria have a symbiotic relationship with leguminous plants. For this reason, it is important to have a rotation program that allows legumes to be planted periodically, especially before a greens crop is planted.

Phosphorus is critically important for the growth of plants. It is needed for cell division and is a carrier of energy to the plant. It promotes flowering and fruiting, crop maturation, root and stem development, and some disease resistance. It can counter the effect of too much nitrogen. Phosphorus deficiencies are uncommon and hard to diagnose. It is not needed in as big amounts as other macronutrients. It is not as available either. Most phosphorus is fixed or tied up in soils and unusable to plants. It is also highly mobilized in the plant. Phosphorus is also not available in alkaline soils. High iron, aluminum oxides, or high available manganese inhibits its availability. Calcium also antagonizes it. The introduction of humus helps reduce this fixation and oxidation so plants can absorb it better. Good sources are found in bone meal, rock phosphate, bat and sea bird guano, and fish residues. Vegetable and fruit skins are high in phosphorus and can be composted to make it available.

Potassium helps roots and stems grow. It is good for potato yields. It balances out other minerals and aids in the development of chlorophyll. It also stimulates seed development and that is important for grain and seed production. Potassium is susceptible to leaching from water drainage. Microorganisms compete for this nutrient. Like nitrogen and phosphorus, a large amount of all three of these are insoluble and unavailable to plants. A lot of it is removed when plants are taken from the ground. Of course, the answer for this is to compost them and put potassium back into the soil. Good sources for potassium are rock powders of feldspar and granite dust or green sand. Manures and charred wood, especially of fruit trees, contain measurable amounts of potassium also.

Sulfur is essential for amino acids and the development of proteins in the plant. It structures protein and actively converts inorganic nitrogen to protein. As a result, legume plants have a high sulfur requirement. It promotes nitrogen nodules on the roots of legumes. It serves as a catalyst for chlorophyll production. Sulfur directly makes soils acid. Sulfur combines with minerals such as iron, copper, nickel and is more abundant in soils with poor drainage. Because it is negatively charged, it is easily leached out, especially in sandy soils. It is more sensitive to temperatures, slowing down in cold and speeding up production in hot. It needs oxygen and does poor in wet soils. Organic matter is a reservoir for sulfur and helps store it until needed. In the southeastern United States, sulfur is stored in the subsoil. Sulfur is found in the atmosphere, which makes rain a common source for it. With the added supply of acid rain, it is even more abundant.

Calcium is another important mineral that does not get much attention. Calcium plays a major role in soil structure. High calcium can contribute to very tight soil. Too much can create a hard pan. Earthworms are very attracted to it and can help reduce excess amounts if you are lucky enough to have a plentiful supply. Calcium regulates the flow of nutrients and maintains chemical imbalance. It can neutralize cell acids, build cell walls, and helps to prevent grains from lodging. It is unavailable to plants in acid soils. Plants can show signs of calcium deficiency only because of acid soils locking it up. High levels of magnesium, ammonia, iron, and potassium reduce its uptake. It can compete with magnesium for crop uptake. It needs to be in balance with the amount of magnesium.

Calcium requirements are around 60 percent, whereas magnesium is around 10 to 20. Calcium can affect the uptake of zinc, copper, iron, boron, phosphorus, and potassium. Its best sources are lime in the form of calcite or dolomitic lime. This way you are changing the pH while also providing magnesium. Gypsum is often used, but it has been shown to contain heavy metals. Bone meal has a good supply also.

Magnesium is necessary for photosynthesis. It also manifests enzymes for metabolism. It is a carrier of phosphorus, sugar synthesis, and nutrient control. Magnesium increases iron utilization, carries a chlorophyll molecule, and aids in nitrogen fixation. It improves soil structure and reduces leaching of nutrients in general. Too much can cause soil compaction. It has also been shown to reduce weeds. Magnesium is unavailable in acid soils below 5.5. High manganese reduces its uptake, so it is depleted by acid rain. The best sources are dolomitic lime.

Iron is an important micronutrient because of its role in chlorophyll development and function. It also contributes to the plant's energy transfer. It is a major constituent of enzymes and proteins. It aids in respiration and metabolism and nitrogen fixation. It is more available in acid soils. Organic matter improves its availability, so it needs an aerated soil.

Micronutrients can be very complex. Too much phosphorus can inhibit iron. A zinc deficiency can increase iron in the soil and vice versa. The same is true for manganese. High molybdenum can reduce iron uptake;

low potassium interferes with it also. High saline and alkali soils are low in iron. It is not advised to attempt to introduce trace minerals to the soil for these reasons. Well-made compost and a diversity of organic sources can provide trace mineral compositions that are intact.

Boron is another important micronutrient. It maintains balance between sugar and starch. It translocates sugar and carbohydrates in the plant. It is needed for pollination and seed production. It is also important for cell division, nitrogen metabolism, and protein formation. It helps transport potassium. High phosphorus levels reduce its uptake. It is affected by water uptake. It is leached by rain and excess water drainage. Drought also reduces boron. This further reduces root growth. High calcium and zinc can inhibit boron. If nitrogen is low in the soil, the need for boron will be less.

Copper is also a necessary trace mineral. It is a catalyst for photosynthesis and respiration. It is needed for enzymes in converting amino acids to proteins and protein metabolism. It provides structure and strength to cell walls. It affects sugars and storage ability. It is more available in acid soils. High organic matter can sometimes reduce its balance. It is dependent on oxygen, so water-logged soils reduce it. High zinc and phosphorus inhibits its availability. Too much nitrogen affects its transport. Low nitrogen in soils decreases the need for copper.

Manganese helps carbon dioxide assimilation during photosynthesis and contributes to chlorophyll. It transports electrons and the separation of oxygen and hydrogen. It aids in the assimilation of nitrates and the transformation of nitrogen to plants. It likes acid soils with low pH. High iron can reduce its availability as does water-logged soils with little oxygen. Molybdenum is the micronutrient that is least needed. It plays a role in photosynthesis and is very important for converting nitrates into amino acids for protein. It aids in nitrogen fixation and converts inorganic phosphorus into organic phosphorus. As well, it binds with sulfur and is easily leached out by rain. A higher pH increases its availability. High sulfur can inhibit availability of molybdenum. It is a catalyst for legumes.

Zinc produces growth hormones and helps with the reproduction process of plants. It activates protein enzymes and breaks down sugars and carbohydrates. It also supports root development and is necessary for seed and stem formation. One of its most important roles is in the formation of chlorophyll. Zinc contributes to the outer cell development. This gives plants strength when dealing with extreme weather conditions. Its availability is increased in acid soils. High amounts of phosphorus can inhibit zinc from being available. Organic matter offers enzymes and chelates for zinc to develop. Copper can inhibit its availability and vice versa. Manganese is antagonistic to it. Magnesium can increase zinc availability. Heavy metals also prevent its uptake. With all this in mind, it sounds like there is no way to have perfectly balanced soil chemistry. With a healthy soil, flora and fauna, and equilibrium of soil mix, you have the catalysts for making this possible.

A pH that is around 6.5 is ideal. Seven is neutral, so this is slightly acid. The pH refers to probable hydrogen or potential hydrogen. The more hydrogen in the soil, the more acid it is. In wetter areas, like the southeast United States, the soils are fairly acid. In New Mexico, we had a very alkaline soil and it was deficient in phosphorus. It is easier to bring up the pH by adding some lime. Keep in mind that it can take six months for the lime to take effect. It is best to spread lime in the fall if it is needed. Acid soils often show a nutrient deficiency simply because the minerals are not available to the plant at a low pH. A good example is blossom end rot of tomatoes or squash, the result of a calcium deficiency. The calcium is in the soil, but it is not available at a low pH.

Alkaline soils are much harder to deal with. Many more nutrients are unavailable when the pH is too high. Sulfur is the solution. Sulfur is often supplied with good rainfall where I live. Berries and azaleas like a very acid pH, so I often add sulfur when planting. It is best to get the soil tested through your local cooperative extension service. Guessing can cause serious problems. There is no sense in adding a lot of nutrients when the plant cannot take them up. Understanding your soil is very important. Soil classification involves determining what combination you have of basic components. Clay is most common and hard to work, but it is beneficial because it is full of minerals. However, it is lacking in organic matter and aeration. This translates into the need for compost and cultivation. Sandy soil is easier to work yet harder to rectify. It needs body and does not hold structure. A loamy soil is a nice combination of the two. Sand has a greater particle size and so breathes well. Clay is composed of very fine particles; thus, it has much more surface area. Because of their elasticity, these particles stick together and form clods. Adding organic matter coats the surface and helps prevents this.

Soil fertility is a marriage of everything. Soil building is an amazing thing to watch. It does not happen overnight, but in a few seasons some of the most damaged soil can become vibrant and alive. One of my fondest soil building projects was at the Albemarle Community Garden in Atlanta. It was intriguing to see what could be done over several years of work. We started with a place where even weeds had a hard time growing. There was red clay for a topsoil and brick foundations for subsoil. It required a pickax and a mattock to remove all the brick and rubble. After a couple years of incorporating heaps of organic matter into the soil (mostly in the form of compost), life began to flourish. After four or five years, it hardly needed to be double dug as the fork would sink down about eighteen inches with little effort.

Many people got involved in the beginning. Many of them thought I was crazy to put all this work into a piece of land that I was squatting on. It was state-owned land that was destined to become a highway. There were folks who would get involved but suddenly remember something else they had to do and leave, never to be seen again. Some of them would even cross the street when they saw me in town to avoid getting involved with the crazy gardener. The ones who stuck around saw the results of an interesting soil development project. During the nine years of this garden, it became an education resource center that carried with it a lot of history. Couples met, children were born, and lives went through the changes of life. The area around it changed dramatically also. But the soil became stabilized like that of finished humus. It nurtured those who worked in it and taught those who visited it. It also fed those involved spiritually with the life force that flowed through it. This is what biodynamics is really all about. It is more than the giving and taking. It is a dance to the rhythms of life that surround us all, bringing us together and giving us purpose.

Soil and Bed Preparation

Preparing the soil is one of the seasonal rituals of the coming of spring for most gardeners and farmers. It is good to view soil as a fragile living entity. It is important to move into it with a measure of sensitivity. Develop an intimacy with a bed so that you can know it well. You are venturing into a world that you do not live in. This requires a lot of respect and obedience. The cultivation of land enables it to breathe and open up to the forces above. It allows gases to be released and to take in what the atmosphere sends down. You may be able to smell it on a damp day. Most minerals in the atmosphere are deposited with rainfall. This is why plants seem to grow well after a good rain.

Eighty percent of what we breathe is nitrogen. The atmosphere is full of it as well as other nutrients. Rain washes it down to earth. The longer the wait between rains, the more nutrients come with that rain. Particles that are heavy in the air settle down onto the soil. It is very important to treat the soil gently and keep in mind that it is a living organism made up of many living organisms.

Exposure to the elements—sun, wind, rain—will exhaust the rich life of the soil. The wind is more drying than the sun. The sun bakes the life out of the soil if allowed to do so. The rain washes away all the topsoil. This is such a large part of the agricultural history of the entire planet. Treating it as a living, sacred entity is not only important, it is vital.

As I prepare beds, I keep the ground covered with mulch if it has to be open for any length of time. There are many schools of thought on cultivation. Along with this are many misconceptions. For instance, covering the soil with black plastic is referred to as solarization. This is used to kill weeds. In doing so, it also kills beneficial bacteria that need oxygen. It is very harmful. Trenching the paths to create a raised bed is also a ludicrous act. Never dig away the topsoil. It is like robbing Peter to rob yourself. Topsoil is precious. Trenching accomplishes none of the benefits of a raised bed. Beds and growing areas move from season to season. Over time, that path will become a growing area except without the topsoil you moved away.

Boxes are an interesting phenomenon. A lot of time and money for materials are spent for no gain. It separates the bed from the rest of the garden. The garden is one ecosystem. It does not end at a certain place. The sides of the box prevent the soil from breathing. The wood gives off foreign substances that are not beneficial and often toxic. The wood also covers potential growing space. It is possible to get a case of lettuce along the side of a ten-foot bed. It demonstrates an attempt at controlling the garden to protect it from nature. In working with nature and being perceptive to it, one can learn from it every day. That is part of the beauty of doing this work. Bringing in topsoil is also dangerous. First of all, anyone who is crazy enough to sell you topsoil cannot be trusted. Second, you get to buy someone else's mistakes. It is a good way to bring in lots of interesting diseases, insects, weeds, and toxins that have been manufactured all over the world. No till is a very popular concept, and something for every gardener to aspire to. It is accomplished over seasons of hard work.

In *The One-Straw Revolution*, Masanobu Fukuoka did not start with a piece of land that was never cultivated, but one that was cultivated for generations. He had the foresight and vision to go beyond what his elders saw. This is a level of optimum health that is acquired with an investment of time, hard work, and a lot of organic matter invested into the soil. With minimal cultivation, the soil can begin to replenish the mycorrhizal fungi. The long filaments of these fungal bodies are easily destroyed with cultivation. Soil remediation is a process of developing the life of the soil by introducing beneficial bacteria and fungus in their living state. I prefer to introduce these as I am subsoiling. This way I am building the soil from the bottom up.

The process of double digging is an intense way to get quick results. It allows you to maximize the use of a given amount of land. I can grow on a half-acre what would take two and a half acres using conventional farming with a tractor. For the average person, lay out beds to be four feet wide. This allows me to reach out in the middle without stepping on the bed. For shorter or taller people, the beds can be made accordingly. The length depends on your needs and the space available. If the bed is too dry, it is best to water it down lightly the night before.

Soil moisture content is very important. A very dry soil will not hold structure. It will look like dust when you dig it. Soil that is too wet should never be dug. This can destroy the structure of the soil. You will force out the air and create something you can make adobe bricks out of. This could be useful for building a house but not a garden. The weeds or top growth can be mowed or cut to make it easier to dig this into the soil. If the soil is too wet, wait for it to dry out. Put a tarp over it when it rains. If it is too dry, put a sprinkler on it for five to ten minutes a day before you dig. Start the process of double digging by digging out a rectangular trench about a foot and a half wide, as you may need some elbow room. Some folks dig only a foot wide across the width of the bed. Dig down usually about a shovelful deep. If you have measurable topsoil, dig only that deep, so not to bury the valuable topsoil. As you dig out the first trench, put the soil into a wheelbarrow. This is the only soil that will be moved. At this point, you can examine the soil profile and see what you are getting yourself into. This is a time of great excitement or alarming discouragement (see figure 4.5).

Next, dig the fork into the subsoil as deep as the tines will allow. You can dig this very rough. Loosen yet leave it in big chunks. Never pulverize the clay particles into tiny pieces. They will stick back together to make clods. Clay has the smallest particle size. By leaving it in chunks, you create air pockets. Now air and water can flow through this area and it becomes a place that life can inhabit. This is what has been missing. Take organic matter and throw a layer down. This coats the clay preventing it from sticking back together. You are introducing life into an area that has been devoid of it. The organic used can consist of compost, the growth you cut off the top, green matter (especially grass or clover), leaf mold, leaves, basically anything that will decompose and attract worms and microorganisms. I often use a combination of compost, cover crop, and rotted hay.

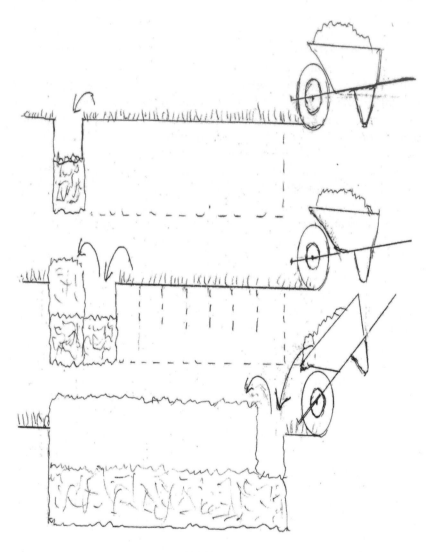

FIGURE 4.5
Double Digging

It is preferable to chop up cover crop first. Run it through a lawn mower with a bag and put this in the subsoil. Then, add compost and/or partially decomposed material like brewery waste or whatever organic matter is available. This way you have mixed in other microorganisms to speed up the decomposition. This process is like building the soil from the bottom up. Next, dig out the next trench and move it into the first trench that was dug, tilthing the soil and breaking it up lightly. Tilthing refers to tilling. Break up large clods into smaller pieces. If planting small seeds, like carrots, break the soil up more. If planting large seeds, like beans, you can leave it in larger chunks. Moving the soil into the trench previously dug allows you access to the next area of subsoil to open up and repeat the process. As you move along you are stepping backward. Once you have reached the end of the bed, take the soil placed in the wheelbarrow and fill in the last trench. The bed will be automatically raised from all the air you introduced. Then, rake the bed even and put at least a couple inches of compost on top. Immediately, fork the compost into the bed so it is not exposed to the sun. This would make it lifeless. Then rake it out again and sprinkle it down with water lightly. It is ready to plant. It is quite an accomplishment. Keep in mind, the next time you dig it, it will be a fraction of the effort you put in the first time. The double digging process is very intense work with intense results. It destroys the fungi in the soil only to build it back up later several-fold. It manifests chaos to bring about order. It introduces life into the soil at a depth that was possibly never used before. When the plants grow they now have one and a half to two feet depth for their roots. This allows you to plant much closer together. The plants can grow a lot bigger. They can store water much deeper, which is useful in drought conditions. There is much better drainage as well.

As growth matures, the beds become intense with life. As the bed takes form, it develops a capillary structure that many life forms flow through easily. This capillary is a very important aspect of the bed structure. It starts out with protozoa, rotifers, and other soil insects. Earthworms are a big player in creating the capillary channels. Sometimes snakes and other reptiles can travel through and open up even larger holes. It is ideal for plant roots to grow in, because it holds water well yet drains well. What that means is that it holds the correct moisture content for healthy root development. The soil breathes and receives water easily through a capillary structure.

The bed should not be walked on. Your feet will sink down and destroy the work that was put into it. When people step on my beds, I usually go soprano. People often comment on all the wonderful things that grow in my garden. I tell them that I don't grow these things. The soil does, and I produce the soil. Digging into healthy soil is like diving into the mysteries of nature with all its riches. The soul of the soil is a constant stream of energy like a gentle breeze or a flowing waterway.

Cover Cropping

Besides the use of compost, the second way to build soil is with cover crops, sometimes referred to as green manure. Using cover crops is like putting money in the bank. The cost of using them pays you back big time. Cover crops make sense on many levels. They stabilize and protect the soil when you are not using it to grow a crop and of course prevent erosion. You are better in control of the area when you get back to it for planting. Cover crops benefit the beds by adding nutrients during growth. They increase microbial development along their roots and do an excellent job of choking out and keeping out weeds. They provide an incredible green manure when they are dug in. In the summer when you are between crops, cover crops can be used to reserve and build the soil until time to plant. For example, after late broccoli or lettuce is harvested, it may be too late to plant whatever else you had in mind. You could plant some cover crops while you wait until fall or late summer to plant a fall crop. This is a good time to use buckwheat mixed with clover.

It works best to plant most cover crops in the fall to protect and add nutrients for next spring. It is ideal to use a mix of vetch, annual rye, and clover, sometimes oats. Grasses such as rye, wheat, or oats contain high amounts of silica. Silica balances polarity with calcium. They allow filtered sunlight to reach the soil. The roots spread outward and the seed heads open out into the sun. Legumes move in an opposite direction. They cover and protect the ground like an ocean of green. The roots penetrate deep into the soil. Flowers fold inward like a butterfly resting. All grasses from corn to bamboo to field grasses contain high amounts of silica. Fava beans (*Vicia faba*) are an excellent source of nitrogen, although they can perish if it gets too cold. We used them extensively on the West Coast of the United States. Austrian winter peas are also an excellent source of nitrogen. They need to be placed down into the soil. A stick can be used for a small area. Rape is a good leafy source. Oats are another excellent source, especially combined with a legume. Ideally, it is good to turn this crop in when it is between four to six inches tall. Plants can get much taller during a mild winter, or if you are busy you might not get to that area soon enough.

Again, a lawn mower can be used to chop them up; then you can dig them into both the subsoil and the top layer. Ideally, it is best to do this two or three weeks before planting, so they rot a little. But you can do this at various stages, and if you put chopped cover crops into the subsoil, the plants you are growing will not send roots down that far for some weeks anyway. This is a wonderful source of nutrient base for the soil and the plants help cultivate the soil. There are farmers who plow in spent greens after they are finished. This is a very good way to increase worm populations in the soil, as long as there are no diseases present. Cover crops harbor beneficial insects and microorganisms. Anything planted that can be put back into the soil will bring good results. The more you put in, the more you get out.

The soul of soil is a constant stream of energy that moves like a gentle breeze or a slow flowing waterway. Creating cultured soil is the best way to create a healthy place to grow. Cultured soil involves encouraging its biological capacity, keeping it planted, and aerating it with plants to maintain the pulsation of its life force. Biodynamics equals life force. This is the true science of nature. Treat it as if it is a fragile gift of life. For it is. A living soil breathes. This way it can receive what the universe gives it, to evolve into a lush place to grow. Like anything alive, it is always in a state of movement and change. This is the true spirit of life.

5

Plant Culture

No occupation is so delightful to me as the culture of the earth, and no culture comparable to that of a garden.

—Thomas Jefferson

OUR DEEPEST CONNECTION TO THE earth is usually through the plant world. They provide for us in so many ways. They are the substance of life. They have the amazing ability to reach to the skies and collect energy from the sun and transform it into food for animals and insects without which we could not survive. They nurture our bodies as they nurture our souls. The earth smiles with their flowers while providing an ocean of oxygen for us to breathe. They are the delicate essence of the beauty of life. They are the best recycler of water and soil.

To work in a world surrounded by plants is a beautiful place to be. I love my relationship with them and learn a little more about them every day. People often think one gets into this because plants are so easy to work with. It tells something of the personality of gardeners. If the plants are not happy, they just die. Yet they have an incredible will to live. The relationship between plants and gardeners is a special one. Plants are very sensitive and invite intimacy. This is where the soul of the gardener meets the soul of the plant world. They open us up to a special part of the universe that is subtle, yet grand.

Plants are also great teachers, just as children are. They provide an environment that feeds me spiritually. Growing plants is both a science and an art that interacts with all humans on a daily basis. Each plant family has its own way of taking form and utilizing the resources from above and below the ground.

Diverse Adaptations

The cactus is an interesting example. Its entire above-ground surface can photosynthesize the sun's rays—it collects the energy from 360 degrees. It has a vast root system that can travel hundreds of yards. So when it does rain in the desert, it does not miss a drop. It also stores water incredibly well for long dry periods.

Plants have distinct smells, tastes, and textures for interacting with nature. Establishing a garden with some blind gardeners offered me insight into how to communicate with plants. These gardeners taught me how to experience communication with my eyes closed. This can be used as a teaching tool for children's gardens. Plants are very diverse and work well in a diverse environment. As a garden or farm evolves, so does the environment around it and throughout it. Plants help create their environment as they interact with nature. Plants are the best indicators of what works well in your given area. Each area has its own unique set of dynamics.

As our planet has gotten smaller, so have the unique varieties of each area. I have seen nonnatives strewn across the global landscape. Some are very invasive. You can find lantana in Indonesia, *Acacia longifolia* in Brazil, scotch broom in California, and water hyacinth all over the tropics. In Georgia, we have the wonderful kudzu plant that was brought here to check erosion on the land that was being cotton farmed to death. One of my first jobs in Georgia was working with the county cooperative extension service. I found some old pamphlets in the back storeroom promoting kudzu as something every family should be planting, but I was told we would not be giving those out. They dated back to the 1950s. Standing on the hillside in Georgia, it is amazing to think that hundreds of years ago we would be standing ten feet higher, before the land eroded into the Gulf of Mexico or the Atlantic Ocean depending on which way the creeks flowed.

During the process of growing heirloom plant varieties and collecting the seed from them, it is good to recognize where they are from. There may be Italian beans and garlic, Russian tomatoes and kale, or New Mexican chiles and hot peppers. This is a little strange when you consider that beans are from North America and tomatoes and peppers are from South America. These seeds have traveled and would have wonderful stories if they could talk.

I have lineage from most European countries; I guess we all have a little hybrid vigor in us. When using seeds from season to season they become more adapted to their own microenvironment. It is easy in a kitchen garden to become somewhat attached to your garlic varieties, tomatoes, melons, and so on. Or to feel a sense of ownership for cleomes, nigella, or larkspurs, as they become a part of a place. Yet do we really own them or are we just borrowing them as they pass through our hands? Seeds are nothing more than a gift from nature. I save many of my seeds and they acclimate to my garden. Yet each season comes and goes. The garden exists for that season and those seeds do also. It is the idea of expressing yourself in your work. So it really comes down to lifestyle and perspective. This is part of the connection with plant culture.

As we become set in our ways, we savor and hold on to things like seeds. The plants take on certain characteristics that make them desirable. Seeing plants as more than just what they offer as food gives us a different appreciation of their being. Flowers can be beautiful and magical regardless of size. The national flower of Belize is a tiny black orchid and it is just as beautiful as any found in Malaysia. A cauliflower is a rich floribunda that is a grand sight to behold.

Flowers are the messengers of the genetic makeup of the plant. Each one is exquisite with its own unique form. As people have traveled around the world so have the seeds and plants of their homeland. I enjoy the stories that followed their linage. But I am not an anthropologist. The work I do in horticulture and agriculture is justified in just doing it. As a grower one would be more interested in the plants' traits that serve them, like how well they produce, disease resistance, storage of roots and fruits, and, of course, the taste, smells, and textures that I learned about from my blind gardener friends.

Plants' physical nature is an efficient system of capturing and storing energy that becomes food for them and us. As a seed germinates, it forms first a radical; then it forms a hypocotyl, cotyledons, plumule, and root hairs. Until this takes place, it is relying on stored food in the seed itself. Visualize the plant upside down to understand its growing trait. Lateral roots stabilize the plant as the root tip continues growing into new territory. The root tip maintains constant cell growth due to abrasion with the soil it is traveling through and because this is where the new growth takes place. This is the meristematic region at the root tip. The apical hormone relates to plant growth and is a crucial messenger. The further down it grows, the further a plant grows up toward the sun.

The interaction with the soil involves a series of symbiotic relationships primarily with the root hairs. Roots absorb nutrients through epidermal cells. Yet root hairs are responsible for most absorption of water and nutrients. They are short-lived and regenerate quickly. Root hairs are most vulnerable to damage during transplanting. Loss of them sets the plant growth back. This is why it is best to minimize their damage. Woody stem plants are best planted during their dormant stage for this reason. They do not regenerate as quickly. Besides the adsorption of water, several chemical and biological interactions occur. Root exudates attract beneficial components and repel undesirables. Of course, this does not always work or there would not be disease and insect problems. A good example of repelling is French marigolds and African black oats that are effective in warding off root knot nematodes. Other root exudates attract rhizobial activity and beneficial bacteria like actinomycetes, azobacters, azohizobium, and other beneficial bacillus forms. This symbiotic relationship is important for healthy soil plant relationships, for the soil is the intestines of the plant world. The flora and fauna produce soluble nutrients from organic matter in a form that roots can assimilate. Fungal threads, called hypae, form a cover around roots and sometimes penetrate the root itself. This is important for the plant's growth. If you introduce salt-based fertilizers, like 10-10-10, the salts and other synthetic ingredients are toxic. They inhibit and actually destroy these biological life forms. What you are doing is creating a dependency on synthetic chemical-based fertilizer because you have essentially killed off the natural order for doing this. It really comes down to short-term gain versus the long-term development of your soil.

Plant Nutrition and Assimilation

Plant nutrition is important in understanding how plants function. As nutrients are absorbed they travel upward through the xylem, out through the petiole, and into the leaf. The xylem provides a channel for water and the nutrients absorbed in it. The leaf contains chloroplasts that help manufacture food from sunlight. Stomata cells located on the bottom allow the leaf to breath and release water during hot days (referred to as transpiration).

These also work as guard cells to protect the size of what comes in. Foliar feeds work by spraying solutions that can be absorbed this way. Plants produce carbohydrates that are sugars in the leaf. These sugars are sent to other parts of the plants as needed. This is called translocation. It is sent down through the phloem. The excess food is stored mainly in the roots.

Of course, the whole process is much more complex than this. There are many nutrients that play vital roles in photosynthesis. The least of which is molybdenum along with chlorine, zinc, iron, manganese, copper, magnesium, and nitrogen. About 18 percent of the protein of the plant is made up of nitrogen. It is important as a protein builder and stimulates chlorophyll and green growth. Stem and leaf growth depends on it. It also is necessary for the formation of growth hormones. Nitrogen deficiency is indicated by yellowing of older leaves and overall stunted growth. Too much nitrogen causes a buildup of amino acids in plant tissue. The plant becomes more susceptible to plant diseases. This is the nutrient that most often needs to be replenished. It is used up quickly during the growing season. Legumes used as cover crops and composted manure, both animal and green manure, are a good source of nitrogen.

Phosphorous has the main role of facilitating energy metabolism. It plays a role in cell development. Again, compost and cover crops provide the best source of phosphorous and potassium. Phosphorus also stimulates flowering activity and seed germination. It is important for photosynthesis, protein formation, and energy metabolism of the plant. It forms bonds against bacterial diseases. A primary source of phosphorus is bone meal. Rock phosphate is another source, but not a sustainable one. It comes from mines. Deficiencies show up as purple stems, leaves, and flower drop.

Potassium is an activator of many enzymes. It aids in the formation of sugars, starches, proteins, and carbohydrates. It helps with cell division and activates various enzymes. It is necessary for protein synthesis. It also stimulates strong stems and roots. If you live in a place of granite, then you have access to granite sand and can cycle it through the compost pile or sometimes put it directly in the soil. Mottled, spotted, curled, or scorched leaves and burnt leaf margins and tips indicate potassium mineral deficiencies. It can show up as a temporary condition on young plants.

Sulfur is also a builder of proteins and amino enzymes. It aids in chlorophyll production and is more available in areas of high rainfall. Rainfall contributes to hydrogen. This correlates to a more acid soil or lower pH (probable hydrogen). Arid areas can suffer from a lack of sulfur. Deficiencies are similar to nitrogen deficiency with light green leaves.

Calcium helps build cell walls. So it is important to all parts of plant growth, especially roots. It supports water movement in the xylem and helps facilitate the uptake of nitrogen. Deficiencies include yellow leaf margins. Calcium and boron deficiencies contribute to excess sugars and amino acid buildup in the leaf and stem. Fungal diseases release enzymes that dissolve the lamella that bonds cells together. Calcium inhibits this activity. It forms bonds against bacterial disease. Calcium is not available in low pH soils, so liming is the best solution. The calcium is tied up at a low pH. Deficiencies can cause flower and fruit to not mature properly; this is known as blossom end rot.

Magnesium is an activator of chlorophyll. It also produces many enzymes and aids in phosphate transfer and enzymes for carbohydrates. It helps sugar and fruit production development and seed germination. It is usually readily available in a mineral balanced soil. If you need to add lime to the soil to raise the pH, use dolomitic limestone to incorporate the magnesium.

Next are the micronutrients; they are generally readily available in most soils. Iron is a catalyst for chlorophyll. It is necessary for photosynthesis and stimulates new growth and respiration. It shows deficiency through yellowing between the veins of leaves (chlorosis).

Manganese activates enzymes for photosynthesis. It helps chloroplasts function. It aids in the metabolism and respiration of the plant. It also aids in the metabolism of nitrogen.

Boron contributes to calcium uptake, the translocation of sugars, movement of hormones, and the formation of pollen. Deficiencies show up as brittle stems and leaves, hollow heart in potatoes. Boron also helps produce defense compounds. Borax can be a quick fix for boron when needed.

Silica helps protect leaves from fungal penetration. It is used widely in biodynamic preparations, in both 501 (the horn silica) and 507 (horsetail herb tea). Silica can be produced by using grasses, such as rye, oats, or wheat as a cover crop. I use a lot of bamboo for trellising beans, tomatoes, peppers, and eggplant. When the bamboo starts to crack it goes into a burn pile. The ash is used in composting as a source of silica.

Copper aids in the metabolism of enzymes for proteins and carbohydrate production. It supports photosynthesis. Deficiencies cause dye back of shoot tips.

Zinc plays a role in auxin hormones. Auxin hormones affect the direction of growth in the plant and are located at the growth tips. Zinc is another component of photosynthesis. Zinc activates and metabolizes amino acids. If deficient, it can cause little leaf or rosetting. This inhibits the internodes to grow properly. If you prune side shoots, it stimulates auxin hormones to grow upward. Pruning the top of the plant also stimulates horizontal growth.

Molybdenum is the smallest nutrient found in plants. It helps break down ammonia and is essential to photosynthesis. Deficiencies affect nitrogen uptake in the plant.

Chlorine is necessary for osmosis and water transport in the plant cells. It is rarely deficient. Nickel helps break down urea. Nitrogen, phosphorus, potassium, calcium, sulfur, and magnesium are macronutrients. All others are micronutrients.

It is best not to add or try to adjust micronutrients. They are needed in minute amounts. Adding them can be antagonistic to other nutrients. Excess copper or sulfur may affect molybdenum uptake. Excess zinc, manganese, or copper affects iron uptake. Excess phosphorus can cause a zinc, copper, or iron deficiency. Excess potassium affects manganese uptake. Excess iron, copper, or zinc also affects manganese absorption. So you see, it gets rather tricky to be a soil chemist and farmer at the same time. If you are feeding the soil a balanced mixture of life-giving properties as found in rich compost that is fully decomposed, it will provide a plentiful variety of nutrients. Seaweed is another source of micronutrients. Beyond that, the microorganisms in humus digest all the nutrients that the plants need. A balanced source rich in humus works best.

Most of the plants grown in the garden or farm are angiosperms. They contain built-in ovaries where seeds develop. Gymnosperms produce seeds on the outside. Pines are an example of this. Plant families make it easier to understand their individual needs. *Phaseolus vulgaris,* such as beans, and its relatives, peas, clover, peanuts, lentils, and related legumes, are nitrogen builders. They actually absorb nitrogen from the atmosphere and fix it. The nitrogen nodules can be found on their roots. They are native to North America. These plants are givers and help build up the soil; they will grow in many conditions. They tolerate some shade, but prefer sun and a neutral pH.

Plant Families

Asparagus officinalis is not related to other plants commonly grown for food. It originated from the western part of Europe. It is a coastal plant so it tolerates salt air quite well. It likes a bit more of an alkaline soil, pH 7–7.5, and grows along a rhizobial pattern with strong root development. It functions well where there is a lot of fungal growth. Plant it in a permanent location. If cared for it can last for several years.

Beta vulgaris (beets) are in the family of Chenopodium along with spinach, chard, lamb's-quarter, and quinoa. They are medium to heavy feeders on the soil. They are a European native that likes a rich loamy soil and neutral pH.

Crucifers are a large group of vegetables. Brassicas are a subgroup. The Brassicas can be broken down into many species. The Europeans took cabbage and developed it into broccoli, Brussels sprouts, cauliflower, kale, kohlrabi, and the like. The Chinese took crucifers (the main group) that include mustards and developed them into bok choi, tat choi, mizuna, Chinese cabbage, and several others. The third group of Cruciferae includes turnip, radish, and rutabaga. These are cool weather crops. They are heavy feeders on the soil and need potassium. The leafy ones, like cabbage and broccoli, need lots of nitrogen.

Apiaceae or Umbelliferae are easy to identify by their flowers. This group consists of carrots, parsley, cilantro, dill, parsnips, celery, caraway, anise, lovage, fennel, cumin, angelica, and anything with a similar flower. They are native to southern Europe and enjoy cool dry conditions, very loamy soil, a neutral pH, but they will tolerate some fluctuation in soil types.

Cucurbitaceae belong to the squash family. They produce both male and female flowers on the same plant. If the soil is too acid, they cannot take up needed calcium and suffer from blossom end rot on their fruit. The subgroups are divided into four groups: melons, cucumbers, summer squash, and winter squash.

Zea mays is another vegetable from the Americas. Its common name is corn. Corn has an interesting history traced back to the Incas. It is not totally clear just what or where it came into play. It requires human interaction since seeds need to be planted and they do not store well. It is also a monocotyledon. This means it sends up one leaf and then an alternate leaf, like grass or bamboo. Dicotyledons produce two leaves at a time, opposite one another. Corn needs to be planted in a series of rows in order to pollinate well. If not planted in consistent rows, the ears end up with jack o'lantern smiles with half their kernels missing. Most of the plants in the garden are dicotyledons, sending out two leaves at a time. The dicotyledons fall off once the first true leaves take form.

Alliums consist of onions, garlic, shallots, and leeks. They are also monocots. They have been traced back to Africa, southern Europe, and South America. They like a loamy or even sandy soil with good drainage. They respond well to a soil rich in potassium.

Solanaceae is the most popular family consisting of tomato, pepper, eggplant, potato, and tobacco. It is also related to deadly nightshade. It is native to the Andes mountain region of South America. There are occasional new discoveries of potatoes being dug up to turn into a new garden variety. Although potatoes like an acid soil, the others like a neutral pH. They respond well to a rich soil; the better the soil the better they produce. They are fairly heavy feeders.

Lactuca sativa (lettuce) has been developed into many varieties since Egyptians first developed it. It is in the Aster family like sunflowers and all types of daisy. The seeds are formed in the middle of the flower. It is a light feeder, fond of cool weather, and can accept some shade.

Okra (*Abelmoschus esculentus*) is from west Africa and south Asia. It does well in heat. People often ask, when is it time to plant okra? I tell them when you start sweating. It is a heavy feeder. It is in the hibiscus family and related to mallow plants like hibiscus, hollyhock, and cotton.

Sweet potato is often mistaken for a type of potato. It is not at all related to the Solanaceae family. It is related to morning glory. It does well in poor soils that are cultivated well. Understanding these groups will help you to know what to plant where, and how the plants will interact with one another.

All plant families have unique ways of dealing with their environment and have physical traits for doing so. Leaf structure is a good example of this. Hairy leaves are used for insulation from light frosts. They reduce evaporation and collect moisture. They also protect against some insects. Waxy leaf plants are covered with a coating of lignin that protects against some diseases and insects. Cactus is obviously very protective about who it lets get close.

Plants relate to their environment in a number of ways. Plants can communicate with other plants as well. Researchers at the University of Aberdeen, Scotland, have discovered ways in which plants communicate by sending signals along different channels. First, damaged plants give off odorous chemicals, referred to as volatile organic compounds, that repel insect damage. Secondly, plants use the filaments or hyphae of mychorrhizal fungi to relay messages of danger. Plants also give off vibration patterns to attract bees.

The energy plants put out is very subtle. They are very sensitive to their surroundings. Plants are integral to their environment; they play a role in what is going on around them. Without their presence the environment is altered. Plants like growing in a space surrounded by other plants. They don't like being too crowded to inhibit their growth, but like to be in close proximity with one another.

Understanding this level of sensitivity is important in knowing how to communicate with plants. Handling them in a gentle manner is a good place to start. Young plants are as gentle as their roots. You are a vital part of their environment. As you nurture the growth of the plants, you are sending them positive energy. To enhance the growth of the entire piece of land is to enhance each plant contained in it. They are gracious in their growth. Direct contact with them is something that they respond favorably to. Checking plants for insects and diseases is a form of grooming them. The attention they receive is nurturing to them. As they reach to the sky they also fill the space that they've been given. Most plants we grow are cultivars, derived from their wild cousins. They will need a boost to compete in the wild environment they have been cast out in. Understanding the growth habits of these species will help you prepare for their development into maturity.

The relationships and disrelationships between plants encourage healthy growth patterns. Plants that reflect similar needs can share similar habitats. Plants that support each other's growth habits are a good choice. Plants with long taproots such as lamb's-quarter, dock, or alfalfa are very good at permeating hard soil. Those cultivators help bring needed nutrients to the surface for shallow-rooted plants. Nitrogen fixers offer nutrients for heavy feeders like spinach, cabbage, or corn. Plants that exude strong aromas like garlic or herbs offer a deterrent for plants susceptible to insect damage.

In planning a garden there are many considerations to take into account. Timing of planting is one of these. (The dates used in planting guides are for zone 7b. Add or subtract one to two weeks for each zone accordingly.) Efficiency for the work ahead is another factor. Prevention also needs to be part of the plan. There are other factors to consider like the health of the soil, weather, and so on.

Planting Techniques

There are various techniques for starting seeds successfully based on their needs. Root crops need to be sown directly into the soil. Since they are primarily roots, you don't want to disturb that part of the plant too much. Broadcast carrots, beets, and radish onto a finely prepared bed. The art of laying them down so that there is minimal thinning later takes a bit of skill and practice. It is easy to oversow the seed. Carrots and radishes need a couple inches, beets a few inches or more. Then, spread a one-half-inch cover of spent compost or leaf mold.

Because of the mild winters in the south, you can plant carrots in early October. They get established in the fall, brave the winter, and provide me with mid-spring carrots that are usually delightful. You can plant turnips in drills. Make light impressions in the soil a few inches apart in staggered rows across the bed and drop a couple seeds in each space and lightly cover. It is easier to keep track of them. A light water with a rose flare a few times a day helps ensure germination. Peas, beans, and other legumes are poked directly into the soil, as are corn and all cucurbits (the squash family). Using a zigzag method down the bed helps fill the squash bed well once the plants mature. A staggered planting is an optimum use of space that would otherwise invite weeds. The weeds will move in during the early phase of bed development, but once the plants mature there will be little space for them. Figure 5.1 illustrates a bed layout for cabbage and beets.

Many of the easy flowers, like marigolds, celosia, zinnias, cosmos, cleome, and sunflowers are easy to direct sow. Larkspur, nigella, and poppies can be sown during the winter. The winter cold triggers them with what they need biologically. In nature, they drop seeds in the fall. After a series of frost, they know when it is time to come up. You can do this artificially by putting them in the freezer to get the same effect.

Many other families are too fragile and need to be started indoors, namely, the brassicas (cabbage family), with exception to kale and collards,

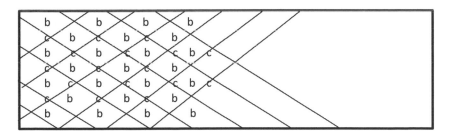

FIGURE 5.1
Bed Layout for Cabbage (c) and Beets (b)

and Solanaceae (tomatoes, peppers, eggplant). Lettuce, spinach, and mustards (Chinese greens) can be directly sown or started indoors. It is preferred to start them as transplants to get an earlier start and prevent loss. It is easy to broadcast kale and collards. Thinning them later provides one with several harvests at various stages of growth. You may wish to start some kale as transplants and direct sow some. It offers a variety that works here.

Perennial flowers are peculiar and often difficult to grow. Many require being planted on the surface of the potting soil and watered with a fine mist. It is good to freeze the seed for 48 hours to trick them into germination after a winter chill. The bag method helps them to germinate. This is discussed in the chapter on propagation (chapter 6). Delphiniums require darkness for germination. Most alliums are started indoors and transplanted with a dibble. You can make one from a hardwood branch.

Garlic is the exception. These are best planted in the fall in my area. Alliums do not do a good job of covering the bed to keep weeds out like other plants. A lot of mulch and diligent weeding is required. Garlic is a high maintenance plant that responds well to the care I give it. Herbs are often easier to grow if annual or biennial. Many of the umbellifers will reseed themselves and come up the following spring. Dill, cilantro, and parsley are good at this. They often reseed themselves, which produces volunteers for the next season. These volunteers are good for providing extra plants that can be moved into empty spaces in beds.

Caring for plants properly brings the same results as caring for anything that is alive. The stages of growth in plants require different amounts of attention. From seedlings to transplant is a fragile time. Plants are tender, yet vigorous. The delicate new life has an excitement and vitality of life about it. They are easy to impact and more sensitive to climate and their environment. This is a time when fertilizing will have the biggest impact. It is also easier to overfertilize; weekly supplements especially during a waxing moon bring desired results.

Fish emulsion, compost, or comfrey tea diluted is good. As plants are developing into maturity, they can and should be in their optimum health. An established nutrient base is most effective now. This is where you see the effects of soil preparation and proper irrigation. New growth is important for the plant to become well established. It is time to train and help the plant create the environment that supports healthy growth.

Once the plant reaches maturity, it moves into the reproductive phase. The shift in energy is toward procreation more than growth. All living things want to reproduce; that is their objective. Seed production is where they are headed. It is easier to see this in annuals. For them, it is one season, one big fast performance. Perennials are less in a hurry and focused more on adaptability. They move in the direction of affecting their environment. Whereas annuals are more affected by their environment, the energy of trees and shrubs has more of a relationship with wildlife, such as birds and small animals. Trees and shrubs can be used to establish boundaries and give definition to the surrounding area. The shift from short-term plantings to long-term ones is like moving from season to season rather than from month to month. They both have their place in the overall scheme of things.

It all begins with planting seeds. Plant seeds in flats at a depth of about twice their width into a mix of your own potting soil. One of the keys to growing from seed is to water often. You can't put a lot of water into a seed. So they don't need a lot of water at one time. Soil temperature is also important; above 70 degrees Fahrenheit is crucial for most seeds. Most seeds will come up in a week at this temperature. At 90 degrees, they will germinate in a few days. When they form the dicotyledons, they are susceptible to damping off fungus. You can deal with this by spraying Roman chamomile tea on the surface after watering. Damping off lives on the soil surface and the tea changes the soil chemistry, so it is not a conducive environment for damping off fungus to live in. Once plants grow their first set of true leaves, the damping off is no longer a threat. When plants develop their second set of true leaves, they are about ready for transplant. It is ideal for the plant to be at least four inches tall. See the planting guide in table 5.1.

Transplant into a well-prepared bed late in the day and keep the sun off the plant for a few days, depending on how much loss occurred to the root hairs. Roots hold water. Sun pulls water from the plant through respiration. So they need to grow new roots to deal with the sun. Water them well after transplanting and try to keep water off the leaves. Watering the leaves actually pulls water from the plant, and you don't want this. Watering well around the base pulls soil in around the roots without forcing out air. A lot of people smash the soil around the plant. This is not favorable. Let the watering pull soil in around the roots. The roots need water and air and a place to grow that is soft, not a cement-like soil. Mulch helps keep the sun off the soil and water in the soil, as well as maintaining temperature in the soil. It helps to water the plants again in a few days if rain does not show up.

TABLE 5.1
Planting Guide

Plant	Planting Dates	Weeks to Transplant	Soil pH/Sun Requirements	Spacing	Companion Plants	Special Considerations
Asparagus *Asparagus officinalis*	1/15–4/1 11/1–12/15	Plant crowns	Sandy loam 6.0–8.0	12"	Tomato, parsley, basil, nasturtium, marigold	Perennial; best to plant from crowns. Harvest second year.
Beets *Beta vulgaris*	2/15–4/1 8/1–9/20	Direct sow	6.0–6.5	3"–4"	Cabbage, onions, lettuce, kohlrabi	Add borax to prevent hollow heart boron deficiency.
Beans *Phaseolus vulgaris*	4/1–6/1 7/15–8/15	Direct sow	6.0–7.5 Sun to part shade	6" bush 8" pole	Corn, cucumber, potatoes, summer savory, rosemary, marigold, nasturtium	Watch for bean beetles. Handpick.
Broccoli *Brassica oleracea*	1/15–2/15 seed 3/1–4/1 transplant 7/1–8/1 seed 8/15–9/15 transplant	6 weeks	6.0–7.5	11"–15"	Dill, celery, sage, rosemary, beets, onions, garlic, thyme, chamomile, hyssop	Watch for cabbage moth. Handpick; spray Bt (*Bacillus thuringiensis*)
Brussels Sprouts *Brassica oleracea gemmifern*	1/10–2/15 7/1–8/1 seed 8/15–9/15 transplant	6 weeks	6.0–7.0	10"–12"	Same as broccoli	Needs long cool period. Best to start early in cloche.
Cabbage *Brassica oleracea capitata*	1/15–4/14	6 weeks	6.0–7.0	12"	Same as broccoli	Use baking soda for downy mildew.
Cauliflower *Brassica oleracea botrytis*	1/21–3/15	6 weeks	6.0–7.0	10"–12"	Same as broccoli	Easier to grow in spring than fall.
Carrot *Caucus carota*	2/15–3/15 8/15–9/21	Direct sow	6.0–7.5	2"	Peas, lettuce, rosemary, sage, tomato, chives	Use rosemary to deter carrot fly. Spray horsetail to deter aster yellows.

TABLE 5.1
Planting Guide (*continued*)

Plant	Planting Dates	Weeks to Transplant	Soil pH/Sun Requirements	Spacing	Companion Plants	Special Considerations
Celery Apium graveolens	1/1–2/1 seed 3/15–4/15 transplant	8–10 weeks	5.5–6.5 sun to part shade	6"	Leeks, tomatoes, beans, cabbage	Watch for aphids. Spray off with soapy water.
Chinese Greens Mustard Brassica rapa	1/21–2/21 2/21–3/21 trays 7/15–8/15 seed 8/15–9/15 trans	4 weeks	6.0–7.0	4"–8"	Catnip, garlic	Use of mulch encourages flea beetles.
Corn Zea mays	4/1–6/1	Direct sow	6.0–7.0	10"	Beans, squash, potatoes, cucumbers	Oil or Bt (Bacillus thuringiensis) in top of ear will deter worm.
Cucumber Cucumis sativa	4/1–5/15 7/15–8/15	Direct sow	5.5–7.5 sun to part shade	12"	Sunflowers, beans, radish, peas, lettuce, marigolds	Spray off aphids with soapy water. Use Serenade for bugs.
Eggplant Solanum melongena	2/15–4/1 seed 4/1–5/15 trans	6 weeks	5.5–6.5	18"	Beans, potatoes, borage, garlic, catnip	Transplant at 1 foot to deal with flea beetle.
Garlic Allium sativum	9/1–10/15	Direct sow cloves	5.5–7.5	5"	Beets, tomatoes, lettuce, chamomile, summer savory	Mulch well with compost tea in early spring.
Kale Collards Brassica oleracea	2/15–3/15 8/1–9/15	Direct sow or 6 weeks	6.0–7.0	8"–10"	Dill, celery, sate, radish, beets, garlic, rosemary, chamomile, hyssop, thyme	Use compost tea for black spot.
Leeks Allium ampeloprasum	1/15–2/15 8/1–9/1	8 weeks	6.0–8.0	6"–10"	Onions, celery, carrots	Plant deep in soil.

TABLE 5.1
Planting Guide (*continued*)

Plant	Planting Dates	Weeks to Transplant	Soil pH/Sun Requirements	Spacing	Companion Plants	Special Considerations
Lettuce *Latuca sativa*	2/1–3/1 trans 3/1–4/1 direct 8/15–9/15	4 weeks Direct sow	6.0–7.0	6″	Carrots, radish, peas, cucumbers, onions	Drainage prevents rots.
Melons *Cucumis melo*	3/1–4/15 trans 4/7–5/15	4 weeks Direct sow	6.0–7.0	18″	Beans, sunflower, nasturtium	Keep fruit off ground; apply mulch; spray off aphids.
Onions *Allium cepa*	2/1–3/15 8/1–9/1	Direct sow	6.0–7.5	4″–6″	Beets, tomatoes, lettuce, chamomile	Mulch well; pull soil back in spring.
Peas English *Pisum sativa*	2/15–3/15 8/15–9/15	Direct sow	6.0–7.5	4″	Carrots, turnips, radish, cucumbers	Trellis well in hoops to discourage birds.
Peas Field *Paseolus vulgaris*	4/1–6/15	Direct sow	6.0–7.5	6″	Corn, squash, okra	It is a good soil builder. Likes hot temperature.
Peppers *Capsicum annuum*	2/15–4/1 seed 4/1–5/15 trans	6 weeks	5.5–7.5	18″	Basil, borage, parsley, chives	Regular water; mulch; limit overhead irrigation.
Potatoes *Solanum tubersoum*	2/1–3/15	Direct sow whole potato or pieces with three eyes	4.5–6.0	12″	Beans, cabbage, horse radish, marigolds, catnip	Change out mulch periodically. Needs good drainage.
Radish *Raphanus sativus*	2/15–4/1 8/1–10/1	Direct sow	6.0–7.0	2″–3″	Peas, nasturtium, lettuce, cucumber	Cultivate soil to discourage flea beetles.
Rutabaga *Brassica napus*	2/15–4/1 8/1–10/1	Direct sow	6.0–7.0	4″	Peas, nasturtium, lettuce, cucumbers	Wood ashes discourage maggots.
Spinach *Beta oleracea*	2/15–3/15 9/1–10/1	4 weeks or direct sow	6.0–7.5	4″–6″	Strawberries, radish, onion, beets, turnips	Likes afternoon shade to prevent bolting; keep weeded to prevent diseases.

TABLE 5.1
Planting Guide (*continued*)

Plant	Planting Dates	Weeks to Transplant	Soil pH/Sun Requirements	Spacing	Companion Plants	Special Considerations
Okra	4/1–6/15	Direct sow	6.0–7.0	24"	Beans, peas, squash	Likes hot weather; spray soap on aphids.
Squash Summer– *Curcurbita pepo* Winter– *Curcurbita maximus*	 4/1–5/15 8/15–8/30 4/1–6/15	Direct sow or 4 weeks	 6.0–7.0 6.0–7.0	 18"–24" 24"	Beans, corn, nasturtium, marigold, angelica tansy	Protect base of plant from squash bugs. Inject Bt into stem for vine borers.
Sweet Potato *Impomea batatis*	4/15–6/15	Start slips 4–6 weeks before	5.5–6.0	12"–18"	Castor bean, sunflower, okra	Cut back excess vines; are edible.
Swiss Chard *Spinachia oleracen*	3/1–4/15 8/15–9/15	Direct sow	6.0–7.0	8"	Radishes, onions, beets, turnips, strawberries	Hose leaves and stems to wash off insects.
Tomatoes *Lycopersicum esculentum*	2/15–6/1 seed 4/1–7/15 trans	6 weeks	6.0–7.0	24"	Borage, chives, onions, parsley, carrots, marigolds, nasturtium, asparagus	Keep leaves off ground. Mulch well. Spray with horsetail and silica. Regular water.
Turnips *Brasica bapa*	2/15–4/15 8/15–9/15	Direct sow	6.0–7.0	3"–5"	Spinach, peas, marigolds	Cultivate to discourage flea beetles. Wood ashes eliminate weeds.
Watermelon *Cucurbitaceae*	3/1–4/1 seed 4/1–5/1 direct	Direct sow or 4 weeks	6.0–7.5	12" 18"	Nasturtium, beans, marigolds, sunflower, angelica	Squash bugs. Use netting at base of plant. Tansy, mint tea.

Succession Planting

Successive plantings provide a continuous harvest. This is important for a market operation. This works better with some plants than others. It works well with the companion planting model. You can plant beans alongside cabbages that are almost ready for harvest to keep the space used well. Another method is to grow English peas in hoops; as they are finished, usually when it gets too hot for them, you can pull the peas and throw a shovel of compost in its place. This makes a nice place for a late crop of tomatoes.

As mentioned before, radishes mature as the lettuce leaves consume the bed space. An early planting of turnips comes out in time for a late planting of broccoli. Time can be a factor if trying to successive plant melons, winter squash, peppers, eggplant, garlic, onions, or sweet potatoes. Peas have a short window to grow here in the South. Try to use successive plantings as much as you can to ensure success. It can be a gamble with the weather, and it is easy to have losses trying to second guess what will work. This is especially true now with our very unpredictable weather patterns.

FIGURE 5.2
Chinese cabbage, bok choi, and mizuna.

Caring for the plants helps keep them healthy. Once the plant has reached maturity, it should occupy the space well. There are generally some weeds that show up before the plants are full size. At this stage, pull weeds. By doing this you have cultivated the soil. Topdress the open soil with compost, water it well, and cover it with mulch.

The timing of weeding is a consideration and should be done a short while before the plant reaches full size. After this, if the bed is planted intensively, there will be no more room for weeds. This is referred to as the living mulch. Use staggered plantings across the bed. Plants are not square and do not fit into a grid. They are round and occupy round spaces well. Over the years I have moved away from straight rectangular beds. The bed layout should fill the needs of the plants, not the gardener.

Plant Layout

Using a staggered planting allows many more plants for a given space. Here are the number of plants you get for a one hundred square foot bed. At 36" spacing, 20 plants (blueberries, blackberries, cardoon). At 24" spacing, 24 plants (tomatoes, melons, squash). At 18" spacing, 40 plants (peppers, eggplants potatoes, basil). At 12" spacing, 112 plants (cucumbers, small cabbage, broccoli, sunflowers, sweet potatoes). At 10" spacing, 144 plants (Chinese cabbage, cauliflower, several flower varieties). At 8" spacing, 200 plants (kale, Asian greens, chard, many flower varieties, celery). At 6" spacing, 345 plants (lettuce, beans, small Asian greens). At 5" spacing, 540 plants (garlic, small spinach, onions). Many small roots, such as carrots, beets, turnips, and radish are broadcast directly into beds and get 2" to 4" spacing depending on variety.

The mature leaves should just overlap enough to keep weeds out and protect the bed. Try to develop a canopy over the bed with the living mulch concept. This is part of the French intensive method. Weeds are really guardians of the soil. If you do not use an area well, they will— and preserve it for you until you are ready to use it. They demonstrate how to use land effectively. Their role is that of being the scar tissue of tilled land. They protect it and help put back the ecology that was destroyed. They become weeds until we discover a practical use for them.

Weeds are good indicators of the soil, as already mentioned in the first chapter. During drought conditions, weeds do a better job of protecting the soil until there is favorable weather you can work with. Of course, there are weeds, and then there are *weeds*. Plants like henbit (*Lamium amplexicaule*), Chinese mugwort (*Artemisia vulgaris*), purslane (*Portulaca oleracea*), lamb's-quarter, violets, clover, plantain, and dandelion are quite welcome, as they are not very competitive plants. They are not only beneficial but also sometimes edible and medicinal. There are also plants that are very beneficial but might otherwise be considered weeds. Sonchus or sow thistle is an aid to tomato culture. This, along with fava beans used as a cover crop, can be dug into the beds where tomatoes are to be planted. Horsetail (*Equisetum arvense*) can be spread on top of the bed below the mulch as a disease preventative.

However, some weeds are not as pleasant to deal with. It is common to have a lot of Bermuda grass (*Cynodon dactylon*) and Johnson grass (*Sorghum halepense*); and occasionally pigweed (*Amaranthus palmeri*) is brought in accidentally. Pigweed is related to amaranth grain and callaloo, a popular green used in Jamaica and Belize cooking. It is hard to pick your weeds, just like it is hard to pick your neighbors. I learned a long time ago to work with what I've got.

I worked as an apprentice in Alan Chadwick's Enchanted Garden at UC Santa Cruz, and later worked as an apprentice at Camp Joy Garden in the Santa Cruz Mountains. Both of these experiences fed me with a lot of inspiration. Plant culture is part of garden culture. The magic of the garden is no more than a human's ability to understand nature. For it to be a full experience, it helps if it is done in complete cycles. This means from compost to harvest and back to compost, from seed planting to seed harvest. These gardens sustain themselves on what they grow as well as on the enthusiasm they create.

These gardens were the ultimate horticultural classroom, full of eager students. It was easy to learn a lot about methods and just as much about appreciating the work that was in front of me each day and for years to come. I would lie awake each night planting gardens in my mind. By the end of the season, they would blossom in my soul. As I formed the beds, they helped form me. All plants have a strong desire to grow. If you nurture them, they usually do quite well. If not, you will learn from them, for plants are also great teachers. The whole environment needs to work together. It is important to view it this way. The fruit trees are important to the garden beds below them. The birds and insects and all life forms are part of this holistic landscape, and you are the facilitator of this magical place.

6

Plant and Seed Propagation

All of nature begins to whisper its secrets to us through its sounds. Sounds that were previously incomprehensible to our souls now become the meaningful language of nature.

—Rudolf Steiner

STARTING SEEDS AND PROPAGATING PLANTS are the renewal of the work in the garden. It is the investment toward the beginnings of a new season. The proper techniques for doing propagation require a greenhouse that has a proper mist system in place. I have almost never been so fortunate, so I will show methods used in huts, bathrooms, and porches.

With seeds, be it sexual or nonsexual, reproduction is the process where the plants either need bees to reproduce, or they are a complete flower. Seeds offer an amazing look into the future. Plants want to reproduce and help their species survive. That is the goal of all living things. The acorn has in it the makings of a tree, patterning itself after the one it came from. Seeds are one of the origins as well as keepers of culture. The keeping of seeds is to put perpetual motion into that culture. Being truly sustainable involves growing your own seed and saving that germ plasm. It adapts itself to the surroundings it is grown in. I have grown some New Mexican hot chili peppers that came my way many years ago. But they are really Georgia peppers because they have adapted to the climate and field that they now grow in.

It is good, when possible, to introduce new origins of the same seed from time to time. This idea lends itself to the development of seed networks. If you pass your seed onto reliable growers, you ensure a security deposit on getting the seed back in case of a worst-case scenario.

When collecting seeds, do not pick the first fruit or pods because the energy being thrust forth may not represent its true characteristics. As the plant matures those fruits are better rounded and produce better seed germ plasm. Hybridization is regression. Using hybrid seeds will bring about results short term, but it is a bastardized approach and leads you away from sustainable growing. True open pollinated seeds tell stories of the past from which they came. They bring with them an evolution of life.

Start with Good Potting Soil

Starting seeds is the first step to making this all happen. In starting seeds, it is important to begin with a good potting soil mix. A common soil mix to work with uses two parts finished compost to one part leaf mold. Leaf mold is best if made from decomposed leaves. Other materials can be used if made from organic matter and fully decomposed. These are shifted through a quarter-inch mesh screen. Add one part sharp sand (very coarse, $\frac{1}{16}$"–$\frac{1}{8}$"). Next, mix these thoroughly on a flat surface while having someone spray water onto it. Doing this adds air and water evenly into the mix. This mix can be made with equal parts for better drainage.

Another popular mix is one part sand or vermiculite, one part leaf mold, and one part compost. This would be a good mix for herbs. Peat moss is not a sustainable product. It is mined, usually from Canada, and is not at all a sustainable product. I build flats from old crates with quarter-inch spacing between slats on the bottom for spring vegetables like brassicas, crucifers, lettuce, and spinach. I use larger containers, four-inch round, for the Solanaceae family (tomatoes, peppers, and eggplant). I either make them or use recycled plastic containers taken from nurseries when they throw them out. For flowers and herbs, you can use a variety of recycled containers that fit the dimensions of what you need.

Seed Germination

Seed germination is the beginning of something magical and new. A seed contains everything needed to start a plant. It contains germ plasm, food, and water all in a protected shell. A seed embryo that swells with water is lush with life as it awakens. Once this takes place, the soul of the plant is alive. The magnetism of gravity pulls the root down, and the radical begins. The hypocotyl is developed, and it moves to find an opening at the surface of the soil and toward the sun.

Growing from seed is the ideal. Growing from cuttings is for security, yet cannot be avoided since so many plants are hard to grow any other way. Most garden seeds are quite simple to work with. Outside air and soil temperature are important factors (see the seed planting guide in table 6.1). At 70 degrees Fahrenheit most seeds will germinate in about a week. At 90 degrees, they can germinate in a couple of days. In January and February, one needs to give a week or more for them to germinate. Bottom heat under the trays or flats works well as long as you remember to water them often.

There are creative ways to provide bottom heat. Many recycled items, such as waterbed heaters, hot water tanks, old gas heaters, or whatever resources are available, can work quite well. In mid or late summer, it is time to start seeds for the fall. In the summer heat, it only takes a couple days for them to germinate. It does not take long before they are up and running. Remember to plant seeds in the soil about twice their width. Root crops and legumes are direct sown and do not need to be started indoors. Herbs are a little more difficult. Parsley and lovage, for instance, can take a month to germinate, usually two weeks or so. Basically, look at the life of the plant. If it has a long life, it will be in no hurry to germinate. Some perennials, such as camellias, may take three months to come up. Flowers vary in their requirements to germinate. Some of the perennials require darkness to germinate, such as delphiniums, phlox, *Centaurea, Salpiglossis,* verbena, and statice (*Limonium*).

There are many more that need light to help germinate, like snapdragons, coreopsis, gaillardia, and echinacea. Flowers are an important part of any garden. Besides being much more profitable than most vegetables, they are an important part of my integrated pest management; they attract a large variety of beneficial insects. And they provide amazing beauty. For me, they are food for the soul. Ralph Waldo Emerson said, "The earth laughs flowers"; hence, our place is called Smiling Earth.

Seed germination rates are no more than what is required by law in order to sell them. Broccoli and all brassicas are 85 percent; beans, melons, mustard, squash, tomatoes, lettuce, radish, and rutabagas are 75 percent; onions and leeks are 70 percent; beets and chard are 65 percent; parsley, parsnips, and spinach 60 percent; carrots, peppers, eggplant, celery, and okra are 55

TABLE 6.1
Flower Seed Planting Guide

Name	Days to Germinate	Temperature	Depth Comments
Achillea (perennial)	7–30	60–70	Surface needs light
Aconitum (perennial)	5–100	55–60	Surface needs light
Ageratum (annual)	10–14	65–75	Surface needs light, or broadcast (direct sow)
Agastache (perennial)	30–90	55	⅛"
Allium (perennial)	30–90	50	Just cover; chill before planting for 4 weeks
Alstroemeria (perennial)	30–100	55–65	⅛"; chill 4 weeks
Alyssum (annual)	7–14	60–75	Surface, or broadcast
Antirrhinum (annual)	10–21	65–75	Surface needs light chill 48 hrs before planting.
Anthemis (perennial)	7–14	70	Surface
Aster (annual)	10–14	70	Just cover; chill 2 weeks
Calendula (annual)	10–14	70	⅛"; needs darkness, or can broadcast
Calliopsis (annual)	14	65	⅛"
Campanula (perennial)	14–28	60–70	Surface needs light
Catananche (perennial)	20–25	65–75	⅛"
Celosia (annual)	7–14	65–75	Surface light, or broadcast
Centaurea (annual)	7–14	60–70	⅛"; needs darkness
Clarkia (annual)	21	70	¼" or broadcast
Cleome (annual)	10–14	70–75	Prechill surface; needs light, or broadcast
Coreopsis (perennial)	20–27	55–70	Surface needs light
Cosmos (annual)	5–10	65–86	¼" or broadcast
Dahlia (annual)	5–10	65–70	¹⁄₁₆" or broadcast
Delphinium (perennial)	14–28	50–55	¹⁄₁₆"; needs darkness
Dianthus (perennial)	14–21	60–70	Just cover
Digitalis (perennial)	14–21	60–65	Surface needs light
Echinacea (perennial)	10–21	65–75	Surface needs light
Echinops (perennial)	14–60	65–75	¹⁄₁₆"
Freesia (biennial)	20–30	65–75	¼"; presoak seeds

TABLE 6.1

Flower Seed Planting Guide (*continued*)

Name	Days to Germinate	Temperature	Depth Comments
Gaillardia (perennial)	14–21	70–75	Surface needs light
Gerbera (perennial)	15–25	70–75	Surface needs light
Geum (perennial)	20–30	65–70	¹/₁₆″
Gloriosa (biennial)	30	70–75	¹/₁₆″ or broadcast
Gomphrena (annual)	6–10	70–75	Surface needs light
Gypsophilia (perennial)	10–15	70	Just cover or broadcast
Helichrysum (annual)	7–10	65–75	Surface needs light, or broadcast
Hollyhock (annual/ perennial)	10–15	60–70	Surface needs light
Hyssop (perennial)	14–40	60–70	¹/₁₆″
Larkspur (annual)	14–21	50–55	Prechill surface; ¹/₁₆″; needs darkness, or broadcast
Limonium (perennial)	10–15	60–70	Just cover; needs darkness
Marigold (annual)	5–14	70–75	Just cover, or broadcast
Monarda (perennial)	10–40	60–70	Just cover
Nicotiana (annual)	10–20	70–75	Surface needs light, or broadcast
Nigella (annual)	10–15	65–70	¹/₁₆″ or broadcast
Papaver (annual)	10–25	55–60	Just cover; needs darkness, or broadcast
Penstemon (perennial)	16–21	55–60	Surface needs to chill
Phlox (annual/ perennial)	20–30/30–100	55–70	¹/₁₆″; needs darkness, or broadcast

percent. Knowing this, as well as the age of the seed, helps determine how many seeds to put in a hole. The cooler vegetables germinate at slightly cooler temperatures, around 60 degrees Fahrenheit. Warm season vegetables prefer around 70 degrees. Flowers have specific requirements (refer to table 6.1). Perennials do best started in the spring and planted out in the fall to flower the next season. One of the keys to germinating seeds is to keep them slightly damp. They do not need a lot of water. Seeds cannot hold much, so once a day is important. If it is hot and dry, water perhaps twice a day so that the surface does not quite dry out. Once the seedlings have developed their first set of cotyledons, you have a choice to trim them down to one or prick them out. Pricking them out is delicate work. It is best done before watering when the soil is a little dry. Use a kitchen fork to reach under the whole mass. By placing them on a flat surface, you can gently separate them from the roots up. Then hold the plants by the leaves and dance them about gently so the roots loosen until they become unattached from one another. Move them into a nice potting soil mix and water them in well. At this point, they need to be out of the sun for several days. Tomatoes work well for this. Eggplant and peppers do not. Lettuce, spinach, and brassicas are fairly easy, as are cucurbits and basil. Perennials such as herbs and flowers have specific requirements depending on their family.

The best thing you can do to make your garden or farm truly sustainable is to save your own seed. It takes time to find varieties that have all the characteristics you want. Most plants lend themselves to collecting seeds easily. The seed will be more acclimated to your microclimate as well. The major consideration is that you are limited by how many varieties you can grow without them cross-pollinating. Even tomatoes and their family that are self-pollinating will cross. Try telling the bees they are not needed there. It doesn't work.

There are folks who plant over a hundred types of tomatoes. None of them will be true come harvest time, but they usually don't get it. What about some hot bell peppers? If you plant three varieties of tomato and one cherry tomato variety spread out over a half acre that is enough room to keep them true. If you have four types of peppers, two eggplants, a couple melons, a couple cucumbers, and a few beans, then you have a lot of variety. This allows the seeds to stay true. It is good to target the plants that have the characteristics you are looking for early, like good overall growth, size, disease and insect resistance, color, taste, and good production. Mark them with a ribbon and wait for the fruit to get a little overripe. Mark at least two or three plants so that there is diversity in your seed selection.

Tomato seeds are supposed to be fermented. Cut them up and put the pieces in a jar with a little water if they are not very juicy. Swirl the solution and let it set. After about a week, a mold will form on top of the liquid. Strain off the liquid with any seeds on top and discard that. The seeds on the bottom are strained, rinsed, and laid out to dry. Of course, most seeds will germinate without that process, but it helps and gives you mostly good dependable seed.

Beans, peas, cucumbers, melons, squash, peppers, eggplant, okra, and corn can be taken directly from the very ripe fruit or pod. Carrots, cabbages, beets, chard, lettuce, spinach, turnips, mustard, onions, leeks, and radish produce seed in their flowers. The stems with flowers can be cut, placed in a bag, and shaken to collect the seed. Collecting seeds puts you in closer relationship with the varieties you grow, saves you money, and gives you more control of the garden and its resources. Dry and store them in tight containers, mark them with dates, and put them either in a fridge or freezer. Most seeds will keep for a number of years if stored well.

Seeds have different lengths of storage life. Carrots and corn keep for about a year; peas, spinach, chard, and beets for two or three years. Tomatoes, peppers, and eggplant are good for three years. Lettuce, melons, squash, and beans are good for three or four years. Turnips, radish, mustards, collards, and kale keep for several years. It is good to periodically do a seed test to determine the viability of the seed you have. The common method is to roll them up in paper towels, like the ones used in public restrooms. Lay them on a dish and keep them misted. You can, of course, place them in a pot of soil as well. Soaking them overnight in a jar of water and rinsing a couple times a day, as is done with sprouts, will work for big seeds like beans and peas.

Eventually, you can meet other gardeners in your area that wish to exchange seeds. This supports sustainable community development. There is a great need to develop resources like this. This is a good way to meet others to exchange many resources with.

Asexual reproduction is where you are producing the plants in a controlled environment. Honoring a plant by spreading its presence is one of the best ways to show respect for it. Another reason for propagation is because in some plants, natural dissemination can be curbed by changes in the environment. Weather affects how well a plant will reproduce. Encouraging desired plants helps create the environment conducive to your vision. Plants with hairy stems and square stems take well from cuttings placed in water. This is also called cloning. A square stem puts it in the mint family. Tomatoes are also good for this. Tomatoes produce suckers that come up in the base of the petiole near the stem. These can easily be cut off and rooted in water for a late season crop.

When taking fresh cuttings, try to cut about five inches of tender growth. Anything that has stiffness will be hard to root in water alone. When using water alone, change the water at least every couple days. For all cuttings, grafting, and the like, it is important to use materials that are sterile. Using clean sharp knives and alcohol is very helpful in preventing bacteria and fungus from entering the cutting. Sweet potatoes are pretty easy to start from slips. Take last year's potatoes or purchase some organic ones (free from fungicides). At least two months before you wish to plant them, place them in a warm place. As the potatoes start to sprout, place them in containers so they are half submerged in water. They can be laid either horizontally or vertically. As the sprouts grow, leaves will form. Six inches or so of growth make an ideal slip. A little shorter can also work. Cut these off with a little potato still attached. Place them in water with the cuttings about halfway out of the water. In a few weeks they should have some healthy roots. Keep them in a sunny window. It works well to plant them when it is getting warm but not too hot.

In the piedmont of Southern states, try to get them in the ground in mid-May. They do well in hot weather since they originate from Africa. Irish potatoes that originate in the Andes are often grown from potato parts containing eyes. I plant the potatoes wrapped in comfrey leaf. It helps to contribute calcium and potassium for healthy growth.

There are several ways to propagate those plants that are a little harder. Woody stem plants can be divided at the roots. Layering works well for stems that can be bent or sit close to the ground. Vines can often be laid down in the soil to grow roots. Start with tender growth that is still attached to parent plant. Scrape the undersurface of the branch or stem about a sixteenth to an eighth of an inch and a couple inches long. Place it in the soil and cover it with an inch or so of soil. Place a rock on it to hold it down and mark the spot and keep wet. This works with marjoram, oregano, thyme, rosemary, sage, and many vine-producing plants. Give it a month or so and check on the progress. Once there is a well-established root, it can be separated from the mother plant. It is best to move it into a pot for a month or so before sending it out into the field.

Root cuttings can be done on certain plants, such as horseradish, hollyhocks, rhubarb, yarrow, comfrey, figs, raspberry, and blackberry. You must dig down along the side to prune off sections to root, preferably with some stem attached. Fill back in as soon as you are done, preferably with a little compost. Place the rooting in soil and keep damp. Fig stems and elderberry will also root in water if kept warm. Woody stem plants that have many stems coming from a base of crown can be divided. Be sure to have some roots and above the ground leaves to work with. This works well for all the plants listed above as well as all bulbs and rhizomes, such as irises, ginger, and turmeric.

Stem cuttings are another method for woody stem plants. It is best to take perennial cuttings between fall and spring equinox. Take a cutting of a branch that is about a pencil thickness with several nodes. Cut each piece to about four to six inches long. Make sure there are about three or more nodes on each cutting. Put them in a damp place; plastic bags work well. Wrap the cuttings in a damp paper towel and then place them in a plastic bag. Keep the cuttings horizontal and check every couple weeks to make sure they stay damp. This can take a couple of months before you can plant it in soil. This method works well for some hardwoods.

Air layering is another form of propagation that I am very fond of. It works well with several hardwoods. First, locate a branch that is growing in a horizontal direction. It does not have to be exactly horizontal, preferably new growth. Take a sharp knife and cut along the bottom. The key is to cut beyond the bark and into the cambium layer only slightly, maybe one-eighth inch. Use about a five-inch swath, more or less, about an inch or so wide. Next, take a spongy medium, soak it in water, and wring the water out. Place this around the entire stem. Wrap it with a solid sheet of plastic or aluminum foil. Close it tight at the ends so it resembles a large burrito. The idea is to keep the moisture in mixed with air. Sphagnum peat moss is generally used. You may have decent luck with dried fern leaves and fronds. Other alternatives are moss, collected from a ground cover, Roman chamomile, and ground bark. This process takes about three to seven weeks. If you do not see substantial roots after three weeks, close it up and wait a few more weeks. These methods work better in the spring and fall, when the plant is putting on new growth. Grafting is usually used on trees and most hardwoods. Almost all fruit trees you buy have a small graft near the base of the stem. It is important to leave this above the ground a few inches when planting. The type of rootstock used determines the size of the tree. What is above the ground determines the fruit. It is possible to have several varieties of apples on one tree. You can also have a plum, a pear, and an apple on the same tree.

Most people have no idea how many varieties of apples, pears, plums, and so forth there really are. That is because the selection in the store is so limited. These fruits are grown for production, cosmetics, shipping, and most of all storage. Once I was with a group collecting scion wood for grafting in California. We visited an apple collector in residential Richmond, California. This guy had a backyard that was a little bigger than most with five hundred different varieties of apples. He had them on two-foot centers. He had collected the trees from old ghost towns that were once booming during the Gold Rush. When the gold was gone, so were the people. The trees were left to fend for themselves. He had some old Thomas Jefferson varieties. We grafted them onto a variety of rootstocks.

In California there is more flexibility in terms of resources, but there are fruit collectors in all parts of this country. One of the best-known organizations is the North American Fruit Explorers Exchange. There are lots of local groups that have access to fruit varieties to sell or trade. This can be an amazing experience in the diversity of fruit tastes. Most people have no idea of the complexity of tastes that apples have, not to mention all the other fruits. It is good to be able to grow about fifteen different fruits, mostly for personal consumption. This ensures some success rate even on a bad year. You may find trees from local growers where you can discover the best varieties for your given area.

Grafting

Grafting is an acquired skill. The best way to get good at it is to practice. You can practice on trees you have no attachment to. Various grafting techniques generally apply to different ages of the stock plant you are grafting onto. T-budding is done on very young trees. The advantage here is that younger plants are more prone to taking to the graft. It is also best to work with younger plants because they will grow up and adapt better to their surroundings. The scion wood is a cutting from the tree with the desired fruit type you want. Cut a young branch that has a healthy bud on it. Keep this in a bag and refrigerated until use, but use it soon after it is taken. Cut a horizontal line about one quarter to a half an inch long on the stock tree that is in the ground. Cut a vertical line down about a half inch below to resemble a T. Cut off a fresh bud from your scion wood. Make it a clean cut just under the bark to capture a thin layer of the cambium. Cut this piece small enough to fit into the T cut on the stock tree. Gently slide it in and try to make a smooth seat so that both pieces mend together well. The two need to have a good bond. Take a budding rubber or plastic budding strip and wrap the top and bottom to secure the bud stays in place and is held together with a tight seal. Make sure the bud is exposed. If it takes, it will start growing in the coming months. Once the bud has some size to it (at least a few inches), you will need to cut off the tree above the graft so that the bud becomes the above- ground main trunk of the tree.

Chip budding is very similar. It works well on vines like grapes. Make a cut into the stock wood at a slight angle, down about three-quarters of an inch. The cut needs a lip on the bottom like a little flap. Cut the bud from your scion wood to resemble the piece you cut out of the tree. Cut a horizontal blunt end on the bottom. Place the bud down onto the cut with a good surface seal. Wrap the bud well, top to bottom, with the bud exposed.

There are several different methods for grafting trees. Cleft grating is best used on wood of one to four inches in diameter. Scion wood cut at two to three inches long is slid down into the cut and banded together with rubber or plastic grafting tape. This is done during the dormant season. It is a good method for restoring old trees with top damage. Cut the entire tree at about three or four feet. Take a machete or meat cleaver and cut a clean wedge vertically down into the cut right across the middle. Scion wood of one-half inch in diameter works well. Cut a tapered end on the bottom. Push the scion wood down into the cut. Place it out near the perimeter of the tree just a short distance inside of where the bark is located along the cambium. You generally place one graft per tree.

Whip or tongue grafting is useful for young trees. Take two pieces of scion wood exactly the same size in diameter. Make a cut of one to two inches long on both pieces, so they match. A notch can be made to hold the fit. They are then banded together with a rubber strip or grafting tape.

It is necessary to make a good seal with the tree. So the angle of the scion wood is very important. With all of these grafts, try to be as sanitary as possible to avoid infection. Anything that gets in the way of the bond will prevent it from happening, including air. Commercial nurseries use rooting hormones. I have heard of organic growers using willow, honey, comfrey, and nettles for this purpose. I have not had any need for these. I am also not a commercial nurseryman. It is very important to do a good job with the graft by being clean and making a good bond between plants. This is the key to its success. Establish what your needs are and plan for several extra grafts, if you have root stock to work with, to ensure that one of them will take. In the best-case scenario, you will have extra to trade or give away.

Strawberry culture is done differently than with other berries. Strawberries are a perennial, grown for three or four years before starting over. The first year they become established. The general idea is to remove most of the blooms so the plant can put its energy into vegetative growth. This is an important time to keep them weeded, topdressed, and mulched. Strawberries respond well to a good mulch layer. That is easy to remember because of their name. The mulch is important for keeping the fruit off the ground.

The second year they should be good producers. It is good to grow two types. A day-neutral variety produces two or more crops; an everbearing variety is practically the same but produces continually throughout the summer. April or June bearers that come in during a two- or three-week period are good for putting up fruit. In the South, a June bearer is actually an April bearer. Their growth habits are about the same. They are planted in a bed in a staggered planting about a foot apart.

Strawberries prefer a loamy soil with good drainage and eight hours of sun. As the mother plant matures, it produces offshoots that are good producers. Evaluate their growth during the third year. Either at the end of the third or fourth year, you may dig up the offshoots or babies. These are then moved into a new bed to start the process over. The best plan is to have beds that are developed on alternate years. This way there will always be a crop in their prime. Pick off dead or decayed leaves. Watch for slugs. Try to remove grubs before planting. If birds become a problem, netting can be used to keep them out. Strawberry plants also do well along a wall. But this can be a problem if you have slugs.

Other berries vary in their ability to propagate. Blackberries and raspberries are relatively easy. They are best taken from suckers at the edge of the bed. Dig down and separate the root. Dig up the cane with a healthy root system and move into a new location. They can also be divided, but suckers works best. Blueberry is usually propagated from softwood cuttings. Take tip cuttings about six inches long, no bigger than a pencil. Make cuts at a 45 degree angle and place halfway into a rooting medium. The medium should consist of sharp sand, half- decomposed wood chips, perlite, or a mixture. Rooting hormones are generally used to stimulate root growth.

These rooting hormones are not the least bit organic. A healthy alternative is to use tea made from willow. It can be made from the bark or the new young shoots. Fresh willow stems from weeping willow *(Salix baylonica)* can be put in a glass of clean water for a few days to allow the sap to flow into the water, or make a tea from very young new stems. You can experiment with this method and may need more time to determine its success. Another option is to use the bag method. Water the plants well and place a bag over the container to keep the moisture in. This method can be very effective for hard to start perennial seeds like delphiniums. This is put in a sunny location with a mist system.

Hardwood and softwood cuttings are very difficult but can be fun to experiment with. The mist system can be made out of an old lawn sprinkler valve. At best, it is time-consuming and messy. This can be done in the bathtub with limited success. Place three to six inches of medium in the bottom of the tub. I prefer coarse or sharp sand. Commercially, perlite is used. Place the cuttings into the sand with an angled cut. This provides more surface area to root. Place the angle of the cut in a vertical position. If the watering source is from a well, there could be bacterial problems due to the water not being totally clean. This is where city water works best.

But generally I would recommend purchasing hardwood and softwood plants from a nursery. When buying in quantity, it helps to be able to locate nursery plants from a commercial grower that is smaller and less expensive. They need to be kept watered after transplanting out into the ground. Some hardwoods or semihardwoods can be propagated by division or layering. This also applies to blackberries and raspberries. Gooseberry is also easy to propagate by division and layering.

Garlic is another wonderful plant. It is demanding to grow because of its high maintenance, but it is well worth it. There is an attractive garden culture that surrounds it. Garlic works well in many types of cuisine and can be a good market crop. In a supportive market, one can sell garlic braids that are very attractive with a few dried flowers bunched at the top. Finding a good seed crop takes time. It is best to solicit help from other local farmers. Garlic needs to be broken up into cloves for planting. It works to use a triangular piece of cardboard that is five inches in diameter. That provides the pattern for planting. Garlic does not fend well against weeds. It also never covers the bed like other plants and therefore needs to be weeded. Using thick mulch helps with weeds and conserving soil moisture. Most crops will cover a French intensive bed after one weeding with a thick canopy that keeps weeds out. Not so with garlic. It also needs to be fertilized a few times during its season and that starts in the fall. Planting time is in early October. That means about a month or two before the first frost. The garlic plant needs to be established with at least a six-inch growth before the onset of severe cold weather. In the spring, it starts to grow. Its yield depends on a good rich bed to grow in. It is often placed in a bed previously used for legumes. It also needs good regular maintenance consisting of weeding, topdressing, mulching, and watering when it is dry. It also depends on good weather that is not too wet and not too dry in the spring with a dry month before harvest. The taste and size will follow suit with its parent crop. Garlic stores well in a cool dry place. It will often start to dry up when the heat is turned on in the house during cold winter months.

The only other plant that is grown in this manner is shallot. These plants multiply at the bulb. Shallots can be started from seed. This holds true for tulips and several other flower bulbs. Flower bulbs are easy to deal with in a solid stand and that is the best way to plant them. Some will multiply while others will perish. The ones that do multiply need to be separated to prevent them from overcrowding. Overcrowding will prevent them from flowering the following year. This way you can keep a consistent planting by replanting into the empty areas.

With exception to garlic bulbs, flower bulbs are susceptible to mole damage. Different roots are propagated in different ways depending on their classification. Onions, garlic, leeks, tulips, and daffodils are grown from bulbs. They grow in layers. Tulips and daffodils multiply. In a bed, some will multiply and others will perish. The ones the multiply will eventually overcrowd and stop blooming. By digging them up, you can fill in the bare areas to keep a consistent flowering pattern. It helps to put a pinch of bone meal in each hole to encourage flowering. Onions and leeks are best propagated from seed.

Tubers, such as potatoes, sweet potatoes, dahlias, and daylilies, produce along the stolon. Many tubers are not only edible but delicious as well. Dahlias are a good example. They are propagated through reproduction of the roots. This is where they store food, more than with other roots. In other words, they reproduce for you. You harvest and put some back. Rhizomes are ginger, iris, turmeric, and rhubarb. Rhizomes spread out under the soil laterally, making it easy to harvest and propagate. Pieces can be separated and rooted in containers or often replanted with a lot of success. Corms are gladiolas, crocus, freesias, yams, and bananas. Division is the best way to propagate them. As the plant multiplies, it sends up shoots that can be separated along with roots for easy relocation. It is important when using division to have a healthy crown. The part of the plant at the base of the stem, above the roots, is where the life of the plant exists. Without it there is very little to work with.

Asparagus is an exception. The plants, which are male and female, propagate best from seed. The males are sought out as the ones to harvest the savory shoots. Females produce berries that contain a seed that can be planted once it is dried. Growing asparagus from seed takes at least a year longer to produce a crop than purchasing crowns. The only reason for growing from seed is because so few are desired or for the experience of doing it. It can be an interesting experience once. The rhizomes can also be divided in the dormant period. Purchasing the crowns from a reliable source is a good investment. Start by preparing the bed well. They can live for several decades and can outlive the gardener. Asparagus is unrelated to other vegetables grown in the garden. They prefer a more alkaline soil with a pH of around 7.5 to 8. They are adapted very well to coastal areas because of their tolerance to salt air. Well-rinsed seaweed would make a good fertilizer if you happen to live near a clean coastal area of the world. Plant the crowns by preparing a hole with the soil hilled up in the middle. Place the crown on top of the hill so the roots can flow down it. Cover with a few inches of soil when the bed is leveled. Plants are placed about one foot to eighteen inches apart in a double dug raised bed. Planting in the late winter is best. Do not harvest the first year and sparingly the second so that the plant can devote its attention to good root development. Harvest the fresh shoots in the spring for a month or so. Refrain from cutting beyond that so that the ferns can grow up to receive nutrients from the sun.

In mild climates, the tops can be cut down early to produce two harvests a year. It is best not to be too greedy about this. Weed in the spring, top-dress after that. After you are done with harvests, give them a thick layer of mulch in the spring and fall. Cut the top to the ground in late fall when they have died back and compost the tops. They can be enjoyed for many years with very little problems. There is an asparagus beetle, but it is rarely a serious problem.

Growing trees is a special way of perpetuating the future. Some trees are generally grown from seed commercially. This is the principle means by which trees regenerate themselves. Tree seeds require one or two dormant periods to germinate. There are a few ways to trigger that process. Stratification involves placing the seeds in a medium in a tray maybe five or six inches deep. Sphagnum moss is often used. Dried out fern leaves can be used as an alternative to sphagnum moss. I have done this with sand. The seeds are spread apart so they don't touch and placed in cold storage. I will freeze them briefly, and then move them into a fridge and keep them at 40 degrees for a few months. Another method is scarification. Take a shard rock or dull knife and scar the seed lightly. The idea is to break or sever the outer casing without damaging what is inside. This is useful for very hard shell seeds. Pouring boiling water over them can also soften the outer coat to allow them to open up. Seeds can be planted directly out into the field or into pots. This is a good learning project to do with groups to explain how the forest reproduces. It is difficult to dig up trees in the forest without damaging the long taproot. The entire root is needed for most trees to survive and should be done during dormant periods. This is best attempted with very young tree seedlings.

Growing trees from seeds or even cuttings requites a lot of vision. The results of a mature hardwood from your work may not be experienced in your lifetime. It is like when I used to conduct tree-planting programs of small bare root trees. I often told the participants that they were not planting them for themselves so much as they were for their children and even more for their grandchildren.

When planting trees, either root ball or bare root, it needs to be done with permanent intentions. So do it like you are doing it only once. If you have a twenty dollar tree, plan to put it into a sixty dollar hole. Dig a hole three feet in diameter and at least two feet deep. All the soil that comes out of that hole will not fit back in it. Take about half the soil and put it onto a piece of plywood. Mix the soil with about 30 to 50 percent compost. Put this in around the tree. Make sure the tree graft remains above the soil level. I use a stick tied just below the graft to keep it at the right level. Situate the tree so it is straight. Use excess soil to build a well around the perimeter. Water it in slowly (about one gallon per minute) until the well fills with water. Lay down a good layer of mulch. This should be done while the tree is still dormant or is just leafing out.

There is a wonderfully inspiring book called *The Man Who Planted Hope and Grew Happiness.* In the book, Elzeard Bouffier, an old sheepherder, would take a hundred acorns or other tree seeds and drop them in a bucket of water before going to sleep. In the morning, he would place them in a bag, fling it over his shoulder, and set out to herd his sheep. He would make holes with his staff and place a seed in each hole as he walked on his journey. Over time, he replanted an enormous area of valleys and regenerated life where it had been abandoned.

Even with a low success rate and a lot of diligence, the results over several years can be staggering. There is so much energy spent on destroying land that very little is spent on regenerating it. The book is a wonderful study on what is possible if we focus a little of our energy on the impact we can have with a positive effort. The impact we can and do have on our surroundings is beyond our grasp. There are amazing groups in various parts of the United States and around the world conducting tree planting programs in their community. Although very inspiring, the work is often unrecognized outside the community where it is done.

Children's Learning Projects

Here are some other fun projects to do with young children used in teaching propagation in schools. These experiments are for them to understand how plants grow, move nutrients through their vascular system, and reproduce. Seed germination experiments are a good place to start. Find an old aquarium, perhaps one that leaks. Fill it with soil and plant a variety of seeds along the glass wall. Tape a piece of paper along the outside to keep light out. This way the plant roots will grow along the glass and make it easy to examine the different root patters. Roots always grow away from light. Bring in seedpods and dried flowers to let the children collect their own seed. Plant seeds of things they might be familiar with, like peanuts or corn. Hollow out a potato and leave an inch of potato on the inside wall. Fill the potato with soil and grow small plants like greens. Watch the potato sprout along with the seeds. Cut a carrot with two or three inches left on top. Make sure the top of the carrot greens are cut but not destroyed. Hollow out the center. Turn it upside down and make a hanging planter out of it. Fill it with soil and plant something small like arugula. The top of the carrot, which is on the bottom, will start to grow upwards. Growing seeds in a variety of containers can be used to demonstrate recycling, like using eggshells as planters. Lay out a paper towel and spread out a variety of small seeds, especially flower seeds. Spray the paper towel with water until thoroughly damp. Place the rolled up paper into a ziplock bag for a week. Examine the different characteristics of seeds germinating.

Lay a sweet potato in a tray half-covered with water to let it sprout and make slips. This can be done with a variety of roots. Plant a tulip in a container upside down. Dig it up later to see how gravity tells it which way to grow. There are wild jonquils in my area that would work for this also if dug up and let to dry out for a while first.

Watch how vascular systems work by cutting a few celery stalks with some leaves attached. Place them into cups with different colored water in each one. After several days, the stalks pump the colored water into their leaves. This works with white flower cuttings as well. Also, try it with pale lettuce leaves from the inside of a head of lettuce. Plant tops of carrots or beets into soil to see if they root and start growing new tops.

Take a leaf cutting of coleus, begonia, or African violet. Pin the leaf flat onto the soil to create a smooth surface mat. Make a few cuts about a half-inch long across the main leaf veins. Spray the leaf often and after a while it will sprout roots; have patience.

Seedpods are easy to start. Take avocado or mango. Place them upright half-submerged in a cup of water. The pod swells and sprouts into a little tree. A more industrious venture would be to make a sprout collage. Lay a cloth down on a large, long tray. Create a design with bands of different sprout seed. Alfalfa, clover, broccoli, radish, and any small sprout seed works. Spray them a few times a day. They will grow into a green design that is creative and fun to eat. The whole thing is very imaginative and fun. Learning needs to be fun, and developing a closer relationship with nature fosters healthy children. And just maybe, you will plant the seed of a future gardener.

7

Holistic Entomology

Insects and diseases are the symptoms of a failing crop, not the cause of it.

—Dr. William Albrecht

INSECTS ARE A BIOLOGICAL LINK between plants and the world around them. Many gardeners and farmers view insects as problematic. Insects are no more of a problem than the environment they exist in. The idea of organics is not to get rid of or even control insects, but to coexist with them. This can be a challenging endeavor when you depend on the crop you planted. Many people get into growing not realizing that a big part of this work is to have relationships with insects and diseases. Unfortunately, having an insect problem is how many of us are educated about insects. They are vital to living with a natural order. A healthy garden not only has many insects, but hopefully, most of the species available in your given area. The problem occurs when a certain insect or disease grows or over-populates relative to others in their surroundings. Insect problems are no more than indicators of an imbalance. These insects are yelling at you that there is a bigger problem than just them, and you need to correct it.

As you are trying or not trying to figure this out, they are causing a lot of destruction. Most of these problems were preventable and caused by the farmer. Here is an example. I have often seen (many more times than I would have liked) a person clearing a large piece of land to put in crops. By destroying the land, they also destroyed the ecosystem. The result is many problems to come in the months and years to follow. Ecosystems are to be observed and respected at every level. Go back to the design chapter. Learn what is there and how it works before you dive in and muck it up.

Another way to look at it is, for every action there is a reaction. This is the karma that comes from abusing land. We need to realize that we are just another species in here and find our place and how to fit into it. First year gardens and farms can be and often are very problematic. As the overall health of the soil and environment gains and becomes balanced, you will find your place. Keep in mind that balance is fragile and always in a constant flux. So populations can be blown out of proportion. Learning how to facilitate the ecosystem is your role. The weather can affect change very abruptly. Species that are prone to populate quickly are generally the ones with the greatest sensitivity to things like weather changes. Aphids are a good example. They populate rapidly, yet they are very vulnerable to heavy rain, drops in temperature, and are a popular food to many predator insects. Predator insects usually outnumber herbivores (see the list of predator insects in table 7.1).

TABLE 7.1
Predator Insect List

Predator	Host Plant	Host Insect
Aphidius, Aphidoletes 3–6 wk. cycles; 2–4 days for eggs to hatch; 3–6 generations per year.	Lupines, sunflowers	Aphids
Assassin bugs.	Hedgerows, grasses	Caterpillars, flies, tomato hornworms
Braconid wasp (Braconidae) 10–40 day life cycle.	Umbellifers, caraway, parsley, fennel, mustard, clover, tansy, yarrow	Armyworm, cabbage worm, tomato horn-worm, flies, codling moth, beetle larvae, leaf miners
Beneficial mites (*Metaseiulus occidentalis*) 11-day life cycle.	Sunflower, shasta daisy	Thrips, mites, fungus gnats
Damsel bugs (Nabidae) Eggs hatch in 8–12 days. Nymphs live 2–3 wks; 2–3 generations per year.	Sunflower, golden rod, yarrow, alfalfa	Aphids, thrips, caterpillars, leafhoppers

TABLE 7.1
Predator Insect List (*continued*)

Predator	Host Plant	Host Insect
Dragonflies (Odonata) 3–4 wk. life span.	Aquatic; needs a pond to lay eggs in	Aquatic; needs a pond as a habitat
Dicyphus (*Dicyphus hesperus*).	Digitalis	Whiteflies, aphids, mites, thrips
Damsel flys (Odonata) 3–4 wks. life cycle.	Fennel, verbascum	Insect eggs, larvae, termites, most flying insects
Encarsia formosa Larvae pupates in 11 days. Total development 15 wks. 2–3 wks. life span.	Umbellifers, Queen Anne's lace, dill, fennel, tansy, cosmos, sunflower, yarrow, coreopsis	Whiteflies
Ground beetles (*Pterostichus melanius*) 2–3 generations per year.	Amaranth; likes sheltered areas, mulch	Slugs, grubs, wire worms, aphids, caterpillars, beetles
Hover flies (*Syrphus ribesii*) Eggs take 3 days to hatch; larvae last 3 wks.	Alyssum, wild carrots, parsley, cosmos, chamomile, statice	Aphids, mealy bugs, soft-bodied insects
Ichneumon wasps (Ichneumonidae).	Umbellifers, dill, Queen Anne's lace, alfalfa	Caterpillars, other larvae
Lacewings (*Chrysopa carnea*) 2 generations per year.	Yarrow, angelica, Queen Anne's lace, fennel, tansy, cosmos, coreopsis	Scale, soft-bodied insects
Ladybugs (*Hippodamia convergens*) 3 mo. cycles; 3 wks. to pupate.	Sunflowers, Queen Anne's lace, tansy, fennel, dill	Aphids, mites
Mealybug destroyer (*Cryptolaemus ontrousieri*) Life cycle 2 months; egg to larvae in 32 days.	Umbellifers, fennel, tansy, dill, yarrow, sunflower, coreopsis, angelica, golden rod	Mealybugs
Pirate bugs (*Orius hemiptera*) 5 days for eggs; 35-day life cycle.	Helianthus, sunflower, chervil, Shasta daisy, tansy, Queen Anne's lace, vetch	Scale, soft-bodied insects
Praying mantis (*Mantispa styriaca*).	Spirea, forsythia, bronze fennel	Caterpillars, young grasshoppers, almost anything
Predatory mites (*Phytoseiulus persimilis*) 4–12 days larvae to adult; 1–2 mos. as adult.	Helianthus, Shasta daisy	Mites

TABLE 7.1
Predator Insect List (*continued*)

Predator	Host Plant	Host Insect
Rove beetles (*Aleochara bilineata*) 3 mo. life; lay eggs at roots of infested plants.	Rye grass, mulch	Aphids, flies
Spiders (Lycosidae) Life span 1–2 yrs.	Tall grasses, enclosed areas	Caterpillars, most insects
Spined soldier bugs (*Podisus maculiventris*) 7–14 days larvae to adult life cycle; eggs to larvae 3 wks.; adults live for 1–2 mos.	Goldenrod, millweed, hydrangea, decaying deciduous trees	Beetles, Mexican bean beetle, Colorado potato beetle, grasshopper larvae
Stethorus (*Stethorus punctum*) Egg to adult 2–4 wks.; 3 mos. life span for adult.	Alyssum, candytufts, fennel, Queen Anne's lace, dill	Spider mites
Syrphid fly (Syrphidae; Diptera) 5–7 generations per year; 3 wk. life cycle; 7–10 days for larvae.	Umbellifers, tansy, lupines, sunflowers, *Scabiosa, Ceanothus*	Aphids, soft-bodied insects
Tachinid fly (*Trichopoda giacomelli*) Several generations per yr.	Lemon balm, parsley, alyssum, buckwheat, goldenrod	Caterpillars, beetles
Tiger beetle (*Cicindela campestris*) 1–2 generations per yr.	Amaranth, white clover; likes mulch, brush piles	Grasshoppers, aphids, crickets, termites, grubs, caterpillars, wireworms, slugs, snails, fruit flies
Tiphia wasp (*Tiphia vernalis*) 30–40 day life span.	Peonies, forsythia	Grubs, insect larvae

About 97 percent of insects are beneficial and do not serve as a threat. This is the argument against using pesticides. They kill off the beneficial ones along with the harmful ones. First, it destroys the balance that might exist. In doing this, you become dependent on the pesticides. By killing all the insects you are taking on the role that the predators have and that is a big job. The other thing pesticides do is create insect resistance. If you spray a common insecticide, you might kill most but not all of the insects of that species. The ones that survive have superior genes. The next time you spray you kill a smaller percentage. Eventually, you have mostly offspring from the ones that are resistant. The result is the breeding of resistant genes. Now you will have to find a stronger insecticide as you start the process all over again. It takes some people a long time to figure this out. This makes a lot of money for the companies that manufacture these chemicals. Even if one is using organic pesticides, it is a short-term approach. An allopathic approach does not take the entire ecosystem into consideration. It is just a bandage that does not deal with the real problem, only what is on the surface. If the pesticides were 100 percent effective, these companies would not be around long.

The best way to work with insects on your farm or in your garden is to understand their habits, habitats, and life cycles. Insect families are a good place to start. Here is a list of the most common garden insects that serve as a threat. It is by no means complete.

Insect Groups

Coleoptera or beetles is the largest order of insects. It represents nearly one-quarter of all species on the planet. These beetles are chewers. They have a complete metamorphosis. They hibernate in the soil or in sheltered spots like houses, barns, or in debris. Beetles can be beneficial as well and harmful. The list is large; the following is a list of common garden varieties.

Asparagus beetles (*Crioceris asparagi*) are not usually a serious threat. Eggs hatch in three to eight days depending on temperatures. They feed for ten to fifteen days; then they go into the soil and pupate for five to ten days and emerge as adults. They have a three to four week life cycle. The main predators are beneficial wasps, assassin bugs, soldier bugs, and dragonflies.

Colorado potato beetle (*Leptinotara decemlineata*) is more of a problem in the West. They produce twenty to sixty eggs in a mass under leaves. Eggs hatch in three to twelve days, depending on temperatures. Larvae eat for eight to twenty-eight days, depending on temperatures. There are one to three generations per season. Predators consist of damselflies and dragonflies, pirate bugs, big eyed bugs, and beneficial nematodes.

Striped cucumber beetles (*Acalymma vittatum*) start by feeding on roots and stems for two to four weeks. The adults lay about five hundred eggs that hatch in one to two weeks. They pupate in the soil and emerge in forty to sixty days. There are two generations per year. Predators are bats, soldier beetles, beneficial nematodes, tachinid fly, braconid wasps, and ground beetles.

Flea beetles (*Phyllotreta cruciferae*), with their many varieties, produce eggs that hatch in one week. Larvae feed for two to three weeks. After they pupate, the adults emerge in two to three weeks. There are about four generations per season. They live in the soil and like mulch to live under. Predators are lacewing, braconid wasp, and ladybugs.

Blister beetles (family Meloidae, order Coleoptera) are not a common problem. Adults lay from fifty to one hundred eggs that hatch in one and a half to three weeks, depending on temperatures with no known predators. They also prey on young grasshoppers. So keep grass and weeds cut and get rid of grasshoppers along with blister beetles.

Japanese beetles (*Popillia japonica*) are not as common in drier weather. Adults lay forty to sixty eggs in a cluster, five hundred total, in a season. Eggs hatch in ten days to two weeks and feed for four to six weeks. Grubs pupate during the winter. Chief predators are ground beetles, spiders, birds. Sex lures or traps can keep them away, but do not put them in the growing area or it will have a reverse effect. It is better to put them across a field or even better give them to your neighbor.

Mustard beetle (*Phaedon cochleariae*) can be harmful to crucifers. Adults lay three hundred to four hundred eggs total. They emerge in thirty-five to forty-five days. They pupate for eight to twelve days. Beneficial nematodes are a predator.

Mexican bean beetles (*Epilachna varivestis*) are found in some locations, but not all. Adults feed for seven to ten days. They lay yellow egg masses of forty to sixty eggs. It is not uncommon to have five to six hundred eggs hatch in one to two weeks. Larvae feed for three to six weeks and sometimes longer, if is there is food around. They pupate for seven to twenty days. Their entire life span is thirty to seventy days with several generations. Soldier beetles are their main predator. *Pediobius foveolatus* is another one but not as commonly found. Find the egg masses on the bottom of leaves and squash them.

Hemiptera, suborder Homoptera (meaning an insect with uniform wings), do not pupate so have incomplete metamorphosis. Juveniles resemble adults. They eat by piercing and sucking. They have very diverse subgroups. This includes leafhoppers, cicadas, whiteflies, scale, and aphids (Aphididae). Aphids are a common threat, especially to greenhouse growers. They have a twenty-five day life span. Fourteen days for larvae. They have many predators: ladybugs, lacewings, wasps, hover flies, praying mantis, and mirid bugs (*Dicyphus*). Most predators will eat them. They multiply quickly and are sensitive to weather. An overnight rain or temperature drop can diminish their numbers quickly. They can be hosed off easily. Their biggest threat is as a disease vector, especially on fruit trees. Ants farm them; they carry them on their back and place them onto leaves. The ants feed on the honey dew that is extracted. Soapy water can be sprayed on them as it breaks down outer membranes and they dry out and die.

Harlequin bugs (*Murgantia histrionica*) do little damage but are worth considering. They lay egg clusters of ten to thirteen that hatch in trees for four weeks. Larvae feed for four to nine weeks depending on temperatures. Their main predators are parasitic wasps, spiders, birds, toads, and praying mantis.

Whiteflies (Aleyrodidae) have a fifteen to thirty-eight day life span. These are also a problem in greenhouses. Nymphs develop in eighteen to twenty-six days and pupate for ten days. I have had success putting up sticky boards painted yellow. They attach to them and are easily discarded. The main predator is *Encarsia formosa* and mirid bugs. Both are beneficial in greenhouse management. There are many other predators that feed on them.

Dermaptera in the garden is mainly going to be earwigs. Although they are usually considered decomposers, they also are found on certain leafy vegetables that they eat. Adults lay between twenty to sixty eggs that hatch in seven to fourteen days. The nymphs stay close to mother, making it easy to get rid of them if they pose a problem. They use leaf litter and mulch as a habitat. They take seventy days to mature with one or two generations per season. Earwigs can be beneficial as well as they eat aphids and scale. Their primary predators are toads, birds, lacewings, ladybugs, and spiders.

Hemiptera are also called true insects. They pierce and suck plant juices. They have a shield-shaped body like a stinkbug. Squash bugs (*Anasa tristis*) love cucurbits. Adults can live for two to three months. They lay about twenty dark-red eggs in a cluster that hatch in one to two weeks. The nymphs take about thirty-three days to mature with five stages or instars. In the North they have one generation; in the South, there may be several. The main predators are tachinid flies and parasitic wasps.

Lepidoptera are butterflies and moths. They have a complete metamorphosis. The larvae are caterpillars and are chewers. They are generally seasonal. They are the second largest group of insects. Cabbage looper (*Trichoplusia*) is common on all brassicas. They lay one egg at a time that hatches in three to seven days. The gray larva matures in two weeks. It pupates for one to two weeks. There are three to five generations per season.

Their predators are braconid wasp, *Trichogramma* wasp, mirid bugs, and eulophid wasp. The European cabbage moth (*Pieris rapae*) has a very similar life cycle.

Armyworm (*Spodoptera frugiperda*) has an entire life cycle of sixty days. It shows up in the spring and fall in the South. The adult lays one hundred to two hundred eggs total. They hatch in two to three days. The larvae stage is two to four weeks. It has about three generations in my area. The main predators are braconid and tachinid wasps, damselflies, mirid bugs, and pirate bugs. Beet armyworms are similar.

Cutworms (*Peridroma saucia*) is a problem with small seedlings and transplants, amputating the stem at soil level. The entire life cycle is forty-five days. Eggs hatch in five to ten days. Larvae stage is from three to six weeks. They pupate for two to four weeks, with three or four generations per season. Putting a nail or metal foil around the stem at soil level will prevent them from doing any damage. Their main predators are Ichneumonid, braconid and other parasitic wasps, assassin bugs, birds, bats, reptiles, tachinid flies, and predator beetles.

European corn borers (*Ostrinia nubilias*) are present on corn. Adults lay five to six hundred eggs total that hatch in three to twelve days. The larvae live for about two weeks with five stages or instars. The common way to deal with them is to put a couple drops of vegetable oil in the silks, followed by *Bacillus thuringiensis*. The main predators are ladybugs, lacewings, tachinid flies, parasitic wasps, and birds.

Corn earworm (*Helicoverpa zea*) is also very common. An adult lays single eggs totaling five hundred to three thousand. Eggs hatch in two to five days. Larvae feed for two to five weeks. There are four generations per season. Predators consist of big-eyed bugs, *Trichogramma*, birds, and pirate bugs. A couple drops of mineral oil in the tassel will get rid of them.

Squash vine borer (*Melittia cucurbitae*) lays egg at the base of hollow stem squash plants. They hatch in seven to ten days. They develop up through the stem from the bottom up and emerge after about a month. Their main predators are parasitic wasps and ground beetles. Netting can be place around the base of the plant to discourage the placement of eggs.

Tomato hornworm (*Manduca quinquemaculata*) is attracted to all plants in the Solanaceae family, but prefers tomatoes. Eggs hatch in six to eight days. The caterpillar matures in three to four weeks with five stages or instars. They pupate in the soil for two weeks. The main predators are braconid wasps, assassin bugs, ladybugs, lacewings, and birds. Hornworms, although well camouflaged, can be handpicked.

There are several orders of insects that are not related to common insect families and individually represented in the garden. Grasshoppers (*Romalea microptera*) are related to crickets, locusts, and katydids. They have one generation of incomplete metamorphosis. The nymphs live for fifteen to twenty days with several stages or instars. Adults lay about fifty eggs. Keeping the grass cut low is the best way to discourage them. Their predators are tachinid flies, ground beetles, praying mantis, birds, tiger beetles, soldier bugs, and *Nosema locustae*.

Leafhoppers (family Cicadellidae) are sucking insects. Adults lay eggs in groups of three to twenty-eight. There are many varieties. Their biggest threat is as a disease vector, especially on fruit trees. The chief predators are assassin bugs, lacewings, spiders, pirate bugs, dragonflies, and damselflies. Keeping grass cut gets rid of their shelter.

Twospotted mites (*Tetranychus urticae*) do damage by piercing and sucking. They are not true insects but are arachnids like spiders. They create a webbing that helps to find them. They lay about fifty eggs that hatch in two to five days. Larvae take five to twenty days to mature, again depending on temperatures. They are preyed upon by ladybugs, lacewings, mired bugs, damselflies and *Stethorus* (mite predator beetle).

Scale (*Cochineal*) attaches themselves to the bark of plants and suck the juices. They reproduce without mating. They disseminate by wind or else stay in one place. They are preyed upon by pirate bugs, predator thrips, and parasitic wasps. Spraying dormant oil on them is effective. It suffocates them so they can easily be controlled.

Slugs and snails (mollusks) are slow but able to do a lot of damage. They thrive in wet conditions. They are wonderful decomposers, but as they multiply they can eat holes in leaves to the point they defoliate the entire plant. Slugs and snails are hermaphroditic, as are worms. When they mate, they both become impregnated, so they can multiply quickly. They have a seven to twelve month life span. They reproduce in the spring, laying one hundred and fifty to two hundred eggs in a season. They usually lay twenty-five eggs in a gelatinous mass. They are well-liked by toads, snakes, reptiles, birds, and chickens. Releasing a group of chickens or guinea fowl in the early spring before planting can clean up an area quite well. Ducks are commonly used in the Pacific Northwest. Lay down boards in paths. As the sun rises, they hide for cover. Lift the boards and scrape them into a bucket. They are good to feed to chickens. Diatomaceous earth sprinkled around a bed can keep them at bay. Then there is the old beer method. Put out a small container of cheap beer. They crawl into it and drown. This is useful in small gardens.

Thrips (*Thysanoptera thripidae*) puncture and suck plants. They are carried by wind. Some varieties are predatory, eating mites and other insects. Thrips are disease vectors, especially of some plant viruses. Eggs emerge after ten days once temperatures reach 80 degrees, plus or minus. They have several generations. Nymphs feed for four or five days and pupate for a few days before becoming adults. They have many predators like lacewings, beneficial nematodes, pirate bugs, damselflies and dragonflies, spiders, and mirid bugs.

Ants, bees, wasps, and other colonized insects (order Hymenoptera) are in a class of their own. They are the true link between the insect and animal world. Bees and wasps are very beneficial as pollinators and predators. Ants are a mixed bag. Many varieties cultivate soil and help enhance fungal activity in the soil. Because they are voracious eaters, they can clean an area very well. There are varieties that are known to clean houses in the Southwest. In the southern United States, there are fire ants. These ants have bred with most red ants, and they all have similar traits. Fire ants can destroy plants and are a menace to humans because of their aggressive biting. Ants also farm aphids by placing them on plants and extracting the honeydew-like sap that the aphids secrete. This can lead to increased diseases. Because they are imported, they do not have many predators. Beneficial nematodes are somewhat effective. Queens lay thousands of eggs that hatch into larvae. Ants are cannibalistic. The young larvae will eat others for extra protein. (Other cannibalistic insects include crickets and grasshoppers. Female praying mantis and spiders will sometimes eat the male after mating.) Fire ants are very challenging to work with. There are some isolated funguses that have been affective. One approach has been to be more annoying than they are. With a lot of persistence the ants eventually leave. Dig them repeatedly.

Entomology considers some insects to be neither beneficial nor harmful. I do not believe there are any life forms that are benign. Everything has an impact on what you are growing and it is either positive or negative and sometimes both. This is especially true for anything that is eating and occupying in an ecosystem that is also a producing farm or garden. Many insects are decomposers like sow bugs, snails and slugs, some beetles, worms, and flies. It is not a healthy garden or farm without insect habitats and the vital roles they play.

Integrated Pest Management

Integrated pest management or IPM is a system that integrates a variety of practices and considerations from environmental to economic in order to manage insect and disease populations. The principles are about reorienting yourself about just what is an insect problem. First, it is important to establish acceptable levels of insect damage. For instance, there is a big difference between growing greens and growing cut flowers. Define threshold levels of damage so you know when and what actions to take. Identifying populations involves monitoring with the help of lures and traps. This helps to see when populations rise. The timing of insect cycles can be something to work with once you learn them. Evaluating populations helps to understand where balances are in place and to see holes in where they are not. Seeing damage is one thing. Seeing the actual insect doing the damage brings clarity. Sometimes this involves nighttime investigating with a flashlight since many insects are nocturnal. Prevention through cultural practices is an important key. The grower has usually invited this problem in by his or her practices. When following the insect predator chart in table 7.1, make sure a source of water is present for the insects you wish to attract.

Watering at night encourages diseases, but mulches can discourage weeds and provide habitat for a host of insects. Are they beneficial or not? Allowing the grass to grow provides habitat for spiders. It also invites unwanted insects. By watching what takes place, you can decide the best time to cut down weeds to flush everything out. Keeping insects in motion keeps them from settling in. Plant native grasses to attract native species of insects. Hedgerows are a filter for many life forms. It provides habitat for predators big and small. Mechanical cultivation disturbs insects that pupate in the soil during the summer. But this may not be necessary. It is easier to control insects before the numbers become devastating. Handpicking and insect barriers are more effective. Row covers are popular, but they keep everything out. Netting works well because it keeps butterflies and larger insects out while letting predatory wasps in. Biological controls are a useful part of IPM.

Introducing insects and diseases sounds like a good idea. If you go out and buy insects like ladybugs or lacewings, they will probably not stay for the same reasons that they are not there in the first place. So you must first create habitat favorable for their existence. Start with the four elements. Is there adequate water with movement behind it, sun and shade, and ground covers for certain insects to nest in? Does the soil have a healthy biological composition that is diverse? Growing a variety of cut flowers for market that are integrated throughout the garden provides a biological niche.

Many flowers are host plants for predator insects with bloom times when one needs the predators most. Most ideologies consider an allopathic approach using insecticides that are accepted organically. They are still interested in killing insects rather than understanding why the numbers are too high and how to change that environmentally. If you fall behind on being a good steward, you will have to spray organically accepted sprays as a drastic measure. This is not uncommon. A more holistic approach is to first understand the unique dynamics of your given area, and second, how to alter it in a subtle way to curb populations.

Creating a balance is both challenging and time-consuming. The investment in doing this gives you greater control. It allows you to be the facilitator of a garden or farm that is moving toward becoming a balanced ecosystem. Integrated pest management considers using insecticides as a last resort. My last resort is to become a better student of the principles there are to work with. That means learning from my mistakes so I don't repeat them.

A working farm or garden works on many levels and insects are an important component of this. Monitoring insect populations is important especially during the summer when the most activity happens. Setting traps gives helpful numbers to work with. The bucket method is good when there is a concentration of insects in one area. Take a clean white bucket. Bend the given plant over into it and shake the plant into the bucket. Now you have a count of who is visiting that plant.

Butterfly nets can be used. You may look a little silly doing this, but it works on the white cabbage butterfly quite well. Lay down boards in the paths and turn them over when the sun is high to get an idea of slug populations. Yellow sticky cards are a widely accepted method for researchers. Take a piece of stiff cardboard or plastic. Color it bright yellow. Hang it next to a bed on a hook and cover it with a sticky substance. Vaseline works well, or else anything that will not dry up. This is a good control method for whiteflies.

Try to keep records of species, numbers, and when heavy population increases occur. Insect lures as mentioned above are another tool. Buckets of water collect many insects also, but leaving them around can drown honey bees. Lay floating sticks on the water for bees to land on. It also becomes a breeding pond for mosquitoes, so don't leave them around too long. In a forest, there can be a dominant species. In the garden, there are many. The idea is to make these observations before major damage occurs. Once you have a problem, it is difficult to deal with. It does not matter if you use organic methods or conventional ones. A serious problem is a serious problem and that means loss. At this point, one has to depend on a direct approach. A combination of sprays, traps, and catching means doing whatever works. For small outbreaks, the problem can be countered quickly. Major infestations equate into costly lessons. In the first couple of years on a given piece of land, one needs to be able to accept this as the honeymoon phase. In this way, the garden and the gardener are given time to grow together.

The best way to deal with insect problems is to have a good prevention system. It helps by having catchment areas like tall grass in and around the crop area. You may have a field on three sides of your garden. At given times, or periodically, cut it down to chase everyone out. Keeping everyone on their toes is good for keeping circulation happening. Cleaning up areas and good sanitation is part of maintenance. The lack of movement is stagnation and that just does not happen in a biologically active place.

Create predator habitats. A diversity of mixed plantings of annuals and perennials around and throughout the growing area helps with this. Establishing a mix that imitates nature is much better than a sterile landscape. By creating niches in the landscape you can manifest an ecological wealth. A multilayered approach does a good job of this. Some examples of this are letting beds of crops transition right up to fruit trees. Plantings of flowers and herbs around fruit trees can be very beneficial to both. Design habitats like shrubs where the beds end with vines and a combination of deciduous and evergreen trees. Think of plantings that attract a variety of insects and animals. Soil banks of ground covers can blend into large trees with small shrubs and other underplantings. Small habitats are essential to attracting diversity. And don't forget a bird bath set in amongst it all. It also helps the bees. Landscape design complements a crop of vegetables where the woods meet the field. Flowering plants mixed into vegetables are also wonderful habitats for insects. It would not be outrageous to have a row of fruit trees planted down the middle of a field of vegetables. Hedgerows are one of the best habitats to work with. They can consist of things like blackberries, hawthorn, elderberry, pasture rose, huckleberry, witch hazel, and so on. There are an enormous number of plants that can contribute to habitat and can provide food for yourself as well as a mixture of creatures.

Hedgerows provide habitats for insects and animals as well as a filter for movement across an open landscape. They are an important part of the ecology of open land. We'll talk more about hedgerows in the last chapter. Dead or dying trees are another element to consider. Although they can attract the unwanted along with the beneficial, their presence can go a long way toward bringing a healthy mix into the surroundings. Dead trees are often opened up by woodpeckers looking for insects and later provide a home for owls.

Pollinators are a common problem today because of the decline of honeybees. Bumblebees do a pretty good job of filling in the gap. Mason bees are a good substitute to consider. They do not provide honey but are good pollinators. It is easy to set up a habitat for them. Take a double handful of bamboo canes about seven or eight inches long. Use the small ends that still have holes in them. Bunch them together. Glue or twine can help hold them. Put a small roof over them with bark from a tree and suspend the house from a tree branch with wire. They like the shade of the tree and the wire will last much longer than twine. Providing a water source is a very important part of habitats that is often overlooked. It is often the missing element on a small piece of land.

Having a stream or flowing body of water provides a resource for aquatic insects like dragonflies, damselflies, and lacewings, as well as frogs and lizards that all have good insect diets. This can also be good for mosquito control. Another part of habitat consideration is to set up bat houses. They clean the sky at dusk of many flying insects.

Insect populations change during the course of the year. Having a variety of different habitat niches is a way to provide for that. Climate is part of the dynamics that can be hard to account for. On a very wet year, insect populations and diseases can explode. Climate change is adding the element of surprise. A diversity of crops is one way to be prepared for a variety of challenges. One of the best insect predators is also one of the most annoying. Yellow jackets are a threat to many things. They prey on honeybees when they are full of nectar. They do not hesitate to sting humans without just cause. Yet their aggressiveness also translates into being an incredible insect predator, one of the best. It is good to keep them at a distance where they come to visit once in a while to feast on what the garden has to offer.

Every food crop has a certain amount of threat by insects. I can think of only a small list of plants to rely on even in a bad year. I will give poetic justice to the ones the insects seem to miss. Basil is one; its fragrance calls out to me as I pass it by. Field peas hang out waiting to be picked even when the bean beetles have gone home. Cherry tomatoes continue to produce even when full of blight and rain down with loads of sweet fruit. Radishes grow so fast the insects can't seem to find them. Chard, with its colorful varieties, dances in the corner of my eye waiting to be enjoyed. Sweet potatoes lie hiding for me alone, for they are too good a food crop not to grow.

If growing for food, it is easy to grow more than enough. If growing for production, find the acceptable levels of loss that still put you out ahead and share the rest. Insects are a blessing not a curse. The virtuous farmer is the educated one.

8

Plant Pathology

The soil is the great connector of lives, the source and destination of all. It is the healer and restorer and resurrector, by which disease passes into health, age into youth, death into life.

—Wendell Berry

PLANT DISEASES ARE A SCARY thought to most growers. Unlike insects, disease pathogens are microscopic and, therefore, more of a mystery. Many of these are ever present in the surroundings of where one is growing, yet kept in check by a multiple of conditions. Diseases are the great equalizer in the natural world. It is a way to put nature back into balance by destroying what is not in a healthy state. Diseases take advantage of that, but do not exist for very long. Diseases are the result of a parasite invading plant cells as a host to live on.

Diseases cause a malfunctioning of the plant. This is where a problem occurs. Symptoms can also be caused by nutrient deficiencies, pollution, or extreme environmental conditions (like weather changes). So it is important to identify diseases correctly. Diseases require the presence of a pathogen, a susceptible host plant, and proper environmental conditions. A susceptible host plant can be caused by abnormal growth (can be the result of using synthetic fertilizers), extreme weather changes that damage plants, or toxicity. Plants are also vulnerable when there is overwatering or underwatering. Plants that are weak or cannot metabolize food properly are very vulnerable. When sugars are not transformed by amino acids, they excrete compounds that attract disease pathogens. The best way to counter plant diseases is through prevention.

As in insect problems, serious disease problems are an indicator of an imbalance in the environment and all imbalances usually start and end with the soil. Disease pathogens can be a fungus, bacteria, or virus. Bacterial diseases are single-celled microscopic organisms. They have a nucleus, but it is not well defined. They have DNA but lack chlorophyll. They have a cell wall, can live in a wide range of conditions, and reproduce asexually. They are nonspore producing. Bacteria are much smaller than fungi and more capable of entering through small openings like wounds. Penetration does not always lead to infection. They enter plants through leaf openings like the stomata cells, flower nectar, tubers, roots, or are transmitted by nematodes. They may be vascular, such as those that enter through leaves and travel through the xylem. They may be systemic, entering through wounds and directly invading plant cells.

A plant virus is a simple microscopic parasite that consists of a core surrounded by a coat of protein. They are much smaller than bacteria. They are unable to replicate without a host cell, so they attack nuclei. This is the base of RNA and DNA for the plant. They are not considered a living organism that can live by itself. Sucking insects often transmits them. These are disease vectors. Viruses can spread through the plant rapidly.

Fungal diseases are much more prevalent. Most are soilborne. They are produced as spores, are multicellular, and reproduce asexually. They attach themselves to plant tissue usually through openings. They can be taken up through root absorption or carried in the RNA of the seed the plant comes from. They require special conditions like moisture in humidity and proper temperatures to survive. Roots, flowers, seeds, seedlings, and cuttings can be carriers of these pathogens. They enter leaves through stomata cells and water pores. They can also enter through epidermal cells and damaged plant parts. Fungal diseases are favored by damp conditions where high humidity is very conducive for them to thrive. They produce spores and can grow rapidly in the right conditions. They have a nucleus and cell wall. They are also very sensitive to environmental conditions. This is why fungal problems are not as common in dry areas. But they are the most common disease problem encountered and the easiest to identify on leaves.

All diseases require special conditions. The three components involved are pathogen, environment, and host. Pathogens find a vehicle for attachment then penetration. Once they penetrate the host, the infection invades plant cells and colonization begins, followed by reproduction. Insects feeding on the plant allow pathogens to invade the vascular system. Spores are carried by wind and water. They enter cell walls through natural openings. Once infection occurs, there is cell collapse. Degeneration of specific parts of the plant makes it difficult or impossible for the plant to obtain nutrients and function properly.

Plants do have the ability to develop protective immune defenses. This is contained in their genetic makeup. Plants have receptor proteins that are activated when threatened. Some plants have the ability to develop related proteins and toxicity to the infected area. They develop epidermal layers making it difficult for pathogens to penetrate. Leaf surfaces like the fuzzy leaf of dusty miller (*Senecio cineraria*) or the waxy surface (made up from lignin) of magnolias are difficult to penetrate. Plants may also ward off disease on a cellular level. These plants can sometimes shut off or deaden cells around the infected area causing stress for the pathogen. Plants do not have antibodies. Diseases living in the soil can be held in check by beneficial microorganisms. Remember, soil is the intestines of the plant.

Some diseases are spread or travel by wind, such as fungal spores. One answer to this is to create wind breaks. This can be done with trees surrounding your growing area or by using tall plants in the middle to disrupt any type of mono cropping. Soilborne diseases such as fungus and bacteria can be inhibited by the use of mulch. I have often seen many crops destroyed by disease where no mulch was used. Soilborne disease is splashed up onto the leaf by rain or irrigation. This is common for tomato blights. Viruses usually rely on disease-carrying vectors such as aphids, leafhoppers, thrips, protozoa, and nematodes. The answer here is to get rid of their habitats like tall grass around grapes and to minimize populations by making sure there is a plentiful supply of predators. Diseases transported by water and flooding can be controlled by preventing runoff on open soil and changing irrigation methods.

Contaminated seed is another way diseases are transmitted. Make sure to have good seed sources and do not plant anything known to carry disease. Bringing in infected plants can be costly and introduces a wide range of diseases. It is better to grow them yourself. Animals and the farmer often carry soilborne diseases with soil on the boots or tools. This is a common way to transfer nematodes, which help transfer diseases. This especially applies to the use of cultivating tools. Keep animals in their place and clean tools and machinery after use. Incorporate sanitation practices into your daily routine, especially with animals.

Plants yield to adversity just like all living things. Plant-resistant mechanisms and chemical defenses are built into plants. Plants produce metabolites that include sugars, proteins, amino acids, and nucleic acids. These metabolites aid in the growth of the plant. Secondary metabolites are often involved in plant defenses. Monoterpenoids and sesquiterpenoids are the main components of essential oils. Besides being toxic to insects, they also inhibit fungal and bacterial attacks. Some examples are mints and the mint family, lemon verbena, wormwood (*Artemisia*), and pine resin. Other heavy oil plants like rosemary, thyme, and bay leaf are fairly disease-free. These essential oils can be used to ward off diseases in other plants. These all work toward preventing diseases in the plants. Black walnut produces a chemical that inhibits other plants, since they don't like competition. Phytoecdysones mimic insect molting and disrupt larval development. Phenols are a group of secondary metabolites that are produced as defense mechanisms against pathogens. Flavonoids are one of these compounds. Phytoalexins are isoflavonoids. Phytoalexins are a substance produced by plant tissue in response to a plant parasite. They contain antifungal properties.

Another built-in defense mechanism are defensins. Defensins are antimicrobial cationic proteins found in all plants. They help create plant resistance. They also inhibit fungal and bacterial growth. Plants with a thick cuticle and waxy substance on the outside repel water from settling.

Although this is a common beneficial characteristic, most plants depend on structural barriers between their cells. The cell walls contain structured proteins that mainly consist of polysaccharides and cellulose fibers. The polysaccharides are made up of starches, glycogen, cellulose, and chitin. These are the basis for complex carbohydrates. These structured proteins contain an abundance of amino acids. When there is a disturbance made by a foreign substance like a fungal infection, the cells are triggered and increase growth that blocks the disease insertion and activity.

From a more holistic view, plants even have a hypersensitivity that utilizes host receptors that exist outside the cell membrane. Plants can also release fungi toxic exudates that are antimicrobial compounds that inhibit pathogens. Disease symptoms in small amounts are normal. A healthy plant population has the resources and stamina to deal with this. Serious disease issues are signs of a break in the system allowing it to happen. When plants have an imbalance of nutrients, they excrete compounds. Healthy plants have built-in abilities to ward off diseases. There are other factors that contribute to the disease conditions. A pH imbalance locks up nutrients, making a plant vulnerable to disease. Some diseases, especially a fungus, operates at a lower pH. Toxicity from pesticides and pollution can weaken a plant's defenses. Lack of oxygen and sunlight can be contributing factors. Of course, warm temperatures and air moisture encourage fungal growth.

Cultural Problems and Prevention

Most disease problems are the result of the grower creating the right setting for this to happen by introducing the pathogen and not using preventative methods to deal with it. Cultural conditions are a common cause. When I worked with the cooperative extension service in Georgia, I noticed how all the publications mentioned cultural problems. This was after prescribing what fungicides to use. Almost all disease problems are the result of mistakes made by the grower, so most disease problems are preventable. We usually bring about the conditions that cause the disease and often introduce the pathogen ourselves.

All farmers and gardeners have made or will make these mistakes. That is what makes us human. It is important to realize that there is no such farm or garden that is immune to disease, but a healthy growing environment is less likely to have serious disease problems on a regular basis. Creating the correct cultural conditions is the best approach to the problem. They are often simple considerations like sanitation with tools and the movement of soils. Watering systems are important. Not watering late in the day, maintaining good soil drainage, making sure there is good air flow and sunlight penetrating places in and around plants are good measures. Do not introduce foreign substances. This means, be aware of bringing in plants, hay, soil, animals, and anything else that can harbor disease. In pruning fruit trees, vines, or bushes, try to open it up to allow sunlight and air into the center of the plant. All manures are composted with temperatures of around 160 degrees. It is best not to compost diseased plants, just as a precaution. It is better to burn them. A good design should avoid mono-crops, but instead maintain an integrated system of various plant families. Try to keep down weeds around plants that are a target for leafhoppers, thrips, and the like. This works well to avoid inviting virus. On the other hand, allow for some weeds along beds to invite a place for spiders, which are always very welcome. Putting plants in their most suitable location is a good plan.

The most important thing is to be aware of what is going on by monitoring the development of the farm and garden. You will not have a perfect system to work with and it is always in need of being facilitated and learned from. I notice a lot while I am spraying preparation 501. It gives me time to examine plants. It is a work in progress, as are the skills of a gardener. Diseases are a great educator. Another part of the education is to understand what diseases certain plants are prone to. One of the best cultural practices to use is a good rotation schedule. Refer to the charts in tables 8.1 and 8.2 for reference on certain plant diseases and the best rotation plan to take. In general, try to rotate roots to fruits, to follow with seed crops, and then leaf crops. The important thing is not to continually plant the same thing or the same family members. If nothing else, it exhausts the soil of certain nutrients and that makes plants more prone to disease.

TABLE 8.1
Disease Chart for Vegetables

Disease	Susceptible Plants	Symptoms	Development	Controls	Cultural Practices
Angular Leaf Spot (bacterial)	Cucumber, squash family	Bleached specks become angled holes throughout leaf.	Survives in plant debris.	Copper, bleach mix with 4 parts water.	Use resistant varieties; rotate every 2 years.
Anthracnose (fungal)	Beans, cucurbits (squash family), spinach, beets, tomatoes, peppers, potatoes, onions, gar, crucifers, brassicas, lettuce, asparagus	Brown spots along veins, sunken brown spots on pods, intervein blotches, sunken spots on fruit, dark smudges on neck and bulb, reddish brown lesions on root.	Soilborne and seed, high humidity, wind-blown spores.	*Bacillus subtilis*, potassium bicarbonate, copper, rosemary oil, fungicidal soap; horsetail as preventative.	Clean seed, mulch sanitation, rotation.
Aster Yellows (bacterial)	Carrots, celery (umbellifers), tomatoes, potatoes, lettuce, and many flowers	Leaf tips and entire leaf to stem turn yellow then brown.	Effects phloem, carried by leafhoppers, overwinters in plantain, thistles, wild lettuce, dandelion.	Copper.	Weed control, leafhopper control.

TABLE 8.1
Disease Chart for Vegetables (continued)

Disease	Susceptible Plants	Symptoms	Development	Controls	Cultural Practices
Bacterial Blight (Alternaria) Early blight	Beans, peas, potatoes	Yellow blotches on leaves. Sunken spots on fruit, concentric yellow circle turns brown. Starts on lower leaves.	Soilborne (rain splashed on leaves), horsetail is a preventative.	Bacillus subtilis, potassium bicarbonate, soap shield, copper oxide; kaolin as a preventative.	Thick mulch, rotate every 3 to 4 years, use resistant varieties.
Late blight	Celery, tomatoes	Same as above.		Vinegar and citrus oil, Bordeaux mixture (copper, lime, sulfate), compost tea, hurt oil.	Thick mulch, rotate every 3 to 4 years, use resistant varieties.
Bacterial Scab	Potatoes	Raised scabs on tubers.	Spread by wind and water.	Vinegar solution.	If soil is too alkaline, lower pH with sulfur.
Bacterial Spot	Tomatoes	Dark lesions turn to yellow blotches, black spots on fruit.	Spread by water, rain, handling, seedborne.	Copper sulfate, horsetail as a preventative, compost tea.	Use mulch and clean seed source.
	Peppers	Yellow spots on leaf, dark centers scab on fruit.			
Bacterial Wilt	Crucifers, cucumbers	Yellow V-shaped blotches at margins of leaf turn black.	Overwinters on plant and seed, invades wounds spread by cucumber beetle.	Copper, hot-water seed treatment.	2-year rotations, sanitation, clean seed source, resistant varieties (check county fair).
Blackheart	Potatoes	Black rotted centers.	Lack of oxygen in the soil.		Better cultivation, use loose mulch when hilling up.

TABLE 8.1
Disease Chart for Vegetables (*continued*)

Disease	Susceptible Plants	Symptoms	Development	Controls	Cultural Practices
Hollow Heart (similar to Blackheart)	Potatoes	Hollow center.	Boron deficiency.	Boron.	Add Borax to soil.
Black Leg (bacterial)	Brassicas	Black stem rot.	Carried by seed.	Hot-water seed treatment.	4-year rotation, good drainage.
Bottom Rot (fungus)	Lettuce	Stem is shrunken, brown lesions, white mycelium.	Related to damping of soil, soilborne.	Roman chamomile tea.	Mulch, good drainage, rotation.
Rust (fungal)	Asparagus, beans, cucumbers, tomatoes	Rusty orange to brown blisters on leaf. Leaves curl and die.	Seedborne, overwinters in plant residue.	Copper, sulfur, *Bacillus subtilis*, fungicidal soap, corn juice spray.	Rotation, thick mulch, use resistant varieties.
Verticillium Wilt (fungal)	Tomatoes, peppers, eggplant, strawberries, lettuce	Sourced leaf margins, wilted leaves yellow and drop. Yellow V marks on tomato, curled leaves, scorched leaves.	Soilborne, seedborne, wind-carried spores.	Sulfur, fungicidal soap, compost tea.	Irradiate black nightshade, rotation every 3 years, clean seed sanitation.
Septoria Leaf Spot (fungal)	Tomatoes	Black-spotted clusters start on lower leaves and the leaf yellows.	Systemic seedborne, enters through leaf and wounds. Plant debris. Stake up to 3 years.	Hot-water seed treatment, compost tea.	Irradiate black nightshade, rotation every 3 years, clean seed sanitation.
Yellow Vein Virus	Beans, peas, legumes, potatoes, beets, spinach	Interveinal yellowing in potatoes. Vein yellowing in peas.	Soilborne, carried by aphids.	Compost tea, horticultural oils.	Virus harbors in clover, control aphids.

TABLE 8.2
Disease Chart for Fruits

Disease	Susceptible Plants	Symptoms	Development	Controls	Cultural Practices
Anthracnose (fungal)	Grapes, strawberries, blueberries, citrus	Bull's-eye, dark-ringed blotches on fruit, sunken spots on fruit.	Spores spread by wind.	*Bacillus subtilis*, sulfur, copper, potassium bicarbonate, fungicidal soap, rosemary oil, horsetail.	Mulch sanitation.
Bacterial Spot	Peaches, plums, cherries	Black flecks on leaf.	Develops over winter on twigs, spread by wind and rain.	Compost tea, copper sulfate, horsetail.	Sanitary pruning, avoid excessive fertilizing, maintain good open circulation in trees.
Bacterial Canker	Plums, cherries, apples	Localized wounds, bark and limb dieback, cankers have brown margins. Young trees are more vulnerable.	Spread by rain, thrives in wet areas, enters through wounds, low pH, and nematodes.	Tree paste: $1/3$ diatomaceous earth, $1/3$ compost, $1/3$ rock phosphate.	Maintain proper pH, plant in well-drained areas, prune out infected limbs.
Bacterial Spot	Plums, cherries	Black galls on twigs and branches $1/2$ to $1 1/2$ inches wide.	Spores spread by air and rain, new growth is susceptible.	Sulfur, fungicidal soap.	Remove wild plum and cherry trees. Prune out infected branches and burn.
Black Rot (fungal)	Plums, grapes, apples, cherries, peaches	Purple specks on leaf and fruit enlarged to look like frog eye. Concentric rings, soft rotten grapes.	Overwinters on dead plant material. Enters stomata cells on leaf, spread by wind and rain.	Bordeaux spray (lime, copper, sulfur), compost tea.	Sanitation, proper pruning, control insect vectors, horsetail as preventative.

TABLE 8.2
Disease Chart for Fruits (*continued*)

Disease	Susceptible Plants	Symptoms	Development	Controls	Cultural Practices
Brown Rot (fungal)	Plums, peaches, apples, cherries, grapes	Blossom, twig and fruit blight. Mummified fruit ash, gray powder puffs spread by spores. Overwinters in plant debris on ground.	Spread by spores in plant debris on ground.	Sulfur, compost tea, milk spray.	Sanitation, pruning.
Cedar Apple Rust (fungal)	Apples	Bright orange spots on leaf and petiole. Reddish brown leaf falls later.	Overwinters on cedar tree, spores produced on galls when wet spread quickly. 2 cycle year.	Sulfur, fungicidal soap, *Bacillus subtilis*.	Plant apples away from cedar trees and junipers.
Crown Gall (bacterial)	Pears, peaches, persimmons, apples, plums, cherries, berries, grapes, etc.	Galls form on roots and crowns (dark tumors), stunt growth.	Spread by nursery stock, enters wounds, and then xylem.	Hurt oils, copper, tree paste (clay, compost, and rock phosphate), sulfur.	Good drainage, sanitation.
Fire Blight (bacterial)	Pears, apples, plums, cherries, peaches	Scorched, shriveled brown leaves and stem. Dieback at tips.	Spread by insects, animals, rain, tools. Overwinters on branches.	Copper, Bordeaux spray, kaolin spray or strep-tomycine.	Prune infected parts, use resistant varieties, (kieffer pear), do not over fertilize.
Eutypa Dieback (fungal)	Grapes	Yellow stunted leaves, blossom drop, dark canker and pealed stems.	Enters through pruned wounds, overpruning, spread by rain.	Hurt oils, copper, *Bacillus subtilis*, fungicidal soap.	Prune out infections, paint wounds. Use sanitary practices.

TABLE 8.2
Disease Chart for Fruits (continued)

Disease	Susceptible Plants	Symptoms	Development	Controls	Cultural Practices
Gummosis (fungal)	Peaches, plums, cherries, berries	Oozing, gummy sap from trunks to stems that are cracked, lesions spread around to girdle tree.	Oozing spores infect bark, favored by wet conditions, often result of injury.	Compost tea, copper, bleach, alcohol solution.	Protect openings, paint large wounds, keep pruning tools disinfected.
Leaf Curl (fungal)	Peaches, plums, apples	Mottled leaves curl under, red-dish turning yellow.	Fungus grows between leaf cells, spread by wind.	Bordeaux mix.	
Leaf Roll Virus (fungal)	Grapes	Leaves turn dark, curl down, veins stay yellow.	Can result from infected grafts. Spread by scale to mealybugs.	Hurt oils for vectors, sul-fur, diatoma-ceous earth.	Maintain clean conditions to plant sources.
Pierce's Disease (bacterial)	Grapes	Yellow blotches on leaves with a concentric ring around. Leaves turn brown and scorched.	Spread by leafhoppers. Disease blocks xylem. Plants can outgrow disease.	Compost tea, insecticidal soap for leaf hoppers and thrips.	Control leafhoppers, keep weeds cut back.
Phomopsis Leaf Spot (fungal)	Apples, pears	Brown, burnt apple leaves. Black mottled pear leaves. Brown scabby spots on fruit.	Overwinter on canes, spread by rain.	Bordeaux mix, *Bacillus subtilis*, hydrogen peroxide 10% solution.	Proper sanitary pruning, ensure good air and sun, circulation to plants.
Scab (fungal)	Peaches, plums	Reddish brown round lesions on twigs, freckled scabs on fruit.	Overwinters on twigs, airborne.	Hurt oils, sulfur, plant onion chives around trees.	Causes are cosmetic only.

There are many methods for dealing with diseases that address the problem but not the cause. Solarization, mentioned in a previous chapter, attempts to sterilize the soil. This is completely contrary to building life in the soil. It creates a vacuum for disease pathogens to move into. It is a very backward approach to growing organically.

The use of kaolin clay is helpful in preventing powdery mildew on cucurbits or brown rot on peaches. These take care of threats but do not address the real issue, an unhealthy environment that is prone to disease. Planting for resilience involves creating healthy flora and fauna the same way we use probiotics in our bodies. Microbial inoculants can introduce living elements that help keep pathogens in check.

There are several fermented plant extracts that stimulate beneficial microorganisms and improve the growth of soil organic matter. Plants depend on these microorganisms both below and above the soil. The biology affecting the above-ground parts of the plant is called phyllosphere. The best way to introduce life forms to plants this way is with compost tea. There are products that provide protection, but many growers have been using compost tea since long before they were on the market. A lot of work has been done to develop indigenous microorganisms. The concept is to work with localized organisms that are more adapted to the chemistry of your area. These work more effectively and do not pose a risk of introducing foreign organisms. Indigenous microorganisms are made with a fermented grain, then enriched with a food such as molasses or brown sugar and allowed to ferment again. It is then added to a host of rice or wheat and grown into a medium called Bokashi. This can be introduced to soil or used as a solution to be sprayed on soil or plants to introduce and stimulate proper microbial development.

Studies done at the Department of Virology at Sri Venkateswara University in India found that most macronutrient availability was increased after the use of indigenous microorganisms. Soil pH was more acid. There was an increase in soil carbon and water-holding capacity. There was also a strong increase in protease. Protease is an important contributor to inhibiting plant diseases and the overall plant growth. It works well to use effective microorganisms introduced into the subsoil. This can be done during the double digging process. Its characteristics provide a rapid decomposition of raw materials and introduce organisms that are builders of soil mycology. The idea here is to introduce and encourage the development to mycorrhizal life of the soil. *Arbuscular mycorrhizae* is one of the most effective in curbing fungal disease growth. *Pseudomonas fluorescens* is another that has been effective for blight control.

Both of these are found in compost and compost tea. Soil cultivation disturbs mycorrhizal development because the long filaments of mycelium are broken up. This is a conflict with double digging and French intensive methods. Once an optimum state is achieved, minimal or no till can help preserve these microorganisms without disruption.

The use of plants can inhibit certain plant diseases. Cover crops of mustard and brassicas have sulfur-containing compounds. Residues of these plants release chemicals that inhibit diseases while building up the microfloral populations in the soil that also help curb populations of pathogens. Oats are a nonhost of most plant diseases, thereby starving many diseases. Sudan grass enriches nonpathogenic fungal populations that can reduce verticillium wilt severity in potatoes. Hairy vetch enriches beneficial bacterial populations and has shown reductions of fusarium wilt. Part of this is the result in competition for nutrients between beneficial and pathogenic bacteria. Buckwheat has shown a reduction in verticillium wilt. Many crops, such as timothy, clovers, alfalfa, plantain, orchard grass, and chicory to name a few, have been shown to enrich antagonistic bacteria. Turning in cover crops prior to planting or green manuring can bring about these effects. This is also achieved by mixed plantings of vegetable crops with cover crops planted in alternate rows. The effects of a living mulch inhibits soilborne diseases from traveling via wind and rain. The ecosystem that exists at the surface of these soils enhances a healthier biodiversity. This encourages a healthy balance for soils, insects, and microorganisms.

Another approach is in the development of disease resistance. Disease resistance is usually thought of as a genetically modified breeding tool. But natural resistance works quite well. First, what is called resistance is really tolerance. It is a molecular adaptation that some plants seem to have. Disease resistance is best developed in the soil. Diseases occur mostly when a plant is not functioning properly. They excrete compounds that attract the pathogens. This is a nutritional problem that is made apparent through disease symptoms. Potassium is necessary for protein synthesis and the development of starch and cellulose. Deficiencies show up as thin cell structure and high sugar concentrations in the leaf, making it vulnerable to pathogens. Potassium and phosphorous help form bonds against bacterial diseases. Low calcium and boron contribute to thin cell walls making it easier for pathogens to penetrate. Deficiencies also cause excess sugars and amino acid concentrations in the leaf. Calcium builds soil structure so more air is available.

Fungal diseases inhabit soils that do not breathe well. This is a common occurrence when tractors plow repeatedly, creating a hard pan. Fungi release enzymes that dissolve the lamella that bonds cells together. Calcium inhibits this activity. Boron helps build some of the phenol defense compounds mentioned above. Too much nitrogen has a similar effect of access amino acids and sugars that attracts fungal diseases. Silica is important for building epidermal walls and it aids in translocation of phenol compounds. Silica also helps protect leaves from fungal penetration. It attracts light in a form that inhibits fungal development.

This is how biodynamic preparation 501 works as a disease preventative. Oak bark is also used to put diseases in check. Low potassium slows down amino and sugar process. Any excess of nutrients, especially nitrogen, attracts pathogens. The development of mycorrhizal fungi helps keep many diseases in check, both through competition and by being antagonistic. Compost tea is very effective as a preventative and curbing pathogen populations. Among other things, it contains beneficial nematodes that eat harmful pathogens. It is useful on a wide range of bacterial and fungal pathogens. Homeopathic remedies are being developed to combat diseases. One example is using Silica 6x and Sulfur 6x on downy mildew, or belladonna extract on rust, and *Ocimum* (basil) extracts on tomato diseases. This is something worth experimenting with. It is a fine-tuned approach to treating diseases using the right amounts at key intervals. There is much work yet to be done in developing these methods.

Preventative practices are the best way to keep diseases away. The key is to open up pathways for the ebb and flow of energy, the cycling of nutrients, and the recycling of foodstuffs that feed all forces of life. This applies to the vascular system of the plant, the capillary structure of the soil, and the atmosphere surrounding them both. When these pathways become blocked, the plant becomes vulnerable to disease. This can be the result of imbalances in nutrient ratios, caused by over- or underfertilization. Feeding the plant and not the soil usually causes this. Forcing the ecosystem can also cause this. An example of this would be monoculture plantings. Correcting human error is an ongoing process in evolving a piece of land. Environmental factors can be a third cause, usually brought on by dramatic changes in the climate, causing stress. Viewing the plant and its entire surroundings as being part of a larger organism helps put the dynamics in play in perspective. Opening up these passages to receive and release the energy from the soil and the atmosphere allows movement. The opposite is stagnation. This is even undesirable in composting. Too much of anything creates a deficiency of something else. A problem occurs when damage from a disease or from something else is causing unacceptable damage. There is a threshold that needs to be determined. At this point, it is necessary to use allopathic methods. That means deal with it immediately. Bringing in botanicals and dusts that will inhibit or destroy the growth of a particular disease is something that needs to be addressed when it becomes a serious problem in order to avoid major plant loss. With integrated pest management (IPM) spraying is a last resort, even with organic products. It is important to know when to take this action (see tables 8.1 and 8.2).

The natural order of maintaining a healthy environment involves natural selection. This is the role of pathogens in general. This is a way of keeping the overall state of nature in optimum health. Environmental factors contribute to the culling of its weaker elements. A good way to learn from this is to emulate nature, growing food as a forest. A stacked mulching system of dead and living elements that are in a continual state of decomposition will encourage a rich mycorrhizal presence in perennial beds. Try staggered interplantings of species that provide diversity in structure, composition, and function. A polyculture of plants that protect one another in a symbiotic relationship works well in creating a web work for this to happen. Consider the edge of the woods. Add smaller trees blended with shrubs and small edgings that protect lower areas. The idea of a fruit tree planted in the middle of a vegetable bed seems out of place yet provides benefits in both directions. Working with the forces of nature is the coexistence that invites all living elements into the beautiful myriad of life in the garden.

9

Biodynamics in Practice

You can't ever think that you will attain fertility. It is a commencement
that goes on. It builds on its own laws with the mastery of the horticul-
turalist constructing it.

—Alan Chadwick

IN BIODYNAMICS, A FARM OR GARDEN is viewed as an individual organism. The idea is to foster interrelationships with all the components that
make up a farm or garden. It is a holistic approach to becoming an integral
part of what is going on around you. Take land that is in need of healing
and try to develop it into a balanced ecosystem. It is always a unique and
ongoing learning experience. It requires being sensitive to the living entities that already exist there. In biodynamics, all plants are perceived as an
important part of nature, providing both food and medicine. Every aspect
of life, the plants, birds, insects, and so on, feed us with a vision of higher
evolvement. The force of nature is extended beyond what we can logically
grasp and into the cosmos. The inner connectedness with the entire universe requires us to be totally in our place and a garden is a perfect place to
be. This is where the natural world is embraced with reverence and respect.

Biodynamics is based on the teachings and vision of Rudolf Steiner.
Steiner presented a series of lectures in Switzerland in 1924 at the request
of local farmers after noticing a degradation in the vitality of their farms.

The farms had become unhealthy and out of focus with how they were originally developed. The animals were of ill health and the crops were in decline. This became the beginning of what is now biodynamic agriculture.

Alan Chadwick was tutored by Steiner in his youth. Chadwick was born in England and so was also a student of formal English gardens. He later studied the French intensive methods in France with Louis Lorette. There, he was introduced to the double digging process and intensive horticulture that was popular in the early 1900s. His method was a synthesis of biodynamics and French intensive systems, bringing biodynamics into a more horticultural realm. It encompasses the laws of natural science combined with an artistic perspective that is embraced spiritually. It becomes a marriage with the land and the honeymoon demands a serious commitment. The work is great. It requires a labor of love to see what is possible. Here, the gardener is not made but more a reflection of the surroundings. After one has done a measurable amount of investment into the soil and laid out the design of the garden, it is time to take on the role of a facilitator. This is the architectural formation of the vision of fertility. It is never in a state of completion. Maintaining fertility requires constant input. It is an ongoing process. This is what is referred to as the real work. The work that feeds us spiritually is never fully complete. It perpetuates itself by sustaining us in many ways.

That is the beauty of biodynamics. It aligns this work with a spiritual connection. It works with subtle energies that regulate the living systems—like the use of water that is used as a movement of these energies. The ideal is for a farmer to be operating in a truly subsistent manner. Being able to provide for all your on-farm needs is very challenging. This means raising all the livestock, hay, seeds, timber, manures, feed, plant materials, and so forth. One would in this way be able to trace back everything being used on the farm with little or no outside inputs. This system of self-reliance can be challenging when there are crop failures. Yet a closed system is easy to monitor.

Using the cosmic rhythms involves the science of astrology. Forces of the sun, soil, air, and water feed plants. Of the four elements, water can be seen as a carrier of life, wind as a carrier of change, sun as a carrier of energy, and soil as a presence of stability, an organism that radiates upward and outward. Climate dictates a lot of what is going on above the soil. The nature of life below the soil is more stable and less prone to change, which is why it needs to be protected. A healthy soil is composed of a capillary structure, not unlike the vascular system of a leaf. Activity is most intensive within three inches below the surface and two inches above the surface of the soil.

This is the fragile atmosphere where water and gases interchange. It inhales and exhales just like other living organisms and as it does, there is a lot of life force being exchanged. This inclination and declination of energy facilitates growth. It slows down in the evening as the plant elongates. Encouraging this flow encourages growth. Discouraging it encourages disease, the disease that is ever present and looking to attack weakness. Growth in general is especially favorable during growth cycles, during the night and early morning hours. At the peak of day, it is directed back into the soil. It is a subtle dance that is in perpetual motion. It ebbs and flows with the cycles of the sun, the cosmos, and the atmospheric conditions. It contains the fragile basis of what life is all about.

Using the Biodynamic Calendar

The biodynamic planting calendar is a useful tool to work with. It has a description and is all laid out and easy to use. First, there is a fourfold plant relationship aligned with astrological signs. This relates to the part of the plant being emphasized or what it is being grown for. For root crops, it is good to plant during earth signs. Leaf vegetables and herbs are planted during water signs because of the vascular system in the leaf. Water is very important to leaves and that is how nutrients are transported. Fruits and fruiting vegetables are planted during fire signs. The sun is important for the ripening of fruit. It stimulates the enzymes in the fruit just as it stimulates the nectar in the bee transforming it to honey. An obvious example is how apples will show color on the side facing out from the tree first. Seed plants, like legumes and flowers, are planted during air signs because the air contributes to seed dissemination and development. The other aspect of the calendar works with the moon's location to the sun. This affects the gravitational pull on the planet. Water is drawn upward during the waxing of the moon that is demonstrated with the ocean tides during full moons. So it is best to plant seeds that require a week or less to be planted a few days before the full moon. Seeds, like many perennials, that take a while longer are planted just after the new moon. This is when the energy is waxing. Transplanting is done after the full moon to allow time for the transition and recovery of root hair damage that is referred to as transplant shock.

Plants need time to regenerate root hairs and gain some composure. Even though one could do minimal damage during transplanting, there is still an adjustment. This is the most traumatic time for new plants. The cycles that take place are annual. This is evident with the passing of the seasons.

They are evolving around the full moon monthly. They also evolve daily. The lunar cycles affect harvesting and propagation. The sap flows upward, starting in the night and during the morning hours. This is best for harvesting above-ground crops, when they are most fresh. The energy flows back down during the afternoon. This is the best time to harvest below-ground crops. Taking cuttings for propagation is best during the waxing of the moon. Seed collecting is best during the waning of the moon. Just like our own energy has high and low times, so does the energy of the plants. The magnetic energy has a subtle effect on the growth of all living things. Science has confirmed that metabolism, water absorption, and growth rate are all stimulated by the full moon.

I have seen seeds emerge and a measurable amount of growth during a full moon. Being attuned to the cycles allows for a better connection with the rhythms of life in the garden. It gives more clarity and helps one become part of the flow of nature. This is just one of the factors affecting growth. There are other considerations that play a bigger role, like the weather, of course. If it is time to plant beans and it is going to freeze, then you must wait. It would be better to plant seed just before a rain anyway. This work has to be practiced with reason. Hence, this aspect of work has to be done sensibly. For me, it is a consideration not a mandatory requirement. It is good to experiment with the cycles of the moon to see how its position is played out.

Biodynamic Preparations

Biodynamic preparations are used as a catalyst to enhance subtle qualities in the soil and plant world. The preparations are made and used with strategic formulation to bring about desired qualities that help balance the entire environment both above and below the ground. These preparations are used in small quantities similar to homeopathy. Preparation 500 is used to promote root growth and micronutrients in the soil. It stimulates soil bacteria and humus. It helps regulate pH and macronutrients. This can also be beneficial to seed germination in the soil. It is applied in the late winter or early spring. The substance looks similar to finished compost. A small amount of about a spoonful is added to a few gallons or so of water (preferably rainwater that is not too old). It is best not to use treated tap water.

Once the material is added to the water, it is stirred vigorously in one direction for several seconds to create a vortex. Then stirring in the opposite direction breaks up the vortex. This process is repeated for approximately one hour or less. People have developed mechanical ways to stir. The idea of breaking up the vortex creates chaos in the water. It does this by adding oxygen. Equilibrium in a spiraling force becomes a biomagnetic field in the vortex.

The oxygen in the water is released as it invites the gases in the atmosphere surrounding it. Sunlight penetrates, with its warming effect. Many gardeners generally do not stir this long, although it is a meditative process. The ideal container to use is a clay crock. If one is not available, use a plastic bucket. The preparation is applied to soil just before turning. You may have a difficult time using a sprayer without it getting clogged. If this is the case, use a large brush to whisk the liquid onto the beds on a cloudy day. Taking fairly fresh cow manure makes preparation 500; pack it into a cow horn from a cow that has had a calf. The horn is buried in the autumn with the open end down and left until spring when it is used. The substance can be stored in a loose container like a jar with a loose lid in a cool dark place.

Preparation 501 is the silica spray. It is used to spray on plants to enhance light and photosynthesis. The high silica content of the preparation also creates an environment that discourages pathogens from entering the plant tissue. Stir the preparation with rainwater just like preparation 500. This preparation is applied to the plants on a regular basis as part of regular maintenance throughout the growing season. But it really depends on how much precipitation you are having. Humidity and dew content also affect how often to apply it; these are huge contributing factors in disease development. This preparation is easier to strain and apply with a sprayer on a sunny day, preferably in the morning.

Making preparation 501 is a little more difficult. I find a source of powdered clay. You may find this at a potter's store. A mixture of custer feldspar with silica clay very fine is a good combination. Be sure to use a dust mask when dealing with the dry ingredients. Then, pour in a little water to dampen the silica. Let it sit for a day, and then strain it so it is in the form of a paste. The dry powder can be very dangerous to breathe. So it is important to protect yourself from breathing it.

The paste is then place in a cow's horn like the preparation 500. It is buried in the soil in the spring or early summer and dug up in six or seven months. At this time it can be stored in a glass jar and put in the light to be used the following spring. The preparations 502 through 507 are for compost piles and are used all at the same time. Preparation 502 is made from yarrow flowers. Yarrow is a catalyst for sulfur and potassium. It also helps plants attract trace minerals. The flowers are cut from the plant in the summer and dried. In the fall, they are placed in a stag's bladder and placed in the sun for no more than a few months. The bladder will rot and the flowers will have broken down. The contents can be stored in an earthen container until use. Preparation 502 helps enhance sulfur in the compost pile and later in the soil.

Preparation 503 is made from German chamomile. It helps stabilize nitrogen and assimilates calcium and sulfur in the compost and stimulates microbial activity. The flowers are dried in the summer and placed in a cow's intestines in the autumn. A funnel can be used for this process. The intestines should be buried in the ground and dug up in the spring for use.

Preparation 504 is made from stinging nettle. It also has a relationship with sulfur, potassium, iron, and general soil health. The tops can be harvested and dried in the summer. It is mixed with some compost and buried in an earthen container for most of a year or until use.

Preparation 505 is made from oak bark. It helps enhance calcium and restores balance important in curbing plant diseases and fungus. It can contain as much as 80 percent calcium. The oak bark is ground up and placed in a sheep's skull in the autumn and dug up in the spring. The skull is buried in a wet area where it will retain moisture. Upon digging it up, you will need to let it air out for a while before storing it in a clay container.

Preparation 506 is made from dandelions. Dandelions help attract silica and potassium. The dandelions are collected and dried in the spring or summer. They are placed in a cow's stomach that is folded and placed in an earthen jar and then buried in the soil in the autumn until use the following spring.

Preparation 507 is made from valerian flowers. Valerian helps to concentrate phosphorus in the compost. The flowers are harvested in the spring. The fresh flowers are mashed in a mortar and pestle. Put this mixture in a jar with about four times as much water. Let the jar sit in the sun for about seven days. Filter it and place it in a bottle for later use.

These preparations are used in composting. I add them after the pile has cooled down between the first and second turning. Use the handle of a shovel and make a deep hole in the pile and pour one preparation into it, and then cover it up. Go around the pile and continue making holes for the other preparations. Do this around the top of the pile. The valerian is in liquid form. Place some of it in a hole and pour the rest over the top. Later when you turn the pile the preparations will get mixed throughout the pile. Do not add them to a hot pile.

Preparation 508 is made from horsetail (*Equisetum arvense*). The plant tops are harvested and dried in the summer. It can be made into a strong tea, strained and sprayed on the plants as a disease preventative. It contains high amounts of silica. The tea is steeped for a few hours and stirred for about twenty minutes. It is best to use fresh and not stored.

Another useful botanical that can be used is chamomile tea. This is made from Roman chamomile (*Anthemis nobilis*). A strong tea is strained and sprayed on young seedlings to prevent damping off fungus. Damping off is a common problem for seedlings in the greenhouse that are grown in an organic soil mix. It affects the plant during the cotyledon stage. The fungus lives on the surface of the soil. The tea prevents the fungus growth. Spray it daily until the first true leaves grow out. This plant is sometimes difficult to buy, but easy to grow so it's best to grow some and dry for future use.

Comfrey tea is another useful botanical. Take several cuttings of leaves and stems and place them in a waterproof container with a little water. It works best to bruise and cut up the plant material beforehand. This will need to steep for a week or so. The tea is diluted to a half cup per gallon of water and used as a fertilizer on young plants in the greenhouse or in the garden. It is a good supplemental source of potassium.

Compost tea is also good for young plants as a source of nitrogen and trace elements. The compost is steeped for a week or more. It is then strained and diluted to about one cup per gallon of water. Compost tea is also very useful to both prevent and get rid of many plant diseases. I spray it in a mix of half water to tea. It has to be strained well to go through a sprayer.

There are also some good tree pastes to use for insects and diseases on fruit and nut trees. These are applied on the trunks of trees during the spring and fall. One recipe is to make a slurry of clay, compost, and diatomaceous earth, one third each mixed with water. This is painted onto the trunk of the tree and is used for insects burrowing into the tree or bark. Another recipe is to add clay, compost (one third each), and a mix of rock phosphate, silica, and lime. This is also made into a slurry and painted on the tree trunk. This works well for diseases of woody plants. Ants can also be the cause of disease problems. They carry or farm aphids onto the tree so they can suck the sap the aphids secrete. Aphids are a carrier of many diseases. Tanglefoot can be applied a foot high around the base of a tree to prevent the aphids from moving up the tree. These are best applied as soon as a problem is noticed. It is useful to observe the outcome of using the botanicals listed above. Their results will vary from place to place and season to season.

Dynamic accumulators are plants with attractive qualities to encourage in and around the farm and garden. These plants attract and accumulate vital minerals, which are made available to plants around them. Many of them are used in biodynamic preparation. Clover and other legumes attract nitrogen. Yarrow attracts potassium, phosphorous, and copper. Chives and German chamomile are associated with potassium, phosphorous, and calcium. Horsetail accumulates calcium, copper, iron, magnesium, and cobalt. Alfalfa accumulates iron and nitrogen. Peppermint is a good source of potassium and magnesium. Dock accumulates iron, potassium, phosphorous, calcium, and sodium. Comfrey is an excellent source of potassium, calcium, phosphorous, copper, and iron. Dandelion accumulates potassium, phosphorous, calcium, copper, and iron. Stinging nettle accumulates potassium, calcium sulfur, iron, and sodium quite well. Vetch helps gather potassium, phosphorous, and nitrogen. These are good plants to compost as a way to make these minerals available to the soil.

A healthy environment contains elements of nature that must be interwoven and compatible for relationships in order to create order. The utilization of native plants is often overlooked as a way to connect with nature. Native plants are obviously well adapted to your area and so, easier to grow. They require less water and attention. They work well for attracting wildlife and help tie those relationships together. The connection to nature also helps strengthen the cultivars by having this closer link to nature. They attract pollinators that are beneficial for improving yields of fruiting plants. By starting the process of reestablishing the true nature of an area, the entire place develops into a new dimension. This can be another form of completing cycles of nature. This can also open up new doors of perception, partially for seeing the area for how it may have once been, but also for seeing it as it could be. Helping to restore it to its natural state enriches the whole environment. A rich biological state is at the heart of what biodynamics is all about. It is the foundation of dynamic life and aids in the completion of life cycles.

Circles represent the total existence of life. Concentric circles are an alignment of the constituent parts of those circles. When viable resources are readily available, this helps create tolerable and hopefully favorable conditions to grow in. Poles of opposing forces need an equality to keep balance. Positives and negatives can be seen in everything. They are both needed to provide the polar axis for equal growth. Nature is not perfect, yet fully functional. This is as much a perspective as it is a necessary part of life. Something usually good comes out of a disaster, if nothing more than an expensive education. Thinking of gardens and farms as a cornucopia is something to aspire to. The total mix can be like a beautiful bouquet, one I like to get lost in from time to time. Life is meant to be experienced, and the garden is a wonderful place to experience it.

The garden reflects an evidence of virtue. The more you put into it, the more you get out—if it is a passionate work. It is the real work, the work that perpetuates itself. My role in growing is not to make things grow but to be a facilitator. Humans have an important role with nature. We are the keeper of seeds, the planters and caretakers. More quickly than anyone else in nature, we can be a huge asset in affecting and improving the health of the land. Biodynamics is an intentional act of healing the land. Rather than building a box garden, where one superimposes a garden on top of a piece of land, why not delve into the riches of the soil beneath.

To work with the riches of nature is to unearth its hidden treasures. It can and needs to be a reflection of your love. That is the beauty of biodynamics. It aligns the work with a spiritual connection. Becoming aware of the pulsation of the soil and plants puts you in touch with this growth process. The soil has subtle cycles. There is a pulsation that moves slower than ours. It slows down even more in the winter, yet is still there. To truly enhance the life underground, you need to encourage this pulsation. The deeper the cultivation, the more it can breathe. This encourages the pulsation. Part of this is the exchange of gases and the movement of air, water, and living entities deep down in the soil.

Plants also have this pulsation within them. Their growth is a reflection of this. There are cycles that happen daily, monthly through lunar cycles, and yearly as the seasons run their course. To enhance this pulsation is the best way to develop your soil and the whole of the growing area. Through cultivation and organic matter the process is greatly enhanced. An ideal environment for growing allows this to take place without hindrance. The whole of life in the garden is connected to this. Just as the soil is connected to the atmosphere above, the plants are surrounded by both the above- and below-ground atmosphere. Plants rest for long periods. Insects are keenly aware of this, as are the animals moving around at night. It is good to go out and observe what is going on at night, especially during a full moon when there is greater visibility. Having this connection gives insight to growth patterns. This also causes one to slow down and move in a more flowing manner. There is a needed place for this in our lives.

The seasonal cycles remind us of where we need to be. December, when the winter solstice happens, is a time to take an introspective look back and ahead to the coming season. January is a radical time of new beginnings as the days start to grow. When I lived in a Buddhist society, I was introduced to a gentler way of being, to first find one's place, and then act on it. It allows one to be more conscious of what is going on. Finding balance is where the garden can take you, rather than you taking the garden there. It works in both ways. It also makes me feel good about both my work and what it offers me. Finding balance offers a lot of give and a lot of take. Most people in society today are accumulators of things. It makes them feel good. If you observe and pay close attention in the garden, you will accumulate truths and discover the importance of who you are. A garden is a sanctuary for the mind, heart, and soul.

This goes back to horticulture therapy. Sharing this beauty is a wonderful thing to do. Propagating good land stewards through education is very important as well. There is an enormous wealth of knowledge to take advantage of, and we all have something special to share. When one has an incredible passion for what they do, they cannot help but want to share it. Much of the education in biodynamics in the United States takes place through apprenticeship programs. I have been fortunate to have learned what I know from a variety of sources. It is important to learn from an educated source, so you can make more evolved mistakes. I would suggest looking for teachers who have a hunger for knowledge and have been pursuing that hunger for some time. There is a hunger in society today as people become disenchanted with their environments. The need to connect with nature and bring it into our lives gives meaning to our existence on the planet. As people become increasingly aware of the imbalance in their own lives and want to change it, something wonderful happens. They grow into evolved beings. That is a healthy thing to seek out.

The knowledge to do so is abundant and all around us. The dynamics of nature is a great teacher. In a room full of gardeners and farmers, there is always an amazing amount of collective knowledge. We can all teach each other so much. Seeing so many natural wonders through my travels has humbled me. Most likely anyone who gardens organically understands that the force of nature is the dominant one. As my education continues, I realize the vastness of what there is to learn. This is why I never wish to be an expert. That sounds like I do not have much left to learn and that would be absurd. For that is what makes the future so bright. Sometimes I have arrived in other countries to work and been introduced as Mr. Frank the expert. I respond by saying I just got here, and you are already insulting me. When gardeners stop learning and growing, it might be time to make compost of them.

It is important to understand that all plants, insects, and entire life forms are one big family. Every insect and plant has a purpose that we can benefit from in more ways than we can possibly imagine. Understanding this helps us to see that what we might see as pests are also representatives of the land's personality. The delicate connection between all these living things is part of the language that the garden speaks. When there is harmony, it is like a chorus. The rhythm of the garden can be heard by the buzzing of the bees. When spring is at its peak, the garden smiles with an abundance of blooms. The smell of moist gases, being given off at the soil's surface, reflects the state of its health. The fragile balance is easy to upset, yet constantly being altered. Striving for perfection or even anywhere close is to lose sight of what nature is all about. Finding one's place as a proper facilitator, caretaker, or steward is a long road that is always being redefined. Time and making a serious investment of a few years helped me to find what works and how to work in a confluent manner with nature. This is the defining edge of intuitive gardening. It is like finding my place here just as the birds and insects have.

Culture is cultivated. It comes from desire. Agriculture is a marriage of science and the art that holds that culture. Horticulture is the fine art of agriculture. Doing this work ecologically and sustainably involves a lot of insight. Ecoagriculture requires a high amount of consciousness. Proper application of technique needs to involve sensitivity to nature and obedience to its laws. Reverence to these laws helps us understand how fertility is always in a state of growth. It is never complete and never finished. Fertility is a union of cultivation, fertilization, and propagation.

A community of plants or people generates a lot of energy. That energy is being exchanged constantly. Put it out there and it comes back differently. There is nowhere where that is more obvious than in a garden. It moves in and out of people and plants and all living things. Allowing that flow to happen in a manner that is unrestrained is important. Nature's attraction is its life force. Harvesting that energy is the goal, either in the learning, the food it gives us, or the experiences we have. Getting caught up in it is very fulfilling. Nature regenerates itself amazingly well. To help facilitate that process is a job that offers amazing rewards. It is a special gift to those who surrender to it. Working in a natural setting abundant with life is an incredible place to experience what this world has to offer.

10

Maintenance and Balance

And so it appears that most and perhaps all of industrial agriculture's manifest failures are the result of an attempt to make the land produce without husbandry.

—Wendell Berry

I STARTED OFF AS A MAINTENANCE GARDENER working on estates in San Mateo County, California, south of San Francisco. I just fell into this situation. It was as though it chose me. It was a good place to start my career, partly because I didn't know anything but also because it taught me how to plan a garden from a practical perspective.

Designing for how it will be maintained is a big part of the efficiency of how it works. Once the summer arrives it is time to focus on maintaining what has been planted. Maintenance is a large project that is very demanding and bit of a balancing act. In the South there are three good growing seasons and it is hot in June and sometimes in May. The winter provides for roots and greens outdoors. By early June one can try to squeeze in some late plantings of winter squash, eggplants, late tomatoes, field peas, summer squash, beans, and so on. After that you are counting on the weather to help them get established. It is a gamble with the weather during the dog days of summer if one chooses to keep planting. If you don't get it planted by then, you may have to wait until next year.

Maintenance becomes an important part of daily work. It is a challenging role to be an effective facilitator of everything that has been orchestrated to that point. If done well, it is a matter of maintaining the balance. A healthy environment is always evolving. Nothing stays the same or can be counted on when dealing with living entities. Using time efficiently is important. For instance, refrain from pulling weeds until the plants you are growing are at least half mature. When the weeds are taken out, the cultivated ones will cover the bed and create a full canopy over it to prevent the weeds from coming back. In doing this you are weeding once not several times. The weeds only fill in vacancies anyway. Keep in mind that the plants you are growing started out as weeds. They were later developed into cultivars. There are some that are good to allow if they are worth the benefits they provide. Weeds do a good job of filling in empty space. They are the scar tissue of land that needs to be covered. The sequence of events are as follows: weed, topdress with compost over soil that has just been cultivated, then mulch enough to cover the compost, and water to put it all into play. Because weeding cultivates the soil, take advantage of that by putting compost down when the soil is ready to receive it.

Examine which weeds contribute to their surroundings by being beneficial and which ones do not. It is common to have grasses grow along the edge of the beds. They serve as good spider habitats. This is good for squash, tomatoes, peppers, melons, and somewhat for beans. But the grass is not beneficial for grapes because it also attracts leafhoppers, which are vectors of diseases that grapes are vulnerable to. Small greens like spinach and Chinese greens and other mustards, brassicas (cabbage family), and especially strawberries do not do well with the grasses as they provide a place for slugs to get out of the hot sun. Flea beetles also like the grass so they are not good around eggplant. A few cultivator plants like lamb's-quarter, dock, and dandelions are good for cultivating the soil and bringing nutrients to the surface for shallow-rooted ones. It helps to monitor insect populations and diseases in these areas.

In some situations used newspaper can be used in layers around a few shrubs, especially ornamentals; this is referred to as the lasagna method. A thick layer can keep weeds away. It can also be a hassle for gaining access to the area around the plants. Be sure to keep the newspaper a distance from the stem to allow water to get to the roots. The practice works well for grapes and blueberries.

There are a lot of easy maintenance techniques for insect problems. Lay boards down in the paths for slugs. When the sun is high turn them over.

If there are only a few slugs, it is easy to scrape them off into a can. If there are a lot, use diatomaceous earth around the base of plants and along the edge of the bed. This helps you get an idea of their numbers. Netting is useful for winged insects. Use netting over squash for vine borers. The holes need to be large enough to let bees in to pollinate the flowers. You can also use scraps of netting and cloth around the base of the plant to prevent the eggs from being laid. When you do see damage, you can inject *Bacillus thuringiensis* into the stem with a horse needle. It is a hit or miss tactic that sometimes works if done at the right time. Netting is also good for preventing the white butterfly from laying eggs on brassicas. The netting needs to be secured to the ground to prevent them from getting underneath.

Setting up large gauge wire horizontally for staking various plants like flowers works well. Venidiums, gaillardias, cosmos, *Ammi majus*, poppies, dahlias, and coreopsis all need staking in order to get a good cut flower. A piece of hog wire suspended across the bed eighteen inches to two feet high works well for the plants to grow through. When growing a late crop of spring greens like lettuce, broccoli, and maybe spinach (if you are feeling optimistic), use the wire as hoops over the bed. Cover it with sheets and dampen them during the heat of the day. Depending on the temperature and length of the heat wave, you may prevent them from bolting for a couple weeks or so. This can also be done with buckets placed along the side of beds with old window screens laid across. The same thing works in the late summer when getting cole crops in the ground while it is still a little hot for these plants yet you want to get them established for the fall. Another use for the hoop is to cover plants as disease prevention. When there is heavy dew, plants become vulnerable to fungus diseases like downy mildew on kale, lettuce, or spinach. Powdery mildew on squash or cucumbers is another. Heavy dew can also encourage aster yellows, septoria leaf spot, and rust, as well as many other fungus diseases.

A preventative approach for disease involves spraying silica, horsetail, and/or kaolin clay on a regular basis. This could be every other week or after a good rain. Mulch is one of the best methods for preventing soilborne diseases. This is a must for tomatoes. Insects need to be monitored so that you are aware of population outbreaks.

A good preventative method of insect control is to let your chickens or guinea fowl graze in the planting area for a week before planting. They need to be monitored if the area is not well fenced. This is the same concept as chicken tractors. Of course it is not recommended to leave them out at night.

Some farmers keep successive planting of things like squash to stay ahead of vine borer. This idea does not address the problem of why their predators are not present and how to change that. As a last resort you can take an allopathic approach and spray botanicals and organic sprays. But the real problem of creating a biological balance needs to be addressed. Spraying things like cayenne and garlic are quick, easy, and useful for small insect emergence if done at the beginning, but a continued attack should be sending you a message that something is out of balance. There is a measurable amount of damage that is acceptable. What that means depends on many factors. Are you growing for yourself? If so you can ignore a few holes in a chard leaf.

Growing for market means raising the standard of what is acceptable. Consumers have been sold on looks not taste. That is part of the challenge of being a market grower. Getting the consumers to understand that food should not look perfect is something that requires a lot of patience. This needs to be part of the job of the grower in farmers markets. The job of educating the consumers is an important one. Hopefully this will start to change through direct marketing concepts. When you see someone selling a product that looks totally blemish-free and too good to be true, it probably is. And that is a red flag as to whether they are using synthetic chemicals.

Truck farmers deal with a lot of waste. It also depends on the vegetable or fruit. Tomatoes are very perishable. It is common to throw a lot away yet still harvest the majority of what is out there. This is why most commercial growers pick them at the green unripe stage. You may lose a few peppers to sun scald, but if it is more than a few then you can shade them. One of the biggest losses is to spring greens bolting, or going to seed after an extended heat wave. What is acceptable really depends on the grower, what they are willing to tolerate and what they anticipated when planting. A general rule is to tolerate 10 percent loss of most of what you are growing.

Insect monitoring gives a good idea of when insects emerge and population increases for future reference. Animal damage can be a more serious problem than that of insects. Insects can damage plants. Moles eat the roots, leaving no plant at all. In California there are gophers; North Carolina has groundhogs and voles, which are much worse than moles. Castor beans, also called mole plants, will deter them. Many small growers have had success putting castor beans in the animals' tunnels. Other plants that work are *Artemisia*, elderberry, belladonna, and amaryllis. Larkspur are said to attract Japanese beetles and are also poisonous to them. Traps can be useful also. I do not use traps because I do not wish to grow a crop just for the insects. It is too impractical.

Squirrels can be so annoying that they can be a big liability to your garden's success. Netting can work but it has to be secured extremely well, especially along the bottoms. Spraying cayenne and garlic on fruits will discourage them but it must be applied often and after every rain. Birds of prey can also be an asset. It is important to evaluate the presence of nut trees and oaks around your growing area as to whether you will have squirrels.

Rabbits can do a lot of damage in a short amount of time. They will disappear quickly with the presence of a dog or cat. They are very vulnerable since they are a popular food for many animals of prey.

There are many benefits from bird life in a garden. They can do some damage yet it is a trade-off for all the benefits they bring, mainly as insect eaters. When they become a problem, the use of netting can help. Pie pans can work for a short while. Scarecrows seem to work for a short time if you move them around.

Rats are almost as prolific as rabbits. Rats have litters of five to nine, with the pups being sexually mature in eight weeks. Doing the math is very scary. In the city there are Norwegian rats. They are big and slow. In the country there are field rats. They are darker, smaller, faster, and smarter. We experimented with the bucket method. Lay the bucket on its side and put down some paper inside. On the paper put a scoop of grits mixed fifty–fifty with concrete. You hope that they go off and shit a brick and disappear. Mammals should not ingest concrete. So this will not work if you have guinea fowl, chickens, or ducks in the garden. We had pretty good success with this. Still, they are not to be underestimated. They are incredible survivors. If you poison these animals it will come back to you in some bad ways. The poison kills off the birds of prey. It ends up in the water system. It ends up in the food chain and will likely end up in your food. Dogs are also a damaging animal. A good rat dog will get rid of rats and rabbits, but they do upset an ecosystem, as do cats. So they are a trade-off and something to weigh in the overall plan. Birds of prey are very beneficial. The best way to attract them is by building a birdhouse. It needs to be a lot larger than the average birdhouse. Build it over a foot wide and a foot and a half tall with a six-inch entrance. Mount the house up high, about thirty feet up. A telephone or power pole will work. Be aware that they will not get rid of all the animals, for that would get rid of their food supply. But they will curb the population significantly.

Deer are more common than ever in rural areas and on the edge of towns. They are worse in suburban areas. Their breeding season starts in the fall and that is when they are most prolific. Clearing land for development creates habitats for deer. Not the other way around. Years ago we could not put in a garden until we had erected a seven foot high fence with a strand or two of barb wire on top. Once established, a fence like that will last a long time. Electric fences also work very well. When first experimenting with electric fences, you may wonder if they will work. There are two ideas here that we put in place. First, we baited the fence with peanut butter and jelly wrapped in tinfoil. This way deer are attracted to the fence; they taste the hot fence and stay away after that. They also tell the others. This is behavioral modification. The other method is to put a trip wire that stands about a foot and a half high out a few feet away from the main fence. Deer do not have good depth perception. The first fence trips them, the second shocks them. Both fences are electrified. Many farmers have had success installing two fences running parallel, but the cost of doing this is greater than using a trip wire. You can also experiment with deer deterrents. They all consist of a combination of rotten eggs, cayenne, garlic, and coyote urine. You can make some yourself, but you may not find a coyote willing to urinate in a bucket. The eggs alone would keep any animal and half the neighborhood away. This method is effective, but the mixture has to be put out every week or so and reapplied after every rain.

Succession planting is an important way to provide a continual harvest. If a variety of crops are planted, then you will have a variety of harvests. For instance, if sugar snaps and snow peas get burned up early from a heat wave in May, you will have garlic coming in shortly thereafter and blueberries following that, and so on. Succession planting is a good way to make efficient use of your beds. It is also important for market gardens. In the spring there is enough time to plant about five groups of Japanese turnips about two weeks apart. You can plant three groups of broccoli about two weeks apart. Lettuce is planted in four locations at two-week intervals. This way you are not planting everything at the same time and you are better prepared for a weather problem. The crops are also not in one place. Smaller plantings mean less problems. You can interplant with different crops depending on the time of month. I plant carrots in the fall, around early October. These do not mature before the cold weather and winter over for the following spring. Plant the next crop in February or early March, that way you are usually on top of market demands. Succession planting should be experimental to see what works best for your needs.

What works best one year does not always work the following year. Keep track of rotation schedules so that you do not plant a leaf crop on top of the previous leaf crop. Wherever the field peas or peanuts were last year will be a good site for next spring's cabbage or broccoli. Stay on top of what is happening with a bed by keeping a record of what was there last year and the years before that, along with side notes. Each bed is a little different than the ones next to it. Plant each bed to perform at its optimum. You might find that by growing low-growing flowers like nasturtiums or borage you keep a good biological balance.

Keeping fruiting vegetables off the ground prevents rot. Winter squash and melons need to be elevated or they become targets of fruit worms. Place them on top of pots or stash a big handful of hay under them to keep them off the ground. In double dug beds roots grow deeper and plants grow taller.

Trellising is an art that becomes a necessary part of the season. Work with materials that are available to you. You may have various types of wire, wood, and bamboo. Bamboo is usually readily available at someone's place and they would be happy to have you harvest it. Green bamboo will not work. It needs to dry out first and cure to carry weight. With exception to English peas, most of the spring plantings consist of small bedding plants. There are leafy greens and roots in a large supply. A good method is to plant the sugar snaps and snow peas in wire hoops down the bed. Along the perimeters there is ample space for arugula, parsley, cilantro, and/or carrots. Summer is a more vertical garden. Pole beans need staking. Place bamboo along the sides of the bed and place bamboo poles in the middle that angle to meet the ones along the sides. This way you are allowing sun to get down into the middle of the bed where it is needed. Peppers and eggplant are not as tall. Place shorter stakes along the plants halfway between each one. These stakes are then connected with lateral pieces. The plants will be able to lie across the lateral bamboo as they grow up through it. Each plant gets a triangular opening to grow through. Tomatoes can be staked in many different ways. There are as many ways to stake tomatoes as there are gardeners. Smaller varieties can be grown in hoops. When planting a late crop of tomatoes, it is easy to place them in the hoops where the peas where. Simply pull the spent peas. Throw in a large shovel of compost and plant them in the middle of the hoops. It makes the whole process easy and is a good rotation plan. Larger tomatoes are sometimes planted in square spaces. Make the squares with bamboo run horizontally along the length of the bed and down the middle. The tomatoes are staked with vertical pieces that support them. Use two layers of the bamboo rails. After the plants reach five or six feet, let the tomatoes hang over the top. If you do not wish to get on a ladder to pick tomatoes, then you have to let them go at some point.

Cucumbers can also be staked in a number of ways, but there are two main schools of thought. Grow them vertically or horizontally. Putting down a wire that is horizontal about two feet above the bed keeps them off the ground. Once the plants gain some size, pull them through and let them grow across the top. The fruit will hang below the wire. The picking process involves crawling down the path with a basket. This method protects them from sun scald. With this method you can harvest about four bushels for a twenty-five-foot bed. This method could also be used to grow small melons. The other method of staking is to grow cucumbers vertically. This involves placing a fence along the edge of the bed. The biggest problem here is that the fence needs to be very well staked as it will have to support a lot of weight when the fruits mature. This opens up the majority of the bed for something else, like bush beans. Having full sun on both sides of the plant encourages faster growth. However, the fruit matures after the same number of days. I prefer the former method. It is easier to set up and it produces a lot of cucumbers for market. You can also grow cucumber at the base of sunflowers. This is a good example of polyculture planting. There are many ways to plant in horizontal layers that serve both plants well.

Some of the cut flowers need to be staked. Their tall growth makes them vulnerable to winds. If the soil has a good balance of nutrients and not too much nitrogen, the stalks can adequately support most of the flower varieties. Keep them deadheaded to encourage continual blooms.

Growing raspberries along wires is a common method of trellising. The whole thing resembles a clothesline with the wires placed about four or five feet high. You can mark the primary canes with twist ties. This will make it easier to identify and cut them out in the fall. The secondary canes provide the fruit for next year. These are some ideas to consider. Over the years they have served me well. It is always good to experiment with new methods.

If your fence is not electric, you can use it quite well as a trellis. Cherry tomatoes are grown in so many ways that it is hard to list them all. Researching new ways to stake and trellis and to use plants that support other plants is the ongoing development of a garden.

Using corn to support pole beans is an idea taken from Native Americans. Plant squash at the corners and you have what is called "the three sisters." Curved wire and poles also provide a covered area for greens to get morning shade as you try to get them to last into the summer. The focus of these ideas is to be practical, simple, and esthetic at the same time.

Having a good watering system in place is an important part of any farm or garden. Regardless of how you water or how much you water, it cannot replace the benefits of a good rain. On the West Coast of the United States irrigation is needed because it normally does not rain there in the summer. Where I grow in the southeast it rains at some point. So watering helps only to supplement the rain, not to totally replace it. Rain brings with it all the minerals in the atmosphere. In the spring and late fall you can get by with less rain because of cooler temperatures. This means less evaporation. When watering, it is important to do it in the most efficient way possible. Watering at night will have a bigger impact because there is less evaporation, but using overhead watering can create disease problems. Watering the entire field with overhead systems can be wasteful but easy to set up. Using watering tapes provides water only along the parts of beds where the plants are growing. Drip irrigation is efficient in terms of saving water but more expensive to set up. I water the entire bed that I am growing in with hose sprinklers. That is because I grow on the entire bed. When it is fully planted there is no empty space. Remember to treat the bed as if it is alive. Approach the beds as living entities not growing mediums. Once you put compost in the whole bed keep it watered. Start watering as soon as compost is in place. Drip works well for large plants like tomato, squash, pepper, eggplant, melon, blueberry, raspberry, and so on. A drought year can be devastating. It is important to try to stay ahead of irrigation. It is easy for conditions to get away from you on an extremely dry year. When the water table drops during hot summers, it is a downward spiral. The more organic matter there is in the soil, the better it holds onto moisture. During a severe drought this helps but is not a total cure. Keeping the bed covered with plants or grasses helps hold moisture in the beds.

Blueberries do well in a wide row that is two feet wide. If available, recycle an old hose and turn it into a makeshift drip system. Use a pointed tool to make a small hole next to every plant. It is about the only drip system I use. It is good to periodically water the whole growing area if there is no rain for more than a couple weeks. Drip systems have the advantage of keeping water off of leaves, which is very helpful in preventing diseases. This can be a good plan for growing tomatoes; the use of a thick layer of mulch can also assist in this. It also helps to protect the water in the soil from evaporation.

The morning dew that sits on the plants is the biggest threat for spreading diseases. Try to keep disease off of tomato plants by avoiding overhead watering. Most plants like a watering routine. Tomato plants are especially fond of having the same amount of water on the same day. You can check the soil for moisture with fancy water-testing devices, or you can use your finger, observation, and common sense. After a while you will get to know what works in a given field after working with it for a while.

Deeply cultivated beds allow roots to penetrate deeply. This creates reservoirs for deep roots. Deep beds also provide drainage during wet seasons. A good source of water is equally important. City water is full of chemicals, like chlorine that can burn plants, and it is expensive. In this case it is wise to save rainwater to use as much as possible. There are many types of tanks and systems that lend themselves to different situations. In Belize there are rain tanks on about every structure. They even serve rainwater in some of the restaurants. I have seen bamboo used as a rain gutter. When saving water two ideas help to make it work well. Use gravity to get the water from point A to point B, and keep it simple. The amount of water coming off a roof adds up quickly. For instance, a one thousand square foot roof receiving one inch of rain equals six hundred gallons of water. Most of the beds we use are one hundred square feet for research purposes. So that accumulation of water will provide an inch per bed for ten beds. Water, especially rainwater because of its higher mineral content, replenishes and regenerates life in a garden.

A body of water or a stream provides the biological niche that is needed for balance to take place. Benefits include the presence of amphibians, reptiles, and dragonflies. If soil is the source of life, then water fuels that source and provides movement for the mineral and life forms to mobilize. If the farm or garden is a living organism, the movement of water is the cycling of life that needs to take place in order to make that organism complete.

Pruning is an important part of the maintenance of fruit trees, vines, and bushes. It is done in the late winter after the most severe cold weather is usually past, while plants are still in a state of dormancy. Pruning in early to midwinter makes them vulnerable to heavy frost, which can damage the wounds. In the southeast that would be the beginning of February. This is also when roses are pruned.

There are two main objectives to pruning fruit trees. First, the tree needs to be opened up in the center so light can enter down into the center and air can circulate. The second is to clean up unwanted growth that is unhealthy due to unbalanced growth, damage, and disease. Creating balanced growth means it is also being trained to grow. Cut out dead or diseased limbs as the first priority. Then take out small branches that overlap and make for a cluttered look. Remove the ones growing directly up through the middle; these are called water suckers. Branches need to resemble a ballet dancer with her arms raised in a semicircle. Use limb spreaders between the main trunk and side branches to encourage them to grow out away from the trunk. This is best done at an early age.

Old trees are hard to train and bring back to a healthy state. Cut away anything coming up below the tree graft. A central leader is established as the tallest in the center. This method works well for apples, pears, cherries, persimmons, and jujubes. Another system is the vase method. I try to allow three main branches to grow up to resemble an open hand. With this style there is more emphasis on opening the center. This works well for plums, peaches, figs, pomegranates, and apricots.

Other more involved systems are espalier and cordon. These are very well manicured methods. They involve meticulous pruning that is done often. It is a very efficient use of space and more labor intensive. These methods require continuous pruning of small branches and wires to support the growth.

With large cuts of over one inch it is best to paint open wounds with tree paint or something to help close up the wound, protecting it from disease and insects. All cut branches are put into a burn pile unless you are using them for scion wood. Grapes and kiwis are pruned or trained onto a wire or arbor. This can vary depending on the overall look you are trying to create.

Harvest at optimum levels of ripeness to get the highest vitamin content. Kiwis and pears do not ripen on the plant and so need to be picked when color and size is right; they will then ripen indoors. Other fruit is picked when fully ripe, but not what you get in the store. Being fully ripe is determined by color and taste. It is hard to get it all just right. Planting more than enough makes it challenging to keep it all picked on time. So find friends to share in the abundance.

Sap flows up into the plant in the morning, so I pick above-ground vegetables and fruits then. It is best to pick root crops in the afternoon when the sap is flowing back down into the roots. Many people pick the food and immediately wash it off, but they are losing the best part, the bloom. The bloom is the result of the plant's ripening agents. Its gases are given off to protect it as it meets the atmosphere. This is the essence of beauty in ripe fruits. And you are fortunate to be able to experience it in its freshest form.

Of course temperatures affect taste. Melons do best after a wet spring followed by a hot dry spell in the early summer.

Greens like kale, collards, spinach, and so on develop sugars when met with a frost and taste much sweeter. Starches stored in the leaf are broken down into sugars to make the plant less susceptible to frost. This is triggered by cooler temperatures. Where dew settles, it invites frost and destroys cell structure in the leaf. When the sun comes out it becomes apparent. Carrots that were planted in the late fall, wintered over, and pass a cold season in the ground, gain flavor to be enjoyed the following spring.

You can taste nutrients. The better the flavor is the higher the nutrient content. Seed selection is important for growing quality as well. Heirloom varieties are grown for flavor. Hybrids are grown for other characteristics, like disease resistance, storage, gradual ripening, and cosmetic appeal based on concepts that were sold to the public. To find out what is the optimum time for each variety, try picking at different stages. Squash and cucumbers are better a little less mature. Winter squash is best more mature with a lot of color. Hot weather encourages rapid development. It is easy for the growth to get ahead of you during summer or heat waves. When there is too much rain, the sugars are diluted and this affects the taste. The quality of food produced on a piece of land reflects the quality of the soil. Eating the food you grow will save you a lot of costly health bills. The same thing applied to my children when they were young. We never needed doctor visits unless there was an accident. This lifestyle provides health assurance as opposed to health insurance.

Processing is a whole other phase of the process. Roots do well stored in a cool place or in the ground. Burying a tub with a secure lid and easy access works well or just leave them in the ground until harvest. For everything else it is best to do a combination of freezing, drying, and a little canning. Canning is a lot more work. The vitamin content is more depleted by so much cooking. Drying seems to be the most cost-effective. It preserves more nutrients and is relatively easy. Overplanting and succession planting ensure a continued harvest. Food is the best resource a garden can provide, along with pleasing the soul.

Growing for market adds a whole other dimension. It is a separate job and has extra demands. Keep in mind that food first should be the number one priority. For market, harvests must be better controlled for cosmetics. Produce with too many blemishes and holes that might be acceptable for the table must be separated.

Flowers are grown entirely to be admired and so they must be at their best. It is best to pick them before fully open. Refrain from picking in the heat of the day and preferably in the early morning before the sun is on them. Composite flowers should be picked while the center is still depressed and tight. Always pick them when they are in their prime color. A fully open bloom is better kept for seed or deadheaded. Deadheading is a major part of flower maintenance. It keeps the plants productive. This is where quality control needs to be a primary focus. Place cut stems into very clean, cool water. Stems are put in a solution of one tablespoon of vinegar and one teaspoon of bleach and/or lemon juice per quart of water. Containers need to be sanitized before use and cut flowers kept out of the sun. Grow enough varieties to maintain a continual harvest throughout the summer. Growing flowers is more detailed than vegetables. A keen eye on arranging them is also needed. It can be a nice addition to market. They are mostly nonedible. Yet a well-maintained bed of flowers are food for the soul. Without experience and individual knowledge it is best to start with easy selections like zinnias, cosmos, celosia, marigolds, larkspur, cleome, sunflowers, larkspur, and nigella. With these, seeds can be direct sown. Flowers are very inviting and add to the whole presentation.

With vegetables and fruits the best approach to market is to present your product as gourmet. Freshness and quality is what it is all about. When introducing your food, allow people to sample what you grow at market. This way the food sells itself. If you save your own seed, you won't be able to grow as many tomato and pepper varieties. Growing many varieties would make it impossible to keep the seed from crossing. A big part of being in markets is educating consumers about how it all works and helping them to have a closer relationship with their food. This is important. Finding a market niche is an important process in marketing. Many years ago it was often easier because there were not as many growers, so food, flowers, dried and fresh herbs, dried flower and herbal wreaths, plants, and so on would sell themselves when on display. The dynamics of marketing fresh grown food has changed. There are many more consumers and everyone is more hurried to get on with their day. This requires more emphasis on marketing. It is ideal to have the support of someone who is skilled and enjoys that aspect of the operation.

Belonging to a CSA (community supported agriculture) group and direct marketing is an efficient way to market. The best way is to find a group that has an appreciation for the same quality of life. It also requires upkeep and constant communication with members. A newsletter works well for this. Members will need a bit of education to be able to request the food they want from you well ahead of time, ideally before planting begins.

Restaurants can be a good market for quality food. The relationship with a chef needs to be well developed. This is where the grower also needs to be educated on the needs of a restaurant. Before setting up a market system, it is best to do a market study. This involves visiting markets, talking to other growers, and finding out what will work best for your situation. This also means determining what you need to make it work with the numbers you have to work with. It is best to do research on what and how to make it happen.

Marketing requires a different type of skill and a lot of creativity. It involves a different personality and can require a lot of patience in dealing with people. Many of us enjoy working with plants and soil and nature. Marketing is a different job entirely. It is important to evaluate if being a farmer or a market gardener is the best use of your time. It is much easier to grow your own food then it is to make a living from growing. When growing for market it is easy to cut corners and compromise, which means lowering the quality and integrity of one's work. Marketing is a big job itself. If standards are not set ahead of time for high quality, then it will be hard to maintain them. Consumers usually do not know the difference between what an experienced grower does and what someone who just got into this with little or no training is doing.

There is a huge disconnect in the locally grown movement that is not going to be addressed. It is easy to meet a lot of growers whose focus is on product and not on producing a garden or farm. If you enjoy this work, you may prefer to manifest a healthy place to grow and let everything else be secondary. After all, quality needs to be the number one priority. Integrity needs to be a priority of doing quality work.

Natural signs and indicators are important to understand. When you see goldenrod blooming, it is time to start wrapping up the fall plantings. Water that stands for any length of time is a sign of drainage problems that need to be addressed. A steady wind means changes are coming. There is a lot of folklore around what and when to do things. Here are a few that have some credence. Plant potatoes and peas when daffodils are in full bloom. Transplant eggplants and peppers when the irises are blooming. Squash vine borers appear when chicory flowers open. Plant corn when oak leaves are the size of a squirrel's ear. Plant tomatoes when lily of the valley blooms. Prune roses when crocuses are in bloom. Planting too early is a sign of impatience. The soil temperature warms up about two weeks later than the air temperature. A later planting on the correct time will catch up with the early plantings set out too early. The lifestyle of a gardener or farmer is very seasonal. It gives one a perspective of what you are doing and when you need to be doing it. If you go to a restaurant and they bring you fresh tomatoes in January it is very out of place, and you may not want them. That knowledge comes from eating seasonally.

The months in perspective are as follows. December is a time of reflection and looking ahead as the solstice approaches, also looking back on successes and failures. January is a radical time of new growth and indoor work. It is a time of new beginnings. Ideas and seeds are germinated. In Latin, February means "to cleanse." That is when we dodge the rains while trying to maintain the dance schedule. March is the beginning of spring. It is time to execute best laid plans. April is a very intense time. The whole year seems to revolve around this month. May is catch up and finish what is planned before summer. Spring and early summer offer an abundant return on your investment. June means to shift gears and prepare for the solstice. First harvest is in full swing along with kitchen processing. Planting is all but done. July is the fruits of your labor and plans for the fall. August provides time to start the fall plantings. September is like a second spring and a fall garden. October is a month of changes and second harvests. The beautiful weather is a time to enjoy all that is warranted. November is time to catch your breath as the spiral envelopment moves downward and starts all over.

11

Full Circle

Live as if you'll die tomorrow, but farm as if you'll live forever.

—Old Proverb

TAKING IT FULL CIRCLE MEANS having a complete system that carries all the aspects of what is required to accomplish a healthy environment that nourishes itself and sustains itself. It is a holistic approach that takes into account all the surrounding aspects and is congruous with nature. The purpose of this chapter is to take everything written on previous pages and put it in perspective as a way of going full circle. That means to create a model of how it could all work together. Making everything happen with a fine-tuned system never works as well as a well laid out plan. There has to be room for error and for the unknown elements of surprise. That is what makes life exciting and, of course, how we continue to learn.

It is first important to examine your objectives. Being self-sufficient means creating everything from the land or in-house. This is very challenging yet there are several people who have done this to a large degree. It involves a long list of skills, from timbering, running a saw mill, to carpentry, and of course, producing all that one consumes with some level of efficiency. Being totally self-sufficient is hard to accomplish.

Being sustainable involves some similar avenues to subsistence farming. The focus is for primary components to come from the land or a source that encompasses the community at large. Community needs to be an important part of the working order that completes necessary cycles. The idea that no man is an island works well here. When there is community with the support it brings, there is a greater purpose and connection to what makes it all work. Being a social animal provides a valuable resource not to be underrated. The biodynamic concept depends on community to provide all the essential parts that make it a whole. The approach here is to simply do the best one can and embrace the challenges that come with it.

Decentralized agriculture brings food production back into the community. One view is that small farms cannot grow enough to support a large urban population. Yet many small farms are more efficient than a few large ones. More involvement in food production with the onset of community gardens and community-based farms gives a whole new perspective on what local food initiatives needs to be about. This lends itself to the development of farming cooperatives, which can be a resource for other ideas about education, marketing networks, and food coops. This would allow small farms to cater to more than just the gourmet market.

Sometimes all the resources are not in place, and so I move ahead rather than wait forever for the ideal time. Creating a fully operational system that is sustainable takes a lot of time. Creative planning and discovering all the available resources requires a lot of investment of time and work. Developing a worthwhile project needs to be done in stages.

Making sure that the important components of a piece of land are in place is the first place to start. These elements need to be readily available. A sunny field that lends itself to the vision of a garden is the most important. A source of water is crucial as well. Above-ground water fulfills the need for a balanced ecosystem. Below-ground water as in a well can provide the volume of water to grow enough for market. Watersheds provide the assurance that you are in control of what is coming onto your land. This is especially true for elevated land. It may not always be possible to be in control of one's own watershed.

Uncontaminated water ensures a clean source of water to replenish and cleanse. Soil is often in need of healing and that is the challenge that is always calling out as one approaches a potential new garden or farm. It would help also if the air moving in and out of the surrounding areas has a sweet taste and aroma. Trees provide many resources. They are good for wood, shelterbelts, protection from wind, and other elements. They attract wildlife and an enriched ecological base. A substantial tree growth attracts water in the form of rain. Other opportunities they provide are a source of agroforestry, mycology, and medicinal. Other resources are providing materials for making compost. An integral part of a biodynamic farm is animals. Animals provide food and fertilizer. Growing the food to feed them requires a surplus of land. For instance, a horse needs between one to two acres. It is about the same for a cow. It varies widely depending on details of the land. You'll want to rotate the land between grazing by the animals and planting crops.

Chickens are the most efficient to house. They can be used to clean beds of harboring insects before planting. The chicken tractor concept is a good preventative for insect problems. Before preparing a bed for greens, contain the chickens or guinea fowl there for a few days to get rid of slugs and other large insects. If there are slugs harboring in a bed, pull the weeds with slugs and feed them to the chickens. Goats can self-graze, are great recyclers, and a good source of manure. They will eat almost anything. They can reclaim an overgrown area quite well. Rabbits are fairly efficient, but need to be caged and that does not provide much of a life for them. This is hard if one looks at all life as equal. Larger animals are well suited for grazing on fields where crops have been previously harvested. A rotation system for animals contributes to the biodiversity of the land and prevents overgrazing. The common example of efficient animal husbandry is a dairy. The cow's manure is spread onto the fields, which benefits the grass they graze on. Animals are demanding, for space to house them, food to feed them, and the care they need, especially if they get sick or hurt. Hay is also needed. Animals factor into a large spread of land. Most of this does not fit into a vegetarian lifestyle. Taking that into account, smaller areas can be used for micrograin production. An alternative to animals is growing green manure for composting.

You can take the same hayfield and make compost with a simple formula without the added demands of animals. Cut the hay in the field before it goes to seed in the spring. Harvest and store it and use it for mulch. Using hay for compost does not require keeping it clean. Let the field grow up about halfway again. This time, cut and harvest as green manure by not letting it dry out. After a few weeks and a few rains, you can cut the green material to use as your nitrogen source. Layer the compost pile with the hay previously harvested mixed with the fresh cut green manure. Adding a little soil contributes needed bacteria. An important contributor is the added bacteria and nutrients of manure. But the system mentioned above is much more efficient for composting. Providing a source of meat is important. But if you do not eat meat, it does not justify raising animals simply for fertilizer. It would be better to trade vegetables and fruit for the manure from a reliable source. The hay is an important source of biomatter that is needed regardless of how it is used. In the same regard, produce can be traded or sold to buy grains that are not efficient to grow for personal use. This can be a perplexing situation.

Animals require ample land to graze on. If the land is not available, then they do not fit in. In this case, one can house a small group of animals. Chickens are conducive to small plots. With a little more land, you might afford some goats. This will not provide you with the quantity of manure you will need but it contributes some diversity to a composting program. In this case, the main source of nitrogen for composting needs to come from green manures. Worm beds are another way to generate fertilizer for beds. It's a formula that can be adjusted to fit a particular piece of land. Of course, what works in one place may not work in another.

The first phase of development is to build a compost pile. Place compost piles in areas where fruit trees will later be planted. Start with a serious plan since organization is four-fifths of the work. Start laying out beds and preparing them, but you will need a fence before any planting can be done. You can have good success with a two-strand electric fence. On the outside of the fence run a trip wire about eighteen inches to two feet above the ground and about three feet outside the fence. Both are electrified and baited with peanut butter.

The beginning is when we learn so much about what works and what does not. It is better not to have high expectations or plan to do a big market the first year if that can be avoided. The focus needs to be on fertility and development. All the available resources may not appear immediately, but come over time. Leave time for patterns to manifest and fall into place. As they do, they will revolve into the necessary circles that make the system whole.

This is an organic development. As patterns manifest, the components that build fertility will become apparent and avail themselves to you. Fertility is more of a tool than a commodity. It appears best as a skill rather than a purchased item. In deciding what to grow, find out what works best for that area, what is easiest, and of course what you want to eat.

If it is a market garden, you need to do a market study by visiting markets. If marketing is an objective, than you need to be no more than forty miles from that market. If everyone is growing strawberries, then yours will be grown for personal consumption. Remember food first is the rule for what is most important. In parts of the world with limited resources, it is more challenging to start a farm or garden. Seeds are started with leaf mold harvested out of rain gutters. You may have to use old rotted manure from local farms to get started. In cold climates, you can make greenhouses with everything imaginable. Junk items can be used; an old shipping box or a broken refrigerator can be made into cold frames, or place old windows over dug out soil and hay bales. You can use water heaters and other heating devices to start seeds with four inches of insulation on top to keep the flats from drying out.

I have used cardboard boxes to replace wheelbarrows. Making small pinholes in the bottom of a can turns it into a watering can. In Brazil, we tried to make a digging fork out of burglar bars. It didn't work well. You can start seeds in an endless array of food containers. Recycling is a part of appropriate technology. In a big garden, you will need to set up irrigation systems with strategic watering stations throughout the garden. Using gravity helps it work more efficiently. Rainwater harvesting works most efficiently if done on elevations. Using gravity will let it flow downhill to crops that need it most since it is not a pressurized system. This includes fruit bushes, vines, fruit trees, or any hardwood perennial.

You may not always have structures to harvest water from. Plant first and put up structures later. Soil takes time to develop, which means it can take a while to get established. In the first winter, begin establishing perennial crops on areas that have been previously cultivated. This way, you have given time to build up the soil before putting it into a semipermanent bed. It is much easier to start seeds in the summer for fall plantings. The warm summer heat gives a boost to seed germination. They only need protection from the harsh rains and summer sun. A little shade and a makeshift lath house are easy to put together with branches and wire. Bamboo or old lath works well for this. Fruit trees, vines, bushes, and everything else are installed during the late fall or winter months when they are dormant. It is difficult to get it all done in one season without a lot of input and money. So it is usually done over the course of two or three years. When planning for fruits, plant them out surrounding the main garden. This way they are incorporated into the overall landscape. When planning for vine and brambles, take into account that they require a lot of trellises and arbors. Try to be patient with the process of developing it all. Although it is important to spend a lot of time surveying what to do first, you cannot avoid learning a certain amount after the fact and this is OK since you will never really have it all figured out. As you are able to examine how the air movement flows, you can establish windbreaks as needed and create shade where it can be better utilized. Utilizing berries like blackberry or elderberry is a good example of a windbreak that provides food for you and for wildlife; and can also be grown as a hedgerow. Working efficiently and being resourceful is an ongoing process.

Bees

As the entire landscape starts to take form, you can then introduce honeybees. If that does not fit in with the work required, consider mason bees as an alternative. They do not provide honey, but are very effective as pollinators. Tie together a bunch of thin bamboo pieces about seven inches to ten inches long; place a small roof made from bark or aluminum from cans over it and hang it from a branch. Bees will show up later when flowers are in bloom. Bees are the link between insects, humans, and plants. Bees are one of the most natural introductions into the garden. Keeping bees in a natural state contributes to their overall health. This means using natural combs rather than foundations. Allow the bees to become what they are. This means letting the bees do the work by allowing the queen to be. She dictates the personality of the hive. Another part is keeping their homes natural with wood and putting the bee's health first by only harvesting surplus when there is plenty to support the colony. The difference between good beekeeping practices of a hive and *bee-having* badly is to give allowance to what is best for them without compromise. This means providing for them first and last. The health of a beehive eclipses the entire health of a garden. The sensitivity of how bees operate demonstrates their intricate and delicate nature. The current problems with bees, which is evident in colony collapse disorder, reflects the general health of our environment. They are like the canary in the coal mine. Most problems with bees are brought on by the beekeepers themselves, by not having a clear perspective on doing their work in a sustainable and organic environment. The colony operates with intricate communication channels. They always seem to know what is best for them. Bees make apparent the interconnectedness of a garden or farm.

Seed Saving

Like so many other aspects of the garden, success is a matter of facilitating rather than trying to be in complete control of what is happening in the garden. As the garden takes hold, an important aspect of cultivating sustainability is to start saving seed that has begun to acclimate to the surroundings. This might be hard at first, if you have not already recognized what seeds you want to grow. In that case, you will need time to conduct trials. After a season or two, you will usually have a good idea of some important varieties worth saving. The nice thing about this is that now there are plenty of seed companies supplying heirloom seeds. The process of saving seeds limits the amount of varieties one can grow. Those more susceptible to cross-pollination limit you to just a few. Start with those that are easy to save seeds from. Beans, corn, squash, peppers, melons, peas, tomatoes, and cucumbers are examples of seeds that are easy to collect. Many seeds will keep for an extended amount of time in a refrigerator or sealed up well in the freezer. Corn is the exception as it does not store well. Carrots and onions also have a short shelf life of a year or two. Saving roots and tubers is fairly easy also. Sweet potatoes store well in a cool place until it is time to start slips. Potatoes do best stored in the ground in a buried cage or wooden tub. Bring them into the house a month or so before planting and they sprout quickly. Jerusalem artichokes are replanted as they are harvested with a nice helping of compost.

There is also a chance of meeting others that keep seeds in your area. This provides the possibility of exchanging seeds locally. The relationship one has with those varieties becomes special. This is part of cultivating the culture of a given piece of land. It is good to explore what varieties of fruits are best, based on disease resistance and adaptation to your climate. It is also important to consider how their growth fits into the vision of what you are creating. A final consideration is of course the taste. Hopefully, there are fruit groups or older fruit collectors that can provide scion wood for grafting or canes for rooting. There is a rich abundance of old varieties of fruits, many of which are from your area. Most of these are never seen on the supermarket shelves because they don't ship well, store well, or are not cosmetically correct by commercial standards.

Planting fruit trees or anything perennial such as asparagus implies permanence. You can grow asparagus from seed. It takes a year or two to reach the size of crowns you buy and you often get undesirable females. It is important when buying crowns to get them from a reputable source. Although nothing is forever, the commitment that comes with a long-term vision is necessary in order to create a sustainable existence. The idea of planting such things with that intention is being truly sustainable.

Mycology

Mycology is another area to explore that offers many rewards. Besides being a good food source, edible fungi are very marketable and fun. Oyster mushrooms (*Pleurotus ostreatus*) are fairly easy to grow. They are best grown in a medium of straw. Place the straw in water and soak for a day. Next drain and chop the straw into two to four inch lengths. Boil the straw in a drum for sixty minutes. Steam the bags for sixty minutes. Once the hay has cooled, mix the spore at a rate of about one liter per ten bags. Next, place the sterilized straw into nylon bags. These are easy to work with and reusable. Or maybe a pair of recycled pantyhose would work for this. A good dimension for the bags is three feet long by ten inches wide. Bleach mixed at 5 percent is used to clean everything in contact with the bags, including the bags. Gloves are used when handling everything after it has been sterilized. Stuff the bags with the inoculated hay and tie off the end with a rubber band. Add cotton in the neck where it is tied off to allow it to breath. Incubate in a cool place for one to three weeks at 50 to 75 degrees Fahrenheit, then increase the temperature to 75 to 85 degrees. A fan is good for air circulation. Monitor for contamination and black mushrooms or insect and animal damage. In the tropics, it was easy to maintain high humidity. Elsewhere, a humidifier may be needed. After a couple of weeks, start adding a light spray. A mist system can be introduced to provide about 80 percent moisture. Mushrooms are the fruiting bodies of the fungus growing in the bags. Cut openings in the bags to allow the mushrooms to grow. A 10 percent loss is normal. Harvest until the medium of the inoculated spore is spent. Sometimes the harvest can last a few months. The spent mushroom medium can be put in the soil as a way to introduce microorganisms. The used substrate from the used hay can also be used for composting as a way to introduce fungal properties into the compost. It can be fed to worm beds. It can be added directly to the soil, especially the subsoil when double digging. It can be used as an additive to cattle, pig, and fish feed. Pleurotus compost (made from oyster mushroom medium) is very high in nitrogen and relatively high in phosphorus and potassium. It offers high protein as a feed. Oysters grow naturally on hardwoods during the rainy periods.

Shitake mushrooms (*Lentinula edodes*) are also easy to grow. They are commonly grown on oak logs. The oak logs are cured and are usually four to six inches in diameter and forty inches long. It is best to soak the logs in water for a day or more. Drill holes about an inch to two inches deep and about an inch in diameter. Space the holes about six to eight inches apart. Fill the holes with sawdust mixed with the mushroom spawn. Beeswax painted over the holes will protect them and keep the spawn intact. Stack the logs and keep them wet by spraying them every day. A mist system works well here also. The mushrooms emerge in six to twelve months and can continue for several years. Spores are dormant at temperatures below 40 degrees and slow down above 80 degrees. Mushrooms contribute to a varied market item. They also provide resource for soil mycoremediation. The waste products of mushroom growing can be used to introduce valuable fungus into the soil. This greatly improves the mycorrhizae of the soil. This can be an important contribution to a stabilized and healthy soil rich with life.

You will want to consider how much time you have for projects like these. Spreading yourself too thin can be very overwhelming, in which case you may need to seek additional help. Keeping the work in perspective is important to being able to prevent getting burned out. The art of growing a beautiful garden is the main objective. Never lose touch with your passion. Creating balance in one's life is harder than it seems. We all come from a society that does not endorse or encourage holistic lifestyles. So striving for this can be a real challenge. It is counter to what is going on in most of society, yet it is what most people are looking for. This place becomes a reflection of your personality. Your energy translates into the energy of the garden. It is like the idea that you can take the farmer out of the city, but it is harder to take the city out of the farmer.

Solar Greenhouse

Another important aspect of using land efficiently is to harvest the natural elements to produce needed energy. We live on a planet where there is an abundance of energy available, yet most of us do little to make use of it. Appropriate technology as a movement is an art, of resourcefulness, and a science, of technical skills. The sun is a vital resource. There is no place where this is more evident than with plants that demonstrate the most efficient way to harvest the energy that allows us to live here.

About half of what is grown is started indoors and later transplanted out. So you will need a greenhouse of some form to do this work. A greenhouse also offers the luxury of growing tropical plants like a Meyer lemon or ginger, and a place to store tropical herbs and lemongrass in the winter. It provides a place to dry herbs and propagate plants. A solar greenhouse is a very simple concept. The greenhouse design that is most practical involves a rectangular structure with angled glazing. It needs a roof and three sides that can hold up well to the elements. Using a solar design means harvesting the sun's energy. Therefore, it needs a thermal mass. Use fifty-five gallon drums painted black. They do not actually heat up as much from the sun, but do regulate temperature fluctuations. The angle of the sun needs to be calculated to allow access into the back wall during the winter months. This space is good for propagating plants.

You will want to build a tight structure that is well insulated. Leave an earth floor to provide the option of digging it up to plant in the late fall for winter growing. The most important key to a solar design is ventilation. It is very easy to overheat the greenhouse on a sunny day. Awning windows are placed on the front that can open out to bring in air. A vent that runs the entire length is installed at the top. This can be at the highest part of the roof or at the top of the back wall. This provides an air current moving up through the greenhouse. As the air heats up it pushes out the top by convection. A window on the side and a door on the opposite side provide cross-ventilation (see the illustration in figure 11.1). All openings need to be sealed and insulated during the night. A greenhouse has no natural ways to control pests. Use screens on the windows, vents, and doors to make it a controlled environment. Also be careful with what foreign materials come into the greenhouse so not to introduce insects and diseases.

FIGURE 11.1
Solar Greenhouse

Glass is always better than plastic for the glazing but more expensive. Finding recycled solid pane glass works well. It takes time to acquire the windows. The glass windows will determine the greenhouse dimensions. It is a matter of time versus money. Rammed earth can work as a foundation, but again requires a lot of labor. Rammed earth is clay with a small amount of Portland cement pressed into forms. Stone is another option for a foundation as an alternative to concrete. If the greenhouse is not attached to a living structure, then straw bale walls or cob can help insulate the north side. Cob is a free form made of clay and straw. These structures are very labor intensive to make.

In severe weather or places where temperatures drop into single digits, a woodstove can provide a backup heat source. Stoves made from small barrels can be welded on a frame. A more intricate design is to make a double-barrel stove where the one on top contains water. This can become a heat source for starting seeds quickly with bottom heat. A greenhouse can also heat water by the sun, using shallow black containers. Be careful not to let a seed flat get above 90 degrees when placing them on the heat source.

A lath house is used to grow plants outdoors during the warm months. It is best used to start plants for the fall. A free standing lath house can be used as a rainwater catchment. Instead of using lath, place corrugated clear plastic panels on the frame. Along the bottom, run a rain gutter that empties into a storage tank. The tank can be used to water fruit trees or other fruits. It helps if the tank is elevated above ground level for good gravity flow.

Cold frames are another way to utilize the sun. These can be made from recycled windows and scrap lumber. They are useful either to harden off seed flats for a week or two before going out or to grow cool weather vegetables during the winter months. Set up one with a large picture window. Pallets keep the seed flats off of the ground. Hay bales provided insulation. Plastic tarps layered into the box provided protection both inside and on top at night. A light bulb hung in the corner added extra heat on cold nights. With a six by six foot window you are able to grow about a dozen flats. Cold frames need to be opened on sunny days to keep from overheating. Designs for cold frames include all sorts of ideas based on the materials you have to work with. They can be made entirely from recycled materials (see example in figure 11.2).

Appropriate technology utilizes the tools of nature. The solar food dryer is a good example. The New Mexico Solar Energy Association developed the design shown in figure 11.3. There are several important considerations to ensure its success. First, prepare to dry foods when there is going to be a string of sunny days, at least five consecutive days in a row. Slice the fruits of vegetables a quarter inch or smaller and spray them with lemon juice mixed with water to prevent discoloring. Check the drying process every couple days and turn the slices over to get uniform drying. Fruits with high water content, like tomatoes or figs, are difficult to impossible in humid areas. Place the bottom of the legs of the dryer into used metal cans with concrete and leave an inch or two at the top. The cans can be filled with water to discourage ants. Tanglefoot can be used to further prevent ants from climbing up the legs. The key to its success is to have a steady air draft moving through the drying racks. Corrugated metal, painted black, is used in the collector. Window screens can be used for the racks. Flexible material works well for the glazing, but ridged material can be easily substituted with a little design modification. The fruits with the most success are apples, pears, and most vegetables. I've had no success with figs and peaches. In a dryer climate this could work well for a much broader selection of fruits.

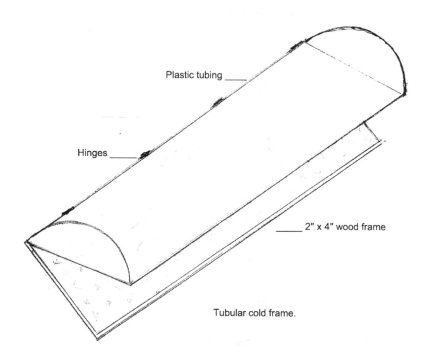

Plastic tubing

Hinges

2" x 4" wood frame

Tubular cold frame.

FIGURE 11.2
Tubular Cold Frame

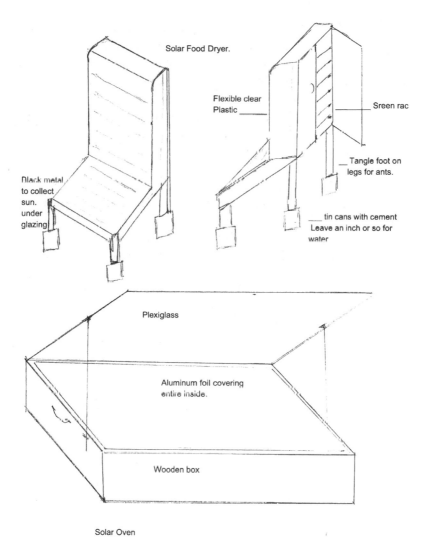

Solar Food Dryer.

Flexible clear
Plastic ___

Sreen rac

Black metal
to collect
sun.
under
glazing

Tangle foot on
legs for ants.

___ tin cans with cement
Leave an inch or so for
water

Plexiglass

Aluminum foil covering
entire inside.

Wooden box

Solar Oven

FIGURE 11.3
Solar Food Dryer and Oven

The solar oven has an amazing capacity to generate mild cooking temperatures of around 250 degrees F. There is a women's collective in Nicaragua that has been building solar ovens with an enormous amount of success. These can be built with recycled materials and plexiglass or regular window glass. Of course, the plexiglass is not prone to breakage so is easier to work with long term. The box needs to be small to retain heat, approximately two feet wide by three feet long maximum or smaller. Keep it shallow, a foot tall or less for best results. Years ago they were made by painting the entire inside black. Research has shown that they work better if lined with aluminum foil with the shiny side facing in. They work best when the sun is high, from midmorning to midafternoon for maximum exposure. It is also good to use black pots with lids that absorb the sunlight. If the food being cooked contains a lot of water, the temperature will not exceed 212 degrees Fahrenheit or 100 degrees Celsius. Celsius is used as a measurement for water temperatures. That is as high as water gets before it boils. The process of solar cooking takes more time than using a conventional stovetop. Cooking at a lower temperature results in more nutritious food content than food cooked at higher temperatures for a shorter amount of time. The same considerations need to be taken into account for dealing with ants and other insects as with the solar food dryer. Creating and using a solar oven requires some experimentation to find what works best for your needs. Foods can be parboiled to help with the cooking process.

A solar shower or water heater is another simple concept. It's best to use this where you have a hillside or an existing building to help support it. Take a sheet of plywood and build a frame around it with 2 by 8s, 2 by 10s, or whatever you have to work with. Line it with black plastic so that the plastic overhangs the entire wood structure. Support the box on two posts on the open end along with a solid post in the middle. This works well with large timbers. Once filled with water, it will have a serious weight. Water weighs about eight pounds per gallon. A hole is drilled in the middle and fitted with a tight fitting drain. Silicon used as caulking around the fittings works well here.

Attached to the drain hole is a piece of hose with the male end hanging down. Then attach a valve with a shower nozzle. The whole thing needs to be tall enough to accommodate a person. Cover the top with a loose fitting piece of plexiglass and fill it with water. After a few hours of direct sunlight, the water will warm to a comfortable temperature. The area of a full sheet of plywood will provide enough water for two or three showers. This system needs to be constructed securely or it could collapse and be very dangerous to those under it. There are many other ways to heat water in the sun based on individual needs.

If one has the fortune of having a creek with lots of flow and drop, you can consider microhydro systems. With as little as two gallons per minute and two feet of drop you can make electricity. Water is a continuous source of power. It flows all day and night, year-round. But this can be a costly venture. On a large scale, the equipment can start in the thousands of dollars. The source of power needs to be near the water flow. It is best to do your research and learn as much as possible about how to do it yourself. The flow of water can be greatly affected by droughts. In most situations, it does not pay for itself but is fun to experiment with on a very small scale. Wind energy is the same. Unless you have a constant wind every month, it will not pay for itself either. But in those unique locations it can provide an abundant resource to tap into. What is more commonly available is wood from the land, and it is easy to burn

Woodstoves are most efficient when being used to simultaneously warm, cook, and heat water. Being efficient is one of the basic laws of being sustainable. Just like companion planting where it is helpful to try to use more than one principle, it is best to utilize every component for more than one purpose. Structures can collect water, house materials inside, be shelterbelts for plantings, and so on.

Small-scale Grain Growing

Growing grains can be done on a small scale with ease. It is not the most efficient use of space since they are inexpensive to buy, but if you have extra space it can be very rewarding. Interplanting works well on small-scale growing and can contribute to weed control. The most popular companions are corn and pole beans or field peas and winter squash. They hold each other together well. Oats (*Avena sativa*) are a high protein grain that is easy to grow, has few pest problems, and produces good yields. Oats can produce over a hundred bushels per acre. Oats are planted in the fall and harvested in the summer; they are harvested when the tops lodge heavily. Clover can be planted at its base. Get the oats up first before planting clover. The tops need to be threshed and winnowed. Millet is mostly grown for birdseed in the United States. It is another highly nutritious grain. Eaten with buckwheat it is a complete protein. Pearl millet (*Pennisetum glaucum*), also known as cattail millet, is easy to grow and is not bothered by marginal soils. It produces fifty to seventy bushels per acre. It can be planted fairly late and needs about three months to mature. It does well when planted in alternate sections with peanuts. It can also be mixed with alfalfa. It is easy to harvest and thresh. I usually grow buckwheat as a summer cover crop. It goes to seed quite quickly. It is supposed to mature in sixty to seventy days but you can get a crop sooner. The seeds are also easy to harvest, but without the right equipment you will have problems getting the seed out of the hulls. It is best to run it through a mill with blades set far enough apart to crack the grain but not mill it. Then it needs to be winnowed. Quinoa is in the genus *Chenopodium*. It is related to lamb's-quarter, beets, and spinach. It is highly nutritious and easy to grow and harvest. It looks like lamb's-quarter and is a close relative but more robust. It can be planted at the ends of beds. It gets quite tall so keep it to the back so as not to shade other plants.

Using herbs grown on the land like comfrey as a calcium supplement, Roman chamomile as a spray for damping off, horsetail (*Equisetum arvense*) as a disease preventative, stinging nettles tea on seedlings, and willow tea for propagation are examples of being highly efficient. All these can be grown in semishaded areas. Most herbs are also more drought tolerant than vegetables.

Ecoagriculture is a system of providing for the welfare of the land as well as the welfare of those that take care of the land. The idea of being truly sustainable involves using what is on the land or in the community to provide all the tools to do the work efficiently. To develop a piece of land into a heterogeneous community that evolves into ecological sustainability is a long continuous process. Agro biodiversity involves maintaining enough variety for the system to depend upon itself. Rather than looking for a level of achievement, it is good to perceive the pursuit as an open classroom. That is also part of one's evolution—to revive the land to its full potential means bringing it to a state of being multifunctional for all beings to cohabitate in. Internal regeneration of inputs that support autonomy can start with something as simple as letting certain weeds grow. Habitat restoration means different things in different places that serve a variety of purposes. This means rocks for lizards and irrigation furrows for horny toads to hide out in New Mexico. This is also seen in biologically rich ponds where bullfrogs sing you to sleep at night in Costa Rica. If you have beautiful bird families that come back in the spring to visit wild cherry and mulberry trees or muscadine vines that climb up through the forest trees, then you are getting recognition for creating a beautiful setting that flourishes with life. Biotic interactions that support the internal regeneration of all species need to be present. Essential functions like nutrient cycling and polyculture plantings are part of this. This is the function of a balance with nature.

At the heart of ecoagriculture is good stewardship of the land. To be a good steward involves continued growth, both internally and externally. Being open to the forces of nature's symmetry is to acknowledge the balanced economy of this interwoven system. It is a system where no living entity is unaccounted for. Making contributions that reverberate throughout the living structure makes a deep connection with this web work of life. For this reason, I avoid tractors. They create compact soils, which leads to hardpans. A garden is a more intimate version of a farm. It is a more efficient use of land and more labor intensive. It needs to be community based to work well. This work when practiced from the heart is harmonious with the life around you and enhances all of life's abundance. Being part of a garden is leaning toward a lifestyle of experiencing wealth beyond money. It is more than an investment in the soil. It is an investment in oneself.

This act is also reciprocal. For the more one puts into it, the more one continues to get out. The most important thing is to give more than you take out. Obey this rule and the land will provide you with glorious abundance. Receiving the riches of its wealth is an honor. Being a caretaker of a piece of land is a noble and very satisfying role in life that I have been very thankful for.

References

Agrios, George. *Plant Pathology*, 5th ed. Amsterdam: Elsevier Academic Press, 2005.

ATTRA Sustainable Agriculture Program. https://attra.ncat.org/.

Buckman, Harry, and Nyle Brady. *The Nature and Properties of Soils*, 7th ed. New York: Macmillan Press, 1972.

Collier, B. D. *Dynamic Ecology*. Englewood Cliffs, NJ: Prentice Hall, 1973.

Cornell University College of Agriculture and Life Sciences, Horticulture Section https://hort.cals.cornell.edu/.

Creasy, Rosalind. *Edible Landscaping*. Berkeley, CA: Counterpoint Press, 2010.

Epstein, Emanuel. *Mineral Nutrition of Plants, Principles and Practice*. New York: John Wiley and Sons [1971, c1972].

Flint, Mary Louise. *IPM in Practice*. Publication 3418. Oakland: University of California Agriculture and Natural Resources, 2001.

Fukuoka, Masanobu. *The One-Straw Revolution*. Emmaus, PA: Rodale Press, 1978.

Hartmann, Hudson Thomas, and Dale E. Kester. *Plant Propagation, Principles and Practice*, 2nd ed. Englewood Cliffs, NJ: Prentice Hall, 1968.

Howard, Albert. *The Soil and Health*. New York: Shocken Books, 1975.

Jeavons, John. *How to Grow More Vegetables*. Berkeley, CA: Ten Speed Press, 1978, 2006.

Kaviraj, Vaikunthanath Das. *Homeopathy for Farm and Garden*. Kandern, Germany: Narayana Verlag Publishers, 2011.

Lappe, Frances Moore. *Food First, Beyond the Myth of Scarcity*. Boston: Houghton-Mifflin, 1977.

Merrill, Richard. *Radical Agriculture*. New York: Harper and Row, 1976.

Mollison, Bill, and Reny Mia Slay. *Permaculture: A Designer's Manual*. New South Wales, Australia: Tagari Publications, 1988.

Odum, E. P. *Fundamentals of Ecology*. Philadelphia: W. B. Saunders Co., 1953.

Olkowski, Helga, William Olkowski, and Tom Javits. *Integral Urban House, Self-Reliant Living in the City*. San Francisco: Sierra Club Books, 1979.

Olkowski, William, Helga Olkowski, and Sheila Daar. *Gardeners Guide to Common Sense Pest Control*. Newtown, CT: Taunton Press, 1995.

Purdue University College of Agriculture. https://ag.purdue.edu.

Richards, O. W., and R. G. Davies. *IMMS General Textbook of Entomology*. University of California Press.

Riotte, Louise. *Carrots Love Tomatoes*. Pownal, VT: Storey Books, 1998.

Steiner, Rudolf. "Agriculture." Biodynamic Agriculture Association.

Sunset Western Garden Book. Menlo Park, CA: Lane Publishing.

University of California Davis, Cooperative Extension Small Farm Program. http://sfp.ucdavis.edu/.

University of California Santa Cruz, Center for Agroecology & Sustainable Food Systems (CASFS). https://casfs.ucsc.edu/.

University of Florida, Institute of Food and Agricultural Sciences (IFAS) Extension. http://edis.ifas.ufl.edu/.

University of North Carolina, ees.ncsy.edu.

Weatherwax, Paul. *Plant Biology*. Philadelphia: W. B. Saunders Co., 1942.

Wilson, Carl, Walter Loomis, and Taylor Steeves. *Botany*. New York: Holt Rinehart and Winston, 1971.

Index

cucurbitaceae, 90, 127
cultivator plants, 38, 92, 166
cultural practices, 131, 141–42, *142–47*
cutworms (*Peridroma saucia*), 128

dandelion, 11, 102, 158, 160
decomposers, 14, 17, 53, 127, 130.
    See also compost and composting
deer deterrents, 15, 170
Dermaptera, 127
design, 20; with beans, 21, 22, 34, 35,
    171, 172; companion planting in,
    27, 32, 36–39; curves and circles in,
    28–29, 101, 161; disease avoidance
    in, 141; edibles in, 4, 33–35, 39, 40;
    flowers in, 41, 93, 177; flow of air and
    energy in, 27–29; of greenhouses,
    185, 189–91, *190*; of learning gardens,
    39–40; for maintenance, 165; native
    plants in, 26–27; permaculture
    principles in, 30–33; for plant layout,
    101–2; plant types and groupings in,
    38–39; preparation and questions
    for, 25–26, 27, 33; restoration and
    recovery process in, 35–36; succession
    plantings in, 35; of water and watering
    systems, 10, 26, 30. *See also* solar
    energy and design
diatomaceous earth, 56, 129, *145*, *147*,
    159, 167
disabilities, gardens for, 2, 40–41
diseases, 3, 5, 131; balance with, 137, 138,
    150–51; biodynamic preparations
    for, 150; chart of vegetable and fruit,
    142–47; companion planting for,
    37–38; compost tea for, 56, *143–47*,
    148, 159; conditions and spread of,
    138–40; cover crops for control of,
    149; cultural practices and, 141–42;
    in forest stability, 13; fungal, 88,
    138, 139, 140, 141, *142*, *144–47*, 159;
    identifying, 137–38; microorganisms
    for, 148–49; mycorrhizal fungi and
    control of, 148–49, 150, 151; with
    nutrient imbalance, 149–50; rotation
    systems for control of, 141–42,
    142–44; tree pastes for, 159–60

diversity, 12, 14, 18, 31, 36, 84–86. *See
    also* polyculture plantings; rotation
    systems
dock (*Rumex crispus*), 11, 38, 92, 160, 166
dormant oil, 129
double digging, 77–78, *78*, 148, 149, 154
drying food, 176, 191–92, *193*, 194
ducks, 19, 20, 129
duckweed fern (*Azolla*), 32
dynamic accumulators, 160

earthworms, 29, 32, 44, 53, 58, 69, 79
earwigs, 127
ecoagriculture, 163, 196–97
ecology movement, 7, 8–9
edible landscaping, 4, 33–35, 39, 40
education, 4–5, 75, 162–64. *See also*
    learning gardens and projects
eggplant (*Solanum melongena*), 40, 91;
    companion planting with, 37; pests
    and diseases, *144*; planting and
    maintenance, 88, 94, *97*, 100, 101, 104,
    105–6, 108, 109, 165, 166, 171, 173,
    178
eggshells, 49, 59
elderberry (*Sambucus*), 28, 29, 186
elephant manure, 49, 57
energy cycles, 26, 163–64
English peas. *See* peas, English
entomology, 5, 121–35. *See also*
    insects and pests; integrated pest
    management
European cabbage moth (*Pieris rapae*),
    128
European corn borers (*Ostrinia nubilias*),
    128

fava beans (*Vicia faba*), 80, 102
feathers, *47*, 70
fences, 19, 170, 172, 184
feng shui, 27
fermented plant extracts, 148
fertilizer: from animal sources, 70,
    183–84; commercial and synthetic, 8,
    49, 86; compost and comfrey tea as,
    59, 94, 159; growth stages for, 94

About the Author

<hr>

Frank Holzman is an organic horticulturist and sustainable farming consultant. Holzman started his career as a landscape maintenance gardener in the San Francisco Bay Area. After studying agricultural sciences at the university, he studied organic horticulture in Santa Cruz, California. He learned about biodynamics in Alan Chadwick's garden at the University of California, Santa Cruz. He worked on farms and gardens in California, Oregon, New Mexico, North Carolina, and Georgia. His work has also taken him to seven countries, primarily in Southeast Asia and Central America, establishing education programs and consulting on creating healthy ecosystems. Holzman also serves as president of Recovery Eco Agriculture Project, working on sustainable land use, education, and research and development.